ZIG ZAG

Other Books in English by Hans Magnus Enzensberger

In Defense of the Wolves, poetry (1957)
Vernacular, poetry (1960)
A Museum of Modern Poetry, anthology (1960)
Braille, poetry (1964)
Poems for People Who Don't Read Poems, poetry (1968)
The Havana Inquiry, play (1970)
Acquittals: Revolutionaries on Trial, anthology (1970)
Poems 1955–1970, poetry (1970)
The Short Summer of Anarchy, novel (1972)
The Consciousness Industry, essays (1974)
Politics and Crime, essays (1974)
Mausoleum: Thirty-Seven Ballads from the History of Progress, poetry (1975)
The Sinking of the Titanic, poetry (1978)
The Fury of Disappearance, poetry (1980)
Critical Essays, essays (1982)
Dreamers of the Absolute, essays (1988)
Europe, Europe, essays (1989)
Political Crumbs, essays (1990)
Mediocrity and Delusion, essays (1992)
Civil Wars, essays (1994)
Selected Poems, poetry (1995)
Kiosk, poetry (1997)

ZIG ZAG

The Politics of Culture and Vice Versa

HANS MAGNUS ENZENSBERGER

THE NEW PRESS NEW YORK

PUBLISHED IN THE UNITED STATES BY THE NEW PRESS, NEW YORK
DISTRIBUTED BY W. W. NORTON & COMPANY, INC., NEW YORK

www.thenewpress.com

The New Press was established in 1990 as a not-for-profit alternative to the large, commercial publishing houses, currently dominating the book publishing industry. The New Press operates in the public interest rather than for private gain, and is committed to publishing, in innovative ways, works of educational, cultural, and community value that are often deemed insufficiently profitable.

PRINTED IN THE UNITED STATES OF AMERICA

9 8 7 6 5 4 3 2 1

CONTENTS

PREFACE

An Advertisement for Myself

WHY BOTHER TO BUY and read my book I am at a loss to say. To ask for an American reader's attention seems preposterous. Is he not a person under the influence, a victim of forces beyond his control? The weekly best-seller list concentrates his mind wonderfully, not to mention the presence of innumerable genial writers publicizing their work on television, all of them waving a copy of their latest book at him. If he were extremely choosy about his reading matter, he might look into the fat volumes (or the slim CD-ROM) of *Books in Print*, which has a few hundred thousand titles by home-grown authors to offer. In the end, however, the chain store at the nearest shopping mall will save him the trouble and come up with a selection of its own, dearly paid for by the publisher.

In such an environment, the marginal utility of self-advertisement is bound to decrease sharply. In recent decades, writers in the United States have become experts in the art of the blurb. But given the concentration of capital in the media industry, I am afraid that such efforts are now past their prime, and I am tempted to say: Good riddance.

In any case, the advertisement for oneself has always been a rather dubious literary genre. Though it can boast a pedigree reaching back to antiquity, the author who tries his hand at it has a stiff aesthetic price to pay, mainly in terms of elegance. In order to make himself heard in the marketplace, he has to raise his voice, and the resulting boom is often less than graceful. This is not to deny that the world is full of gifted showmen who amuse and entertain vast audiences; but this is a talent entirely unrelated to the gift of writing. A well-trained seal juggling colorful balls is a cheerful sight, and there is nothing wrong with people paying a modest fee for enjoying it. Still, it is pastime that bears no obvious connection with literature.

Much has been made of the moral risks involved in self-advertisement. Nowadays, however, it seems a bit quaint to invoke virtues like modesty which belong to another age. In a culture that celebrates celebrity—far above—as its supreme value, no attempt to attain it, however bizarre, can be considered disreputable. Besides, artists have never been demure about their real or imagainary achievements.

The real quandry of advertising yourself as a writer is not to be sought in terms of taste or manners. It is, rather, epistemological in character, or, to put it more bluntly, the problem is that it does not make sense, for the simple reason that no self-description can be trusted. Nobody in his right mind believes a man who begins a conversation by declaring himself sincere, just as no one believes a used-car salesman who insists upon his integrity. There's no such thing as a truthful résumé. Even the most innocuous person applying for a job is a mess of self-delusion, falsehood, and omission. And this of course is perfectly understood by the one who considers him for the job.

The same happens when a writer tries to describe what he has to offer. No matter how hard he tries to give a reasonably accurate account of his work, he will stumble. He may imagine himself a devout Christian, a leftist beyond reproach, a spearhead of the Zeitgeist, a dangerous outsider, or a mainstay of the mainstream—but it will do him no good, for nobody will fall for his claim. Even if someone *were* to be foolish or cruel enough to take him at his word, so much the worse for him—since then he will have pinned himself down. He will no longer be a free agent. He will have to stick to his guns, even if he finds that he has no more use for them. Or worse.

So the safest course appears to be to keep your silence and to let your work speak for itself. After all, you're lucky if it is published at all. Despite the ceaseless din of the media, the noise of the web, the roar of the headlines, it is still a privilege of sorts to have your say in public. Once you are in print, others get to speak their minds—readers and reviewers, friends and enemies—provided there is anyone sufficiently interested in your work, which is highly improbable but not, in the end, entirely out of the question.

Who knows? Out there, perhaps there's a great diaspora of kindred spirits, quite unknown to you, who really want your work, however miniscule the print run and however discouraging the ultimate sales may be. You will reach these people quite without kicking up a racket, on the sly, as it were, by a mysterious process of osmosis. Never mind celebrity.

When all is said and done, it's an affliction and a bore. To keep your cool, to keep your own counsel, is perhaps the best you can do for your work: advertisement by default.

Hans Magnus Enzensberger

Part One

1) SECOND THOUGHTS ON CONSISTENCY

ONCE UPON A TIME THERE was a black American revolutionary by the name of Eldridge Cleaver. He spent some years in jail, wrote a few books, became a Black Panther, went into exile, attempted a comeback as a revolutionary designer of men's trousers, and has not been heard of since. During the 1960s, however, Cleaver coined a memorable phrase. "Baby," he said, "you're either part of the problem, or you're part of the solution."

To many people and for a not inconsiderable period of time, this seemed an apt maxim. Clearcut, unequivocal, uncompromising, it had the deceptively simple sound of a quotation from the Bible. For some years afterward, it was adopted by politically minded people, not only in the USA, but also in Europe and in what is sometimes called rather sweepingly "the Third World." The only trouble with Cleaver's handy dictum is that it does not happen to be true. First of all, the solution is nowhere in sight. There does not seem to be such a thing. Of course, there is a huge supply of quick fixes—zillions of little remedies have been offered by bodies as adverse as IBM, EST, and the KGB—but even their promoters would hardly claim they merit the majestic singular of Cleaver's phrase.

More importantly, however, it has become very clear that everybody is "part of the problem." Supposing, for the sake of argument, that one was able to identify the "good" side in any or all of the many conflicts that beset the world, and granted that one would be willing to *take* it, this would in no way entitle one to a feeling of justification, since one would inevitably continue to participate in the web of situations, arrangements and traditions which are, precisely, "part of the problem." In stating this rather obvious fact, I do not wish to imply that the "baddies" cannot any longer be identified. On the contrary, this is fantastically easy. What I find nearly impossible is the opposite operation. To point out a "goody" does not any longer seem feasible, least of all if a mirror is used.

This is a very disagreeable state of affairs, especially for concerned intellectuals, who for a century or two have thrived on basic tenets like the following: It is good and necessary to establish first principles. It is difficult but laudable to hang on to them at any cost. Compromise in the face of adversity, cutbacks and reaction is bad. A radical should be radical. Opportunism is sinful. Consistency is good.

I should like to think, though I cannot be sure, that these rules were laid down in simpler and harder times than ours. A man who was a devoted socialist in 1912, for example, was certain to be faced with difficulties, but he could hardly be blamed if he thought of himself as "part of the solution." The same may be said of a Spanish anarchist of the 1930s, or of a kibbutznik starting a new life in Palestine. A few of these men and women are still alive, and if you meet them you will find that they inspire a feeling close to awe. Unfortunately, their deep conviction has been inherited by a much lesser breed. Since the early 1960s, a peculiar type of intransigent has made his appearance, a type who is very much a part of our problem, since he is uncommonly close to ourselves, our work, our milieu and our private lives. He is easy to recognize, but difficult to define, since he comes in a great number of varieties. I cannot be sure about America, but in Europe we have seen them all: the stern critic of monopoly state capitalism tucked away safely in a state-run university with tenure for life; the slave of intellectual fashion coming out strongly against intellectual fashion and its followers; the well-endowed bureaucrat of culture with a nauseating fondness for "subversive" artists; the peace research fund director bullying his elegant female office staff, and so on. Needless to say, all these people are full of principles. Indeed, the hazier their identity, the keener they are on the rhetoric of commitment. They all cherish a radical stance, untarnished by considerations arising out of their everyday existence.

Now, it might be thought that there is nothing new in all this. The hypocrite and the pharisee are, after all, well-established and ancient types in the comedy of manners. And indeed, if this were just another instance of self-righteousness and of double standards of morality, we should be confronted with a cast of characters quite familiar from an Ibsen play. The point, however, is precisely that we are not dealing with individual characters or with a subjective deficiency, but rather with an absence of character and with an epidemic of objective proportions. The people I have in mind do not embrace principles because they believe in their inherent truth. They use them as a blunt instrument with which to bludgeon others. Principles are needed only for the purpose of defining others as opportunists, careerists, sellouts; moral, political, or aesthetic renegades. The only person beyond suspicion is the one who has got hold of the microphone and who represents, at the moment of speaking, a higher reality of which, alas, he himself is not a part.

It is hard to identify this sheriff of conviction, this watchdog of basic values; this guru of principle. Indeed, it may turn out to be impossible. Speaking about him involves a moral paradox; this is a phenomenon that one risks becoming a part of the moment one speaks about it. No amount of sincerity will save one from the condition of moral schizophrenia which has become a universal of our intellectual existence. The very claim to a state of superior ethical grace is self-defeating.

Not many people are prepared to resign themselves to such a state of profound and permanent moral ambiguity. There is a heavy demand for idols who refuse to be part of the general quagmire, and a supply-side economy will not fail to provide what is needed. This is why we find, in our cultural marketplace, an unlikely assembly of cult figures who are supposed to be beyond suspicion. What they do for a living is of secondary importance. They may be philosophers or therapists, mystics or ideologues, artists or criminals, gurus or terrorists. The main demand made upon them is that they be part of the solution, not of the problem; that an unquestioned integrity can be ascribed to them that they be untainted by doubt, compromise, and equivocation. The result of this search is a curious Hall of Fame, a Madame Tussaud's of postmodern morality, crowded with figures such as Sid Vicious and Mother Teresa, Castaneda and Einstein, Samuel Beckett and Josef Stalin, Charles Manson and Erich Fromm, John Cage and Henry Abbot, Jian Qing and William S. Burroughs, Karel Woytila and Ulrike Meinhof, the Reverend Moon and Professor Beuys.

What is it, then, that we are so keen on that we want to acquire it at almost any cost, even if it means looking foolish, or crazy, or obscene? It must be something utterly lost. I believe that this something is consistency, the notion that there ought to be a large degree of congruence or at least compatibility between what we are, what we think, and what we do. Consistency is not a simple concept, and I am not sure of its status in Anglo-American philosophy. German philosophy, however, has traditionally been very strong on this notion, for which German philosophers have developed the term *Konsequenz*. This is, first of all, a logical category. In any rational discourse, judgments were supposed to follow from certain assumptions or first principles. In other words, one should not simply jump to conclusions or defend any old phrase that happened to pass through one's head as if it were a valid proposition. Contradictions would have to be avoided, overcome, or at least explained. Very soon, and rather imperceptibly, this rule acquired moral overtones, and finally it became a postulate, an ethical imperative, and even something of an obsession, at least in Germany.

Mine is a culture which historically has been prone to believe that to possess principles and to act them out to their utmost consequences is good. Possibly this has to do with the Reformation, with the turn the Protestant ethic took in Prussia; in any event, it is a recurrent theme in the rosary of German idealism, from Kant to Fichte to Hegel, from Hegel to Marx. But I refuse to believe that we are dealing here with a specifically German obsession. After all, the utopian thinkers of Renaissance Italy, the theologians of Imperial Spain and the French Jacobins indulged quite heavily in the passion for consistency at any cost. And in our own century, dozens of nations, from Korea to Chile, from Cuba to Bulgaria, not to mention Nazi Germany and the Soviet Union, have organized their social systems on the basis of principles that are odiously threadbare and ludicrously hypocritical but which happen to be thoroughly consistent. (It is interesting to note that the models on which most existing one-party systems are constructed are of German origin.)

Entire continents are filled with the monotonous drone of unequivocal speech. In this type of rhetoric, decisions are always "irrevocable," support is invariably "staunch," the laws of history are "iron," and determination is "unflinching." People who long for consistency are notoriously easy to organize in larger groups, in schools, churches, armies, sects, or parties. The man who desperately wants to be "true to himself," will end up, paradoxically, by surrendering to a collective identity. The private resolve to adhere to a set of principles and to follow them to their utmost consequences is no moral safeguard. Indeed, there is often something schematic, something reminiscent of the bureaucrat, about an all too blatant devotion to principle. Those who pride themselves on their loyalty to ideas should remember that abstractions cannot be betrayed, only people.

Consistency, as a logical category, is empty. It is possible to be a consistent vegetarian, a consistent thief, Trotskyist, Mormon, dandy, or Fascist. It is therefore not quite clear how consistency could ever lay claim to the status of a moral postulate. Another little problem arises as soon as one asks oneself whether consistency is to be understood as a demand on thoughts or on actions, or on both. In the first case, the risk to the outside world is minimal, but one may well end up a crank. Schelling's theory of electricity, for example, is entirely based on deduction. It is derived, with a great deal of precision, from the first principles of his *Naturphilosophie*, and is thus quite unblemished by empirical observation. With all due respect to a great mind, it must be said that it is complete nonsense, albeit of an entirely harmless and even entertaining kind. The point here is that consistency places an enormous strain on learning, and makes it exceedingly difficult for a change of mind to take place. If the postulate is then extended to include actions, some real trouble may be the result. The idea of Schelling fixing a lightbulb according to his theories is almost too much to bear. And yet this is a relatively innocuous example. Quite a few brave and decent people, a decade or so ago, concluded from principles which I cannot call unsound that the best way to deal with napalm was to bomb Dow Chemical. Most of them have learned by experience to think otherwise, even at the cost of consistency. Those who refused to pay this price would seem to be in for a lifetime of attacking Dow Chemical with homemade explosives.

But even if one just happens to mind the slashing of welfare or of food-aid programs to desperately poor countries, one ought to think twice before claiming consistency. Any such claim will lead to a particularly obnoxious sort of blackmail which has become very popular in certain quarters. As soon as one voices objections, some horribly well-groomed politician is sure to get up and say: This is all very well, but it is just talk. If you are so keen on foreign aid, or on the welfare of the poor, why not do something about it? Why not live up to your principles? Be consistent! If you happen to be a Christian, for example, the least one may ask for is that you go and spend the rest of your life in an African leper colony instead of sitting here and getting on our nerves. And if you don't like capitalism, why not go away and fight like Che Guevara?

This type of argument is not an argument at all; it is an echo of the voice that can be heard on the streets whenever a potential suicide is crouching high on the windowsill of an office building. It is a mob shouting: What are you waiting for? Why don't you jump? In Germany there was once a most courteous gentleman by the name of Adorno who had an answer to this cry. He said: "The ability to distinguish between theory and practice is a great achievement of civilization."

Now, given the confusing state of affairs I have been describing, I should like to point out some of the advantages and even joys of inconsistency. I do not claim that inconsistency, in itself, is a virtue. There is something neutral and rather unassuming about it, and I daresay that it can be abused. I am not advocating incoherent babble, and I rather like rational discourse. Besides, the case of inconsistency cannot be made consistently without inviting a logical conundrum.

Instead, I would suggest that we owe our lives to vacillation, indecision, and unprincipled action. You would not now be in a position to mind what I am saying, or agree with it, if it were not for the late Mr. Khrushchev, who behaved, as we all know, like a disgraceful opportunist in 1962. Did he not back out with his rockets? Wasn't he simply yellow, as they say? Did he not throw overboard the most sacrosanct principles of Marxism–Leninism? And no one in the whole Kremlin had the guts to stand up and say that selling out to imperialism is bad. No, all those old militants just had one thing on their minds; they wanted to save their own skins, and in the process they happened to save our skins as well. Consistency would have dictated quite a different course of action. It generally does. Let me mention just a few examples:

> Take any economic doctrine whatsoever, apply it, proceed logically with your project, and you will eventually destroy the very economy you had set out to save.
>
> Act out the fundamental tenets of capitalism to their ultimate

> consequences, and you will end up with a state of civil war and/or a Fascist dictatorship.
>
> Attack the social system you live in by any means at your disposal, and you have terrorism; defend it by any means, and you have a Gestapo running the place.
>
> Be a rigorous ecologist and defend nature against man with no holds barred, and you will end up leading a Stone Age existence.
>
> Build communism, be uncompromising about it, and your militancy will take you straight into what is rightly known as the socialist camp.
>
> Pursue economic growth at any price and you will destroy the biosphere.
>
> Join the arms race, be consistent about it, and you will blow yourself to pieces.
>
> Et cetera.

In this sort of situation, which has become quite frequent, principle isn't what it used to be. For those who are still looking around for a maxim to follow, I would suggest this: Consistency will turn any good cause into a bad one. It is a luxury we can no longer afford. For philosophers who are interested in keeping their thinking as straight as possible, this must be an unwelcome thought, but for people at large it will not come as a surprise. In our parts of the world, a vast if not vociferous majority of citizens has come to realize, I believe, that their only chance of survival is based not on one or two Big Ideas but on a constantly changing set of marginal options. They are quite prepared to face a lengthy and contradictory process of muddling through, of trial and error. Even in Germany, a society traditionally much given to principles, the last decades have seen a deep change in attitude. Social scientists have taken little note of this process, perhaps because they prefer to deal in Big Ideals or in statistical data. Nations as diverse as the Greeks and the Japanese, the Swedes and the Venezuelans, indeed most of the peoples who are given a chance to choose, will opt for the blessings of a more or less social democracy—not, I think, because of any deep-seated ideological conviction or loyalty, but because they feel instinctively that a sort of halfway house has become their only alternative to barbarism and self-destruction.

And now a word about ourselves.* I hope you do not mind my using the first person of the plural form. Let us avoid categories such as "the intelligentsia," or even worse, "the cultural workers," and just think of ourselves as a set of people who make a living by coming up, every now and then, with a new idea, a new image or a new shape. It is easy to see why the end of consistency is not something we would relish. The state of affairs I have tried to sketch goes against the grain of our most cherished habits. One of our main satisfactions in life has always been our ability to carry our ideas to extremes. Ever since we have existed as a social group—that is, for at least two centuries—we have been gainfully employed in going too far. Historically, the winner among us has always been the fellow who went further than anybody else. Never has this game been played with greater fervor than in the first half of the twentieth century. In the heroic age of modernism, the logic of consistency was extremely powerful; the whole prestige of the avant-garde depends on its single-minded courage, on its determination to follow an ideological or aesthetic theorem to its very end.

*Enzensberger originally delivered this paper as a lecture at New York University.

It is true that not much blood was shed in the process. The radicalism of the Euro-American avant-garde did not lead to massacres. At worst it led to a certain amount of intolerance, sterility, and dreariness. Thus we can afford to look back without anger to those days. There is even something touching about those black squares on the walls of museums and galleries, and about the critics who saw in them the culmination of art history. Some of us still remember the times when poets who filled a whole book with lower-case "i"s and "e"s were considered the salt of the earth. Treaties were written on the "objective state of composition," as applied to the man who gave a one-hour talk "On Nothing," in front of breathless audiences.

All these games, however, were innocent only as long as they were practised as an indoor sport. When architects started to write manifestos demanding that our cities be scrapped, this gave rise to shrill debates that must have been great fun. When they turned out to be consistent enough to reduce our living space to piles of white cubes, this had rather dire consequences, especially for the unfortunate people who were doomed to live and work in the ensuing concrete dreams. And wherever advanced political theories were consistently applied, things took a decidedly tragic turn.

In the late 1950s, the Political Science department of the University of Paris had become a very cosmopolitan place. All sorts of things were being taught: the political economy of underdeveloped nations; the importance of central planning; the modernization of traditional tribal societies; the dynamics of anticolonialist revolutions. . . . It is therefore not surprising that the lectures and seminars of the faculty were largely frequented by a motley crowd of students from the former French colonial empire, from Vietnam and Morocco, from Madagascar and Somalia, from Algeria and Guyana.

Some of the more radical teachers had come to the conclusion that liberation movements in the poorest parts of the world would have to undo the structure of the colonial societies inherited from the age of imperialism, if they wanted to put an end to the endemic misery of their countries. It was no good, they said, to do away with foreign domination and to take power if existing social structures were left untouched. The radical solution they advocated had three major aspects.

First of all, the relationship between town and country had to be reversed. The urbanization of the poor countries introduced by the colonial powers was disastrous. The parasitic cities siphoned off the productivity of the land. Industrialization would require a huge amount of foreign capital, and it would inevitably favor the local bourgeoisie. It should therefore be postponed. Absolute priority should be given to agriculture.

Second, a poor country must take care not to be integrated into the world market. Terms of trade would inevitably follow the pattern of international capitalism and perpetuate its domination. Isolation for a considerable length of time was the only solution. Economic self-sufficiency must be the goal. A subsistence economy would bring initial hardship for the more privileged part of the population, but it would permit antarchy and thus, in the long run, put an end to exploitation from abroad.

Lastly, it was necessary to protect the underdeveloped countries from the baneful cultural influence of the West. It was held that the educated elites in postcolonial nations posed a threat to independence because they clung to the ideas and values of the metropolis. Merchants and functionaries, teachers and doctors were especially dangerous elements, since they had adopted Western ways in their formative years and would infest the whole nation with their thoughts and their lifestyles. This corrupting influence would have to be ended, and the bourgeoisie would have to be liquidated as a social class.

This program, which was advocated by teachers from North Africa and Asia, and was influenced by the Algerian war and by Maoism, is remarkable for a number of reasons. One of its more baffling aspects is the fact that it is curiously self-referential. Quite clearly, its proponents belonged to the educated elite in their own countries; they had spent their formative years in European schools, and their ideas are in great part derived from Western traditions. It would thus seem that they were, in terms of their own theory, at least as much part of the problem as they may have been part of any future solution. Granted that their ideas were based on the experiences of several poor countries, the empirical data they could draw upon still did not make any sense unless it was interpreted. And for this interpretation they depended on principles they took over from European thought. Being progressive people, they did not avail themselves of the obscure dogmas and the ideological patent medicines the West has produced in great abundance; they did not pick up political messages such as racism, chauvinism and anti-Semitism, which are very much part of our heritage. No, they took the very best we had to offer; the basic tenets of the French Revolution, the teachings of the Enlightenment, the idea that it was both necessary and possible to abolish the extremes of injustice, oppression, and exploitation.

Among the students attending those courses were quite a few who came from Southeast Asia. One of them was called Kieu Samphan, another Jeng Sary, and a third one Saloth

Sar, better known by his *nom de guerre* of Pol Pot. They all graduated with honors, packed up their notebooks, and went home. Fifteen years later they started to put into practice what their professors had taught them. They were very earnest, very devoted; their consistency cannot be doubted. The results are known to everybody who reads newspapers or who owns a television set, and the only open question by now is whether the Khmer Rouge's experiment has claimed half a million or two and a half million lives. I try in vain to imagine what their teachers feel when they happen to think of their former pupils.

Mind you, I am not saying that it is a crime to follow a line of thought, *any* line of thought, to its ultimate logical conclusion. We are all extremely curious people who cannot bear to leave unthought anything that is thinkable, and we dearly wish to know where our latest hypothesis might take us. That, after all, is part of our work. Neither is there anything shameful about the fact that most of our trains of thought will sooner or later take us to a dead end. In a finite world, this is only to be expected. And if some of us feel like spending a lifetime in our respective blind alleys, this may seem a boring exercise, but, as long as it remains purely a matter of theory, I do not see why we should object to it. The little parable I have just told goes to show, however, that some people are unable or unwilling to draw a line between theory and practice. They are so desperately consistent that they don't know a dead end when they see one. The fact that there is no way ahead inspires them to an ever more frenzied activity. The result, as we have seen, may well be murderous.

It must be said that there is a much simpler and less violent way out of a blind alley. Once you are sure that you have reached the end, and with a bit of foresight you can find out well in advance, you can turn around and try another route. The trouble is that people who have been nurtured on principles often feel that such a course of action spells defeat or even betrayal. Many of them have reached positions of great power. I am thinking of Mr. Castro, Mr. Begin, Mrs. Thatcher and Mr. Khomeini, to name just a few. In their respective dead ends, they hang on to their anachronistic dreams—terrifying remnants of those heroic days when a person could still imagine himself to have been in the right, just because history was on his side, and because the baddies were against him. In other words, by being sufficiently principled, and militant, and brave, a person could become, as it were, infallible.

Some of us may deplore the passing of the Age of Consistency. They might find some consolation in military science. The classic teachers of strategy have always held that there is no greater feat in warfare than orderly retreat from an untenable position. Only a fool bent on self-destruction will call such a move an act of cowardice. I would rather go along with Paul Feyerabend when he says: "Stamping out opportunism will not make us better men; it will just make us more stupid. What we ought to get rid of is rather, our tendency to dream up, in our egotistical way, some sort of 'good' or 'rational' or 'responsible' life, which we then try to force down other people's throats in the guise of objective values."

Inconsistency is not the answer to our predicament, but it has its advantages and its attractions. It cannot be preached. It increases our freedom of thought and our freedom of movement. It is good for our imagination. It is fraught with intellectual risks. It also takes a lot of training, but, if you put your mind to it, you may end up not only being less afraid, but even less afraid of being afraid. Inconsistency might even provide a much-needed dose of irony and a measure of gaiety in the face of the prevailing mood of depression. We can never know what we have at the back of our minds, but most likely it is more than our principles allow for, and more than consistency will tolerate. Alas, the end of ideology is not in sight, and its monotonous noise seems to go on forever. Amidst all the static and the clutter, the anachronism and the propaganda, nothing could be more tempting, and, perhaps more helpful, than the forbidden fruit of our brains.

Let me now jump to my conclusion, which may turn out to be quite different from yours. A tirade against consistency, however timely, may well bring comfort to the scatter-brained. Immersed as we are in the daily mush of the media, half-dazed by the relentless passage of trends and styles and quirks and fashions, exposed to the most banal and most routine sort of amnesia, an apology for the jellied mind is hardly what we need. To defend the charms of inconsistency is to ask for trouble. Misunderstanding being an essential mode of communication, some of you must have concluded that I have been making a plea on behalf of the Man without a Memory. I would therefore like to conclude with a tale in praise of obstinacy. Obstinacy, you see, is not a matter of principle. It does not need an ideological framework, and it does not offer justifications. The obstinate man is a modest animal, devoid of missionary ambition. He does not actually depend on a theory, and his deeds cannot be said to be derived from abstract postulates. His thoughts do not show up in opinion polls, and the technicians of political control will have a hard time making him out. He is also very difficult to organize. In short, he is a dangerous animal and, needless to say, there is no guarantee, there is only a possibility, that he will do some good. "You go on talking as long as you like," the obstinate man will say. "I know what I want, and I'll keep my thoughts to myself." Then, when he walks out of the door, he will drop a cryptic phrase. He will say: "There is no other way."

Take the inconspicuous man, for example, who is boarding the express train from Munich to Constance—for, although we can do without idols, we still need examples. Just look at him sitting across the aisle, in the smokers' compartment: a quiet, friendly fellow looking out at the dim November afternoon. It gets dark early at this time of year. He has gray eyes, he is in his mid-thirties, his clothes are old but neat, he looks like a craftsman, you can tell by his deft and slender hands. A mechanic probably, or a joiner. In his spare time he will go to his club and play the guitar or the accordion, and if he has some money left he will spend an evening at the small-town dance hall by the river. No, he does not read newspapers. Every now and then he will go to church on a rainy Sunday, but he does not really care deeply about religion, and neither is he very much interested in politics.

Finally, the train arrives in Constance. He gets off and walks alongside the lake. He obviously knows his way, but he does not seem to be in a hurry. There's an old suburb with overgrown gardens and warehouses. It is now a quarter to nine. In a minute or two, he will have reached the Swiss border. Two officers from the nearby customs post walk up and ask him for his papers. He produces his passport. It turns out that the document has expired a few weeks before, and so they ask him to empty his pockets. No contraband is found, but there are a few shreds of paper in his pocket, and old badge issued by the Red Front Militia ("It is just a memento," he will explain later); some bolts and screws and springs, and finally there is a picture postcard showing the interior of a Munich beer cellar called the Bürgerbräu. The customs men don't quite know what to do with him. In the end they ask him to come along for a routine check.

While he is sitting down on a bench in the office hut—the wall calendar shows the date 8 November 1939, and it is now exactly 9:10 P.M.—a bomb explodes in Munich, three minutes after Adolf Hitler has left, earlier than planned, the beer cellar where the big Nazi November rally had been held. George Elser had spent four months making the bomb before planting it in a pillar of the Bürgerbräu vaults.

Elser, born on 4 January 1903 in Hermaringen, and murdered in Dachau concentration camp on 9 April 1945, Hitler's most dangerous enemy, did not belong to any organized group, nor did he act on the orders of any party. In planning, preparing, and carrying out his attempt to kill Hitler, he was entirely on his own. There is no trace of his story in the textbooks used in German schools. In the scholarly works of German historians, Elser figures in a footnote if he is mentioned at all.

Experts will tell you we are living in a society made up of manipulated zombies, and that there are now entire generations suffering from anomie, narcissism, and loss of self. They may well have a point. But I think that obstinate man is still very much with us, just as he was forty or four hundred years ago. You will meet him at the next street corner if you look out for him. He has no specific sociological location. Obstinacy is not a privilege of the intellectuals, quite the contrary. I believe that it will never disappear, but I cannot offer any proof for this contention. I cannot explain where people like Elser come from, what makes them tick, or what may be the source of their determination. Like most of the things worth bearing in mind, it remains an open question.

1981

2) TWO NOTES ON THE END OF THE WORLD

I

THE APOCALYPSE is part of our ideological baggage. It is an aphrodisiac. It is a nightmare. It is a commodity like any other. You can call it a metaphor for the collapse of capitalism, which as we all know has been imminent for more than a century. We come up against it in the most varied shapes and guises: as warning finger and scientific forecast, as collective fiction and sectarian rallying cry, as product of the leisure industry, as superstition, as vulgar mythology, as a riddle, a kick, a joke, a projection. It is ever present, but never "actual": a second reality, an image that we construct for ourselves, an incessant product of our fantasy, the catastrophe in the mind.

All this it is and more, as one of the oldest ideas of the human species. Thick volumes could have been written on its origins, and of course such volumes actually have been written. We know likewise all manner of things about its checkered history, about its periodic ebb and flow, and the way these fluctuations connect with the material process of history. The idea of the apocalypse has accompanied utopian thought since its first beginning, pursuing it like a shadow, like a reverse side that cannot be left behind: without catastrophe no millennium, without apocalypse no paradise. The idea of the end of the world is simply a negative utopia.

But even the end of the world is no longer what it used to be. The film playing in our heads, and still more uninhibitedly in our unconscious, is distinct in many respects from the dreams of old. In its traditional coinings, the apocalypse was a venerable, indeed a sacred, idea. But the catastrophe we are so concerned with (or rather haunted by) is an entirely secularized phenomenon. We read its signs on the walls of buildings, where they appear overnight, clumsily sprayed; we read them on the printouts spewed forth by the computer. Our seven-headed monster answers to many names: police state, paranoia, bureaucracy, terror, economic crisis, arms race, destruction of the environment. Its four riders look like the heroes of Westerns and sell cigarettes, while the trumpets that proclaim the end of the world serve as theme music for a commercial break. Once people saw in the apocalypse the unknowable avenging hand of God. Today it appears as the methodically calculated product of our own actions, and the spirits whom we hold responsible for our own actions, and the spirits whom we hold responsible for its approach we call reds, oil sheikhs, terrorists, multinationals; the gnomes of Zürich and the Frankensteins of the biology labs; UFOs and neutron bombs; demons from the Kremlin or the Pentagon: an underworld of unimaginable conspiracies and machinations, whose strings are pulled by the all-powerful cretins of the secret police.

The apocalypse was also once a singular event, to be expected unannounced as a bolt from the blue: an unthinkable moment that only seers and prophets could anticipate—and, of course, no one wanted to listen to their warnings and predictions. Our end of the world, on the other hand, is sung from the rooftops even by the sparrow; the element of surprise is missing; it seems only to be a question of time. The doom we picture for ourselves is insidious and torturingly slow in its approach, the apocalypse in slow motion. It is reminiscent of that hoary avant-garde classic of the silent cinema, in which we see a gigantic factory chimney crack up and collapse noiselessly on the screen, for a full twenty minutes, while the spectators, in a kind of indolent comfort, lean back in their threadbare velvet seats and nibble their popcorn and peanuts. After the performance, the futurologist mounts the stage. He looks like a poor imitation of Dr. Strangelove, the mad scientist, only he is repulsively fat. Quite calmly he informs us that the atmospheric ozone layer will have disappeared in twenty years' time, so that we shall surely be toasted by cosmic radiation if we are lucky enough to survive then; unknown substances in our milk are driving us to psychosis; and with the rate at which world population is growing, it will soon be standing room only on our planet. All this with Havana cigar in hand, in a well-composed speech of impeccable logic. The audience suppresses a yawn, even though, according to the professor, the disaster looms imminently ahead. But it's not going to come this afternoon. This afternoon, everything will go on just as before, perhaps a little bit worse than last week, but not so that anyone would notice. If one or another of us should be a little depressed this afternoon, which cannot of course be ruled out, then the thought might strike him, irrespective of whether he works in the Pentagon or the underground, irons shirts or welds sheet metal, that it would really be simpler if we were rid of the problem once and for all; if the catastrophe really did *come*. However, this is out of the question. Finality, which was formerly one of the major attributes of the apocalypse, and one of the reasons for its power of attraction, is no longer vouchsafed us.

We have also lost another traditional aspect of the end of the world. Previously, it was generally agreed that the event would affect everyone simultaneously and without exception: the never-satisfied demand for equality and justice found in this conception its last refuge. But as we see it today, doom is no longer a leveler; quite the opposite. It differs from country to country, from class to class, from place to place. While it is already overtaking some, others can watch it on television. Bunkers are built, ghettos walled in, fortresses erected, bodyguards hired, on a large scale as well as a small scale. Corresponding to the country house with burglar alarms and electric fences, we have whole countries, on the international scale, that fence themselves in while others go to ruin. The nightmare of the end of the world does not end this temporal disparity; it simply radicalizes it. Its African and Indian versions are overlooked with a shrug of the shoulders by those not directly affected—including the African and Indian governments. At this point, finally, the joke comes to an end.

II

Berlin, Spring 1978

Dear Balthasar,

When I wrote my comment on the apocalypse—a work that I confess was not particularly thorough or serious—I was still unaware that you were also concerned with the future. You complained to me on the telephone that you were "not really getting anywhere." That sounded almost like an appeal for help. I know you well enough to understand your dilemma. Today it is only the technocrats who are advancing toward the year two thousand full of optimism, with the unerring instinct of lemmings, and you are not one of their number. On the contrary, you are a faithful soul, always ready to assemble under the banner of utopia. You want as much as ever to hold fast to the principle of hope, for you wish us well: i.e., not only you and me, but humanity as a whole.

Please don't be angry if this sounds ironic. That isn't my fault. You would have liked to see me come rushing to your aid. My letter will be disappointing for you, and perhaps you even feel that I am attacking you from behind. That isn't my intention. All I would like to suggest is that we consider things with the cuffs off.

The strength of left-wing theory of whatever stamp, from Babeuf through to Ernst Bloch, i.e., for more than a century and a half, lay in the fact that it based itself on a positive utopia that had no peer in the existing world. Socialists, Communists, and anarchists all shared the conviction that their struggle would introduce the realm of freedom in a foreseeable period of time. They "knew just where they wanted to go and just what, with the help of history, strategy and effort, they ought or needed to do to get there. Now, they no longer do." I read these lapidary words recently in an article by the English historian Eric Hobsbawm. But this old communist does not forget to add that "In this respect, they do not stand alone. Capitalists are just as much at a loss as socialists to understand their future, and just as puzzled by the failure of their theories and prophets."

Hobsbawm is quite correct. The ideological deficit exists on both sides. Yet the loss of certainty about the future does not balance out. It is harder to bear for the Left than for those who never had any other intention but to hand on at any price to some snippet of their own power and privileges. This is why the Left, including you, dear Balthasar, go in for grumbling and complaining.

No one is ready any more, you say, or in a position either,

to put forward a positive idea that goes beyond the horizon of the existing state of affairs. Instead of this, false consciousness is rampant; the stage is dominated by apostasy and confusion. I remember our last conversation about the "new irrationalism," your lamenting over the resignation that you sense on all sides, and your tirades against the flippant doomsters, shameless pessimists, and apostles of defeatism. I shall be careful not to contradict you here. But I wonder whether one thing has not escaped you in all this: the fact that in these expressions and moods there is precisely what you were looking for—an idea that goes beyond the limits of our present existence. For, in the last analysis, the world has certainly not come to an end (or else we could not talk about it); and so far no conclusive proof has reached me that an event of this kind is going to take place at any clearly ascertainable point in time. The conclusion I draw from this is that we are dealing here with a utopia, even if a negative one; and I further maintain that, for the historical reasons I mentioned, left-wing theory is not particularly well equipped to deal with this kind of utopia.

Your reactions are only further evidence for my assumption. The first stanza of your song, in which you bewail the prevailing intellectual situation, is promptly followed by the second, in which you enumerate the scapegoats. For such an old hand at theory as yourself, it is not difficult to lay hands on the guilty parties: the ideological opponent, the agents of anticommunism, the manipulation of the mass media. Your arguments are in no way new to me. They remind me of an essay that came to my attention a few years back. The author, an American Marxist by the name of H. C. Greisman, came to the conclusion that "the images of decline of which the media are so fond are designed to hypnotize and stupefy the masses in such a way that they come to see any hope of revolution as meaningless."

What is striking in this proposition is, above all, its essential defensiveness. For a hundred years or so, as long as it was sure of its ground, classical Marxist theory argued the very opposite. It did not see the images of catastrophe and visions of doom of the time simply as lies concocted by some secret seducers and spread among the people, but sought, rather, to explain them in social terms, as symbolic depictions of a thoroughly real process. In the 1920s, to take just one example, the Left saw the attraction that Spengler's historical metaphysics had for the bourgeois intelligentsia in precisely this way: *The Decline of the West* was in reality nothing more than the imminent collapse of capitalism.

Today, on the other hand, someone like yourself no longer feels his views confirmed by the apocalyptic fantasy, but instead feels threatened, reacting with last-ditch slogans and defensive gestures. To be quite frank, dear Balthasar, it seems to me that the result of these obeisances is rather wretched. I don't mean by this that it is simply false. You do not, of course, fail to resort to the well-tried path of ideological criticism. And it is child's play to show that the rise and fall of utopian and apocalyptic moods in history correspond to the political, social, and economic conditions of the time. It is also uncontestable that they are exploited politically, just like any other fantasy that exists on a mass scale. You need not imagine you have to teach me the ABCs. I know as well as you that the fantasy of doom always suggests the desire for miraculous salvation; and it is clear to me, too, that the Bonapartist savior is always waiting in the wings, in the form of military dictatorship and right-wing putsch. When it is a question of survival, there have always been people all too ready to place their trust in a strong man. Nor do I find it surprising that those who have called for one more or less expressly, in the last few years, should include both a liberal and a Stalinist: the American sociologist Heilbroner and the German philosopher Harich. It is also beyond doubt that the apocalyptic metaphor promises relief from analytical thought, as it tends to throw everything together in the same pot. From the Middle East conflict to a postal strike, from punk style to a nuclear-reactor disaster, anything and everything is conceived as a hidden sign of an imaginary totality: catastrophe "in general." The tendency to hasty generalization damages that residual power of clear thought that we still have left. In this sense, the feeling of doom does in fact lead only to mystification. It goes without saying that the new irrationalism that so troubles you can in no way solve the real problems. On the contrary, it makes them appear insoluble.

This is all very easy to say, but it does not help matters all that much. You try and fight the fantasies of destruction with quotations from the classics. But these rhetorical victories, dear Balthasar, remind me of the heroic feats of Baron von Münchhausen. Like him, you want to reach your goal lone and unafraid; and to avoid departing from the correct straight line, you too are ready in case of need to leap onto a cannonball.

But the future is not a sports ground for hussars, nor is ideological criticism a cannonball. You should leave it to the futurologists to imitate the boastings of an old tin soldier. The future that you have in mind is in no way an object of science. It is something that exists only in the medium of social fantasy, and the organ by which it is chiefly experienced is the unconscious. Hence the power of these images that we all produce, day and night: not only with the head, but with the whole body. Our collective dreams of fear and desire weigh at least as heavy, probably heavier, than our theories and analyses.

The really threadbare character of customary ideological criticism is that it ignores all this and wants to know nothing of it. Has it not struck you that it has long since ceased to explain things that do not fit our schemas, and started to taboo them instead? Without our having properly noticed, it has taken on the role of watchdog. Alongside the state censorship of the law-and-order people there are now ranged the mental-hospital orderlies of the Left in the social and human sciences, who would like to pacify us with their tranquilizers. Their maxims are: 1. Never concede anything. 2. Reduce the unfamiliar to the familiar. 3. Always think only with the head. 4. The unconscious must do what it is told.

The arrogance of these academic exorcists is surpassed only by their impotence. They fail to understand that myths cannot be refuted by seminar papers, and that their bans on ideas have a very short reach. What help is it to them, for example, and what use to us, if for the hundredth time they declare any comparison between natural and social processes inadmissible and reactionary? The elementary power of fantasy teaches millions of people to break this ban constantly. Our ideologists only raise a smile when they attempt to obliterate such ineffaceable images as flood and fire, earthquake and hurricane. Moreover, there are people in the ranks of natural scientists who are in a position to elaborate fantasies of this kind in their own fashion and make them productive instead of banning them: mathematicians drafting a topographical theory of catastrophe, or biochemists who have ideas about certain analogies between biological and social evolution. We are still waiting in vain for the sociologist who will understand that, in a sense that is still to be decoded, there is no longer any such thing as a purely natural catastrophe.

Instead of this, our theorists, chained to the philosophical traditions of German idealism, refuse to admit even today what every bystander has long since grasped: that there is no world spirit; that we do not know the laws of history; that even the class struggle is an "indigenous" process, which no vanguard can consciously plan and lead; that social evolution, like natural evolution, has no subject and is therefore unpredictable; that consequently, when we act politically, we never manage to achieve what we had in mind, but, rather, something quite different, which at one time we could not even have imagined; and that the crisis of all positive utopias has its basis precisely in this fact. The projects of the nineteenth century have been discredited completely and without exception by the history of the twentieth century. In the essay I already mentioned, Eric Hobsbawm recalls a congress held by the Spanish anarchists in 1898. They sketched a glorious picture of life after the victory of the revolution: a world of tall shining buildings with elevators that would save climbing stairs, electric light for all, garbage disposers, and marvelous household gadgets. . . . This vision of humanity, presented with messianic pathos, now looks strikingly familiar: in many parts of our cities it has already become reality. There are victories that are hard to distinguish from defeats. No one feels comfortable in recalling the promise of the October revolution sixty years ago: once the capitalists were driven out of Russia, a bright future without exploitation and oppression would dawn for the workers and peasants. . . .

Are you still with me, Balthasar? Are you still listening? I am nearing the end of my letter. Forgive me if it has gotten rather long, and if my sentences have taken on a mocking undertone. It's not me who injected this; it's a kind of objective, historic mockery, and the laugh, for better or worse, is always on the losing side. We all have to bear it together.

Optimism and pessimism, my dear friend, are so much sticking plaster for fortune-tellers and the writers of leading articles. The pictures of the future that humanity draws for itself, both positive and negative utopias, have never been unambiguous. The idea of the millennium, the City of the Sun, was not the pallid dream of a land of milk and honey; it always had its elements of fear, panic, terror, and destruction. And the apocalyptic fantasy, conversely, produces more than just pictures of decadence and despair; it also contains, inescapably bound up with the terror, the demand for vengeance, for justice, impulses of relief and hope.

The pharisees, those who always know best, want to convince us that the world would be all right again if the "progressive forces" took a strong line with people's fantasies; if they themselves were only sitting on the Central Committee, and pictures of doom could be prohibited by decree of the party. They refuse to understand that it is we ourselves who produce these pictures, and that we hold on to them because they correspond to our experiences, desires, and fears: on the motorway between Frankfurt and Bonn, in front of the TV screen that shows we are at war, beneath helicopters, in the corridors of clinics, employment offices, and prisons—because, in a single word, they are in this sense realistic.

I scarcely need reassure you, dear Balthasar, that I know as little of the future as you do yourself. I am writing to you because I do not count you among the pigeonholers and ticketpunchers of the world spirit. What I wish you, as I wish myself and us all, is a little more clarity about our own confusion, a little less fear of our own fear, and a little more attentiveness, respect, and modesty in the face of the unknown. Then we shall be able to see a little future.

Yours, H. M. E.

1978

3) THE PASTRY DOUGH OF TIME

A Meditation on Anachronism

The world is nothing but an eternal see-saw. Everything in it see-saws incessantly. I am not describing an essence but a transition, an account of various and changeable chance occurrences, of undefined and even, as it happens, contradictory ideas. Not only does the wind of chance bluster me about, but I, in my turn, move and change direction. And anyone who pays close attention to his point of departure will note that he does not arrive at the same location twice.

—Michel de Montaigne

THE NOTION OF PROGRESS, as a singular process of eternal and inexorable perfection, has certainly seen better days. But we continue to speak of "advances" all the same, and they keep on burgeoning, as rampant as ever. Progress in this plural form has its devotees, and not only among the agents of the media and advertising. Among scientists, too, and economists, technicians, and physicians, progress enjoys an unsullied reputation. In countless little steps it advances ever more quickly in every direction, a process that no one dares control, let alone question seriously.

While the old political and artistic avant-gardes have abandoned the field, the technological fundamentalists, quite unmoved by the catastrophic experiences of the twentieth century, devote themselves without restraint to their visions of the future. Their wild-eyed optimism knows no bounds, not even those of self-preservation. Ultimately their visions are aimed not toward mankind's improvement but toward the destruction of humanity, in order to make way for products that they imagine to be far superior to all biological forms of life. This happy masochism is reminiscent of the time when the splitting of the atom seemed to open up the possibility of a bright future.

But the fundamentalists of the modern age are not the only occupants of the planet. Outside their stringent sects, there is a great deal of nervousness. There have always been laggards holding up the march of progress, but now even the more intelligent business leaders look forward to the promises of technical globalization with rather mixed feelings.

There is a very simple reason for this. With growing rapidity, the number of asynchronicities is also on the rise. Each day, progress leaves more stragglers behind in its race toward the future. It has long since left most people in the dust. But it is no longer a case—as it was in the age of the heroic Moderns—of a majority of perpetual slowpokes, who would like to deny some self-appointed "avant-garde" their following. Such tidy distinctions are no longer viable. Even the trendsetters get tangled in the most peculiar contradictions. The theorist in artificial intelligence moves into a rehabilitated old building. The weapons expert loves to go the opera. The deconstructionist suffers the pangs of love, and the microchip designer develops a weakness for the wisdom of Buddha. Of course, one could dismiss such inclinations as mere compensation, ripples on the surface. But that can be countered with the argument that these "remnants of the past" seem to proliferate just as uncontrollably as progress. The disowned past expresses itself, against our will and without consideration for our ideological preference, in a wealth of somatic, psychic, and cultural symptoms. That allows for only one conclusion: apparently the time has passed when one could believe in the possibility of an up-to-date life.

The much-vaunted postmodernism was just such a symptom, but it was not capable of grasping the deeper dynamic of asynchronicity. The very term "postmodernism" reveals its own dependence on successive thinking, in that scheme in which each epoch follows the last as if on a conveyor belt, only to make way for the next. The central dogma of modernism, enshrined in this shockingly simple image, has withstood all of the shocks and self-doubt of the century.

It is difficult to say how and when the idea of succession caught on in the philosophy of history. Perhaps the famous *querelle des anciens et des modernes* of 1687 provides a clue. What began as a struggle between the ancient and modern ages grew into a protracted battle between the inherited past and the revolutionary new, between tradition and the modern, and finally became a given. It has survived into the present as an either/or, first in cultural settings, and then in the political arena.

Obviously this was a temptingly persuasive model; because from that time forward, everyone could imagine that he faced a simple choice. He had only to pick one of the two sides—the *ancien régime* or the Revolution, origins or progress, the old Adam or the New Man, Right or Left—and then he would be equipped with something he could call a worldview or a firm position. Not only have entire intellectual movements worn themselves out with these oppositions, innumerable millions have paid for their choice with body and soul. Humanity imagined that it faced alternatives of heart-stirring simplicity. The world's incongruities were reduced to a binary system. There seemed to be two and only two options, and from now on one or the other would always lead the way.

When Saint Augustine puzzled, "What is time? If someone asks me, I know; if I have to explain it, I don't know," he asked a question for all philosophers. It is an endless meditation, in which astrophysicists and cosmologists have also begun to take part. As penetrating and complex as most of their theories are, they have not been able to join forces against the most commonplace of all conceptions of time, which takes everything that has happened, is happening, and will happen, and places it on a line, with the present functioning as a moveable point that cleanly separates the past from the future. One could almost envy this idea for its simplicity, which leads directly to such tautologies as "What's past is past." But anyone who embraces this concept of time is defeated immediately by the question of how memory is possible—this simultaneous conjunction of the past and present must be bewildering for such chronologists.

Anachronism, if one depends upon German dictionaries and encyclopedias, is a "violation of the passage of time, of chronology," the "incorrect temporal organization of ideas, things, or people." The English sources express this even more strikingly: "anything done or existing out of date, *hence*, anything which was proper to a former age, but is out of harmony with the present." The accusatory, if not denunciatory, undertone is unmistakable. Woe to the ignoramus who would dare violate the normal passage of time, who organizes his ideas incorrectly or perhaps even does or says something that is *out of date*, out of line with the present. This kind of thing presents an insufferable disturbance to contemporary harmony.

In these definitions, a modernist monomania is quite innocently elevated to objective law. For the person who thinks this way, the rule of the present has become so much a part of nature that he does not even notice it. He behaves as if he could not have a thought or undertake anything without first taking a look at the calendar in order to be sure of what is scheduled. But it is extremely questionable as to whether zombies of this type truly and physically exist. Since the air went out of the historic avant-garde, and not only in the political arena, disc jockeys, lifestyle magazines, and multimedia managers are probably the only ones left who take the time signal on the radio seriously.

The modern concept of time runs aground when confronted with the most obvious of data, so obvious that it is almost embarrassing to mention it. Our genetic code originated billions and billions of years ago; only a minimal part of it is derived from hominization (the evolutionary period in which humans emerged), and thus represents a relatively late development. Thus, our somatic and psychic equipment is invincibly ancient, to say nothing of what comprises our consciousness. We are composed of layers of time, reaching immeasurably far into the past. Our cultural evolution is just as complex, and in this area, too, the portion of newer elements is relatively small. The "violation of the passage of time," a violation called an exception by the discourse of modernism, is actually the rule. The present "new" only skims the thin surface layer of an opaque ocean of latent possibilities. Anachronism is no avoidable mistake, but a fundamental condition of human existence.

Take a square piece of pastry dough, fold it over, and stretch it so that it is only half as long but twice as wide. Then divide the rectangle in half and lay the right half over the left.

Now begin again from the beginning, stretch the dough a second time, cut it in two and piece the halves together again. This will produce a third square, just as large as the first. Only now it consists of four horizontal strips. Repeat this operation as often as you like.

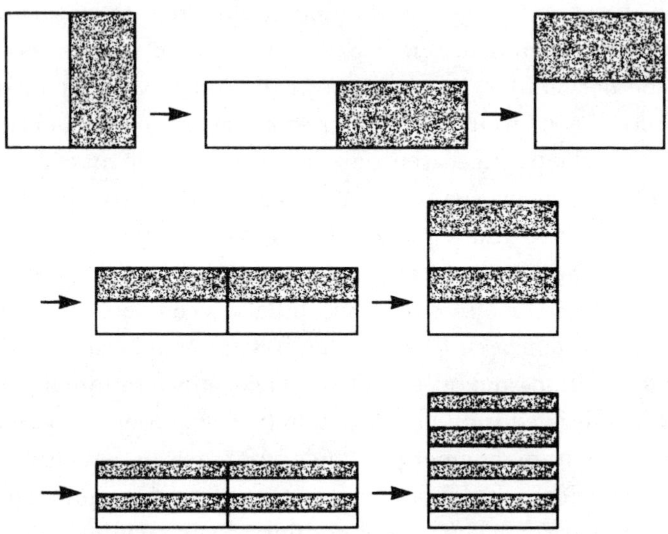

This process has a cute scientific name. It is called the "baker's transformation," and its product is a pastry dough of a particularly good quality.

With every fourth step the structure becomes more refined. After the tenth time the dough will have reached two to the power of ten layers, and after the twentieth we will have 1,048,576 unimaginably thin layers.

Naturally, any baker with an ounce of experience will object that it is impossible to bake a two-dimensional dough. This difficulty is easily set aside. One needs only exchange the square for a cube, and the thing could look like the following figure:

The topological characteristics of the transformation

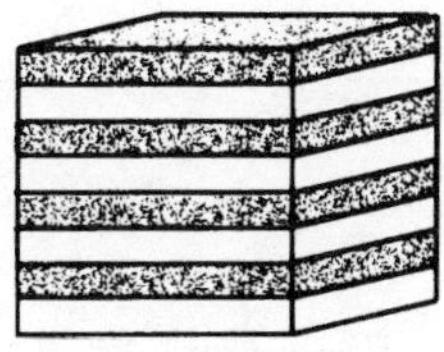

would be the same; it is possible in higher dimensions, as well. But for simplicity's sake, we can stick with a two-dimensional square.

What would happen if we were to apply this simple mathematical model to time or, more precisely and more modestly, to historical time? Just out of curiosity and, if you like, for entertainment, as an alternative to the linear model of time used in classical physics, let's do the experiment. The pastry dough structure exhibits a number of surprising characteristics that are not immediately apparent. How does any given point behave, when the pastry dough is subjected to the baker's transformation? This point A, let's say a granule of sugar or a raisin, wanders back and forth in a bizarre way, like this, for example:

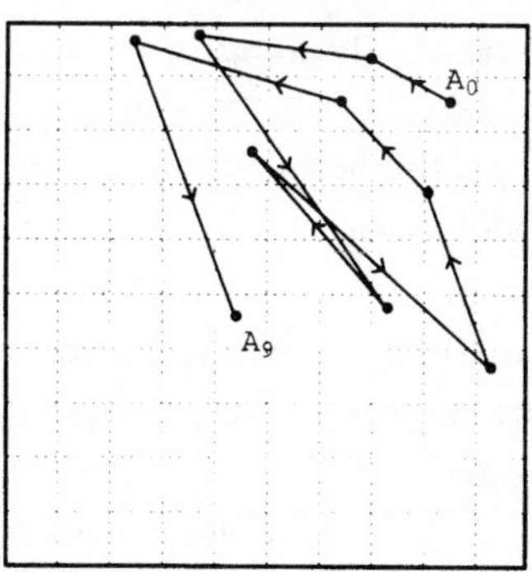

A_0 = (0,840675437/0,840675437)

A second point B starts out nearby, but quickly distances itself from A and blazes a completely different trail:

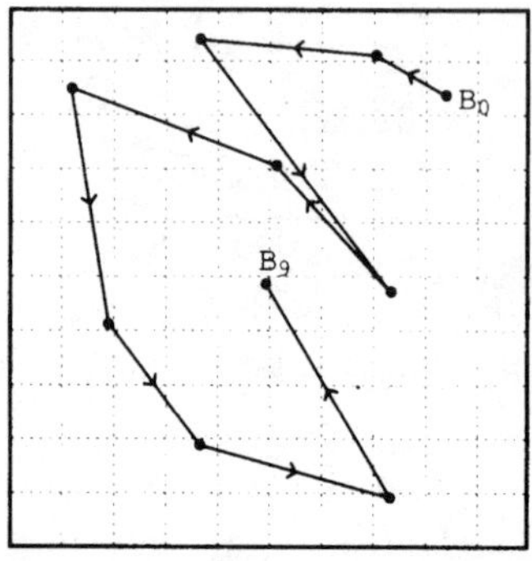

B_0 = (0,846704216/0,846704216)

These two trajectories seem accidental, though they were achieved through a strictly deterministic process. If we have all of the original data at our disposal, we can immediately calculate them.

But since we usually do not work in a binary, but rather in a decimal system, we can make it easier on ourselves if we do not divide the dough into two strips with each step, but ten, from which we can form the respective square each time.

Now if we specify the length of the side of the original square as 1, we can then define each of its points with two decimal fractions: the first of these coordinates indicates the distance from the y axis (the left edge), the second from the x axis (the bottom edge).

A simple trick now will allow us to put aside our pastry dough and simulate the leaps of the points A, B, C . . . with a pocket calculator.

This first point A_0 can be determined with the help of a random number generator: the random key gives us, for example, the values 719260839 and 061492. The corresponding decimal fraction then gives us the coordinates of A_0: 0.719260839 . . . and 0.061492 . . . It is child's play to use these figures to calculate the journeys undertaken by our chosen point A_0, through every step of the baker's transformation. To do it, we need only take the number from the first decimal place of the first figure and put this number into the first decimal place of the second value. In this way we get the next position of

A:	0.719260839 . . .	0.061492 . . .	(A_0
	0.19260839 . . .	0.7061492 . . .	(A_1)
	0.9260839 . . .	0.17061492 . . .	(A_2)
	0.260839 . . .	0.917061492 . . .	(A_3)
	0.60839 . . .	0.2917061492 . . .	(A_4)
	0.0839 . . .	0.6917061492	(A_5)
	0.839 . . .	0.062917061492 . . .	(A_6)
	0.39 . . .	0.8062917061492 . . .	(A_7)

(Mathematics named this trick the Bernoulli shift, after the famous Swiss mathematician who invented it). On the quadratic plane, the movement of A looks like this:

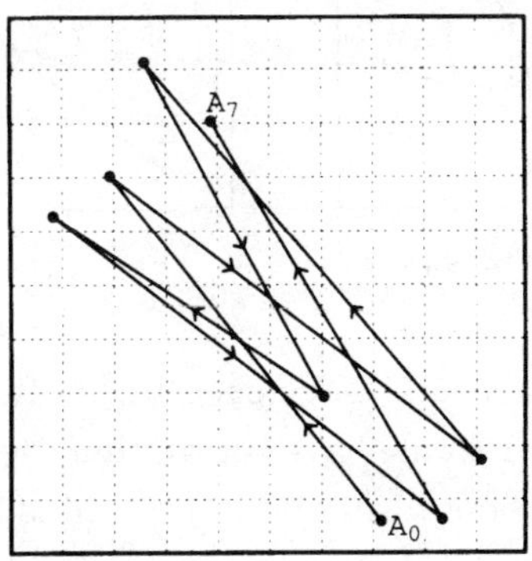

A_0 = (0,719260839/0,061492)

If one knows the origin coordinates with sufficient precision (whether it is a case of recurring fractions, or that the chance number has many decimal places after the decimal point), one can continue the game for as long as one wants, that is, one can predict how the points A, B, and C will continue to behave into the future. But what would it look like if one knew not both coordinates, but only one of them—if there were holes in the information at one's disposal? Then the path of the points seems arbitrary, as in the following examples, and chance takes the place of a calculable occurrence. It becomes impossible for the observer to predict how the individual points will hop back and forth across the plane. (This same paradox, by the way, appears in the operations of the random number generator, which gave us the original values; it too, works with a strictly defined program and nevertheless produces unpredictable values).

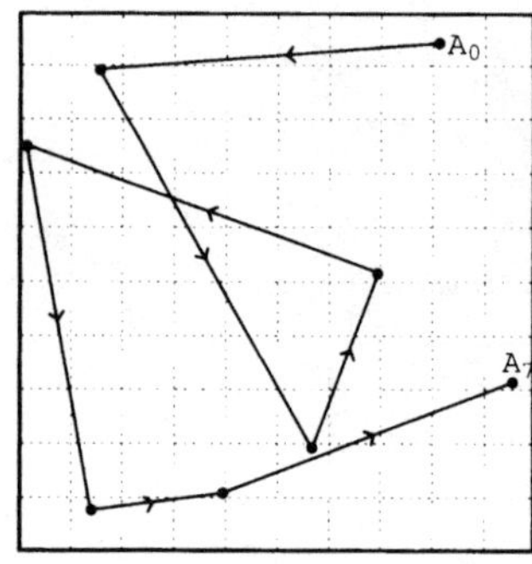

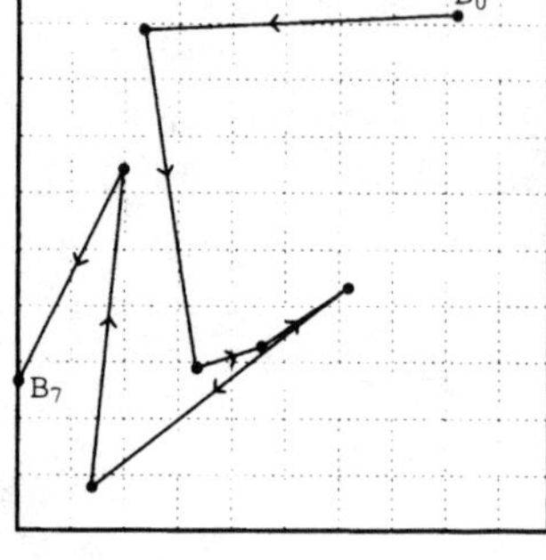

A_0 = (0,815701396/0,945341) B_0 = (0,823462001/0,920311)

Mathematicians such as George Birkhoff, Vladimir Arnold, and Stephen Smale have shown that the baker's transformation is no mere form of entertainment, but a method upon which many real processes can be modeled, such as theoretical astronomy, the physics of phasic transformations, the dynamics of currents, and quantum theory.

Perhaps it could also be used to explain the structure of historical time, its layers and folds, its irritating topology.

There, too, we are not able to derive the future from a linearly conceived past. We know from experience that we do not know the consequences of our actions beyond the next step. Extrapolation fails us. Futurology reads coffee grounds. Long-range market and stock forecasters make fools of themselves with their prophecies just as regularly as politicians.

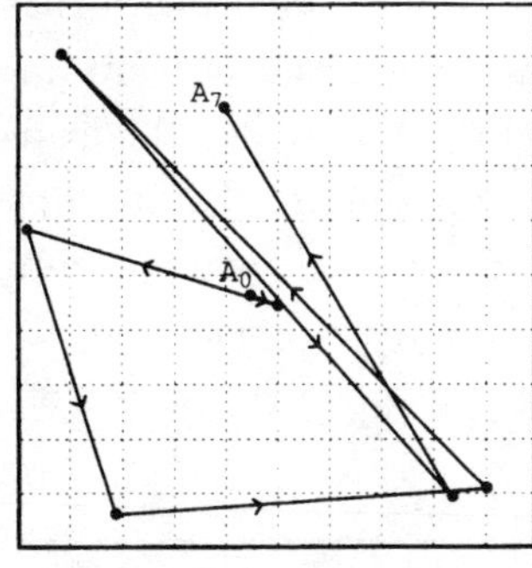

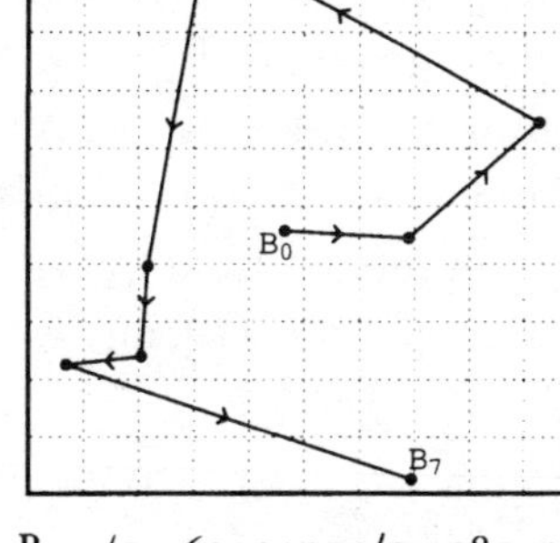

A_0 = (0,450190840/0,465071) B_0 = (0,469322070/0,458113)

Just as in physical situations, the impossibility of making dependable predictions does not negate the power of causality. Even the unforeseeable is determined; it is only that we never have a complete knowledge of all of the premises, not only because the past that comes down to us is inevitably incomplete, but because of principle.

Our contemporary, baptized in the waters of modernization, pulls out his hair. Someone is always disturbing the unison of the present, the goodwill of simultaneity. Entire societies behave obdurately. Rather than advancing along the only possible pathway for growth, many of them refuse to get on the train of time and follow the advice of the International Money Fund. Underdeveloped as they are, they do not want to admit that it is only a matter of time before they achieve the standards of the United States. On every continent there are stubborn minorities clinging to anachronistic ideas. In order to justify their claims, the incorrigibles refer to battles fought several centuries ago, and they gather hundreds of thousands of followers under medieval banners. No modern achievement is immune from being suddenly dissolved into nothing, there are regions of the world in which even the state as an organizing principle has disappeared. The last word has not been said on communism. The talk of a dustbin of history, into which the communists wanted to throw their opponents, has turned against them. Now they are the ones who are no longer running in the forefront but are hopelessly to the rear; and still one can not say with any certainty that this will continue to be so.

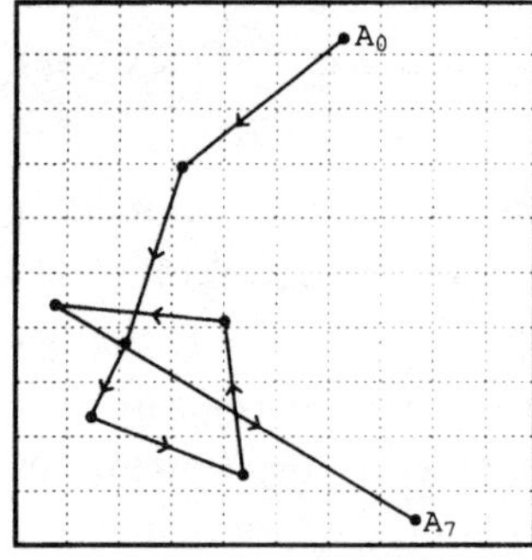

A_0 = (0,632144077/0,931948)

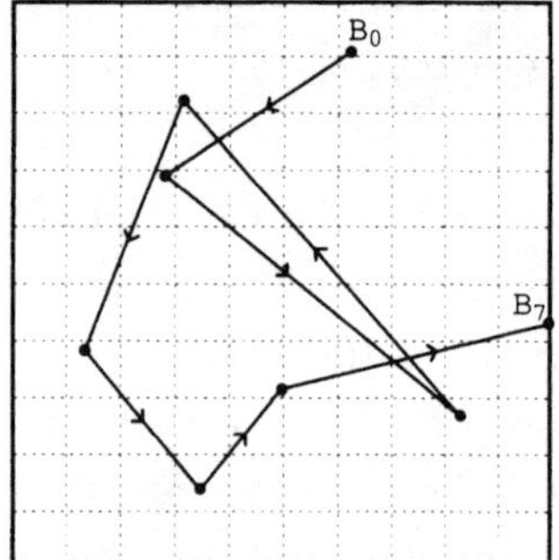

B_0 = (0,628313499/0,912880)

Yet even in the heart of the metropolis the defeat of the outdated does not appear to be fully successful. Superstition, long since unmasked and refuted, has risen again, as if there had never been an Enlightenment. All the things we had settled and disposed of, the great as well as the small, are celebrating their tangled comeback. Furniture that a short time ago would have landed in the dump is now showing up in expensive antique shops. Gregorian chants, which inspirited little more than a dismissive shrug of the shoulders scarcely twenty years ago, now have appeared on the music industry's hit charts. There is hardly a motif, no matter how distant and discredited, of which one can be certain that it will not at some point be presented at the costume ball of culture in the radiant array of sparkling novelty. In short, the "violation of the passage of time, of chronology" is no avoidable accident, but an inevitable fact.

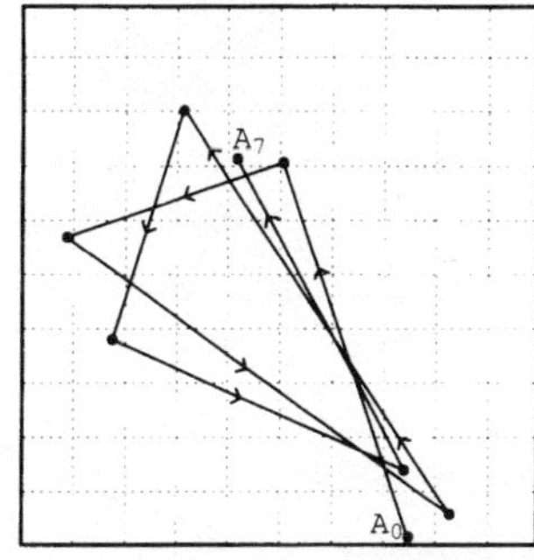

A_0 = (0,750831742/0,012542)

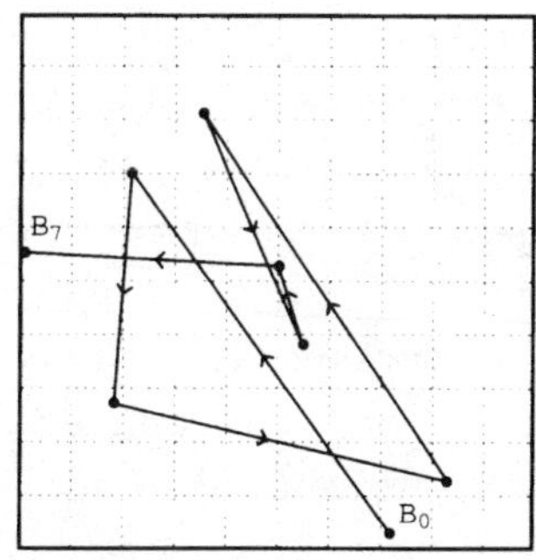

B_0 = (0,721835501/0,025431)

If one could imagine a structure of history besides the linear time of classical physics, it might be easier to grasp the leapfrogging of time. In our pastry dough, memory does not exist along a continuum; it is discrete. In the baker's transformation, the dough dissolves into an innumerable array of leaping points, which distance themselves from one another in unforeseeable ways, only to meet again, who knows how or when, or along what paths. In this way there is an inexhaustibly large number of contacts between different layers of time.

But because this is a dynamic system, there can never be

an identical repetition. The leaping point would only land exactly in the same place in the most unlikely case—instead, it will almost always, at least infinitesimally, diverge from its point of origin. Besides that, it will always land in a transformed context. Thus, the contact between different layers of time does not lead to a return of the same, but to an interplay that produces something new each time, something new for both sides. In this sense it is not only the future that is unforeseeable. The past, too, is subject to continuous change. In the eyes of an observer, who lacks an overview of the entire system, the past is perpetually transformed.

The person who finds this model illuminating will regard anachronism not as a source of irritation but as an essential aspect of a protean world; instead of denying anachronism, he will find it more rewarding to take account of it and, wherever possible, turn it to productive use. In any case, he will no longer be captive to the illusion that it only takes a mere effort of will to escape the folds in the structure of time.

It is because of time's complex layering that every day surprises us with good and evil, with unexpected advances and setbacks, and that all linear projects, whether progressive or conservative, are sooner or later simply sabotaged by history. Reactionaries of every description have failed to lead the world back to the conditions of some—more or less imaginary—golden age, and political, technical, and cultural revolutions have not been able to eradicate the potential that lies in the enormous pastry dough of time. This stubborn reality has been especially difficult for the engineers of the body and the soul, who can only grasp this reciprocal play of anachronisms as a dull resistance to their unambiguous visions. But it is not only the incurable, future-loving reformers who are fixed on linear thinking, but their opposites, who deal in prognoses on the other side of the looking glass.

The preachers of the apocalypse, too, believe in a perfectly predictable future, which allows for no zigzags or anachronism. Their pessimism is just as straight-ahead and unimaginative as the optimism that characterizes the adherents of irrepressible progress.

Yet what the reciprocity between the various layers of historical time actually looks like and what sort of transformation anachronism produces—these are questions that no formal model can answer. On questions of content, the Bernoulli shift is inadequate, and we must draw on experience.

There is no universal answer, but a collection of microscopic and macroscopic examples could perhaps give us an initial hint. Some of these cases are as well researched as they are controversial.

The most famous of all anachronisms is the Renaissance. Nobody knows exactly how to date it. Upon closer inspection, the concept unfolds into a plural. We speak of a proto-, early, high, and late Renaissance; some have even described a Carolingian Renaissance, and finally the term is applied to quite different situations, too.

At the same time, though, there is no doubt that there were people in Europe who, after centuries characterized by quite different interests, suddenly turned back to antiquity with a terrific energy, reading classical texts, studying their philosophy, imitating their architecture, in a word, connecting to a largely lost, "surpassed" tradition. That such a reciprocal moment took place is not doubted by even the most inveterate revisionists, who believe that *the* Renaissance is nothing more than a construct.

Later, every conceivable revivalist movement was given the name "Renaissance," often enough with reference to national traditions, as in the case of the "Irish Renaissance" or the "Catalan Renaissance." In each of these, the "passage of time" is "violated" without a second thought.

While rebirth enjoys primarily a good reputation, atavism is considered a particularly despicable departure from the orderly progression of history. This term, coined by the botanist Hugo de Vries in 1901, was originally meant to describe only "individual regressions to older ancestral conditions." Freed from the biological context, it now serves mostly to brand impulses that resist, more or less violently, the process of modernization. Journalists like to speak in such cases of a regression to darker times, as if ours were perfectly enlightened; the medieval period is usually cited as a dark page of history in this context. Atavism is the opposite, so to speak, of renaissance.

Our judgment of the reciprocity between old and newer layers of the temporal structure vacillates; on the one hand, we have the recollection of the riches of history, and, on the other, the fear of barbarism, which—though it is difficult to say why—seems to be located in the past.

The temptation to judge anachronism on moral grounds is difficult to resist. But perhaps its actual scandalousness lies precisely in its indifference to such judgments. The pastry dough contains *all* possibilities, positive as well as negative, in a topological blending that allows for no clear separation.

Just as the leaping point in the baker's transformation hardly ever returns to its point of origin, the anachronism never quite coincides with the thing it aims for. Instead, it brings out a third thing, something never before seen, in all the possible steps and forms of transformation, from misunderstanding to reprise, from revision to self-delusion, from productive appropriation to falsification.

For that reason the ever-popular "return to our roots" never achieves its object. The Romantic attachment to the Christian Middle Ages, like all regressive utopias, missed its mark. No one would confuse a neo-Gothic cathedral with one from the thirteenth century, or a Palladian façade with a Roman temple. Every religion has had movements that wanted to turn their backs on the decadent present in order to find their way back to the original purity of their founders. The fundamentalist movements among Christians, Hindus, Jews, and Muslims at the end of the twentieth century are some of the crassest examples of this. Far from returning to the ancient forms of religious life, they are shot through and through with the crises of modernism; they would be inconceivable under any other circumstances.

It looks as if misunderstanding is almost a requirement for anachronistic behavior. Projection plays a decisive role in this. The imaginary portion of renaissance/atavism can be larger or smaller, like the distance between the two points of contact in the pastry dough.

English historians, following the formulation of Eric Hobsbawm, have examined the "invention of tradition," a political practice that bloomed in the nineteenth century. In order to achieve legitimacy, governments and parties, defenders of the status quo and revolutionaries, all came up with far-fetched traditions. Whether it was the coronation ceremony of the British monarch or the popularization of supposedly ancient folk customs, national martyrs or heroic rebels—the portion of fantasy in all of these cases was significant. And not all of the participants were as honest as the conservative Catholic Gonzague de Reynold of Switzerland, who urged his compatriots to "keep up the old traditions, and, when necessary, invent them."

From imitation to falsification is just a small step. But even where this line has been crossed, the contact to an older layer of time is the prerequisite for the success of the operation. Every successful swindle has to contain a grain of truth, and so the counterfeiter, too, must have as exact a knowledge as possible of the past. When the Scot James Macpherson wrote his Ossianic songs, all of Europe was enthralled. The author claimed that his work was a translation from the Gaelic, and dated his fictive original back to the third century. For a long time the supposed relic was held to be authentic. This had far-reaching consequences. Macpherson's counterfeit sparked a renaissance in Celtic studies, and the research of Scottish and Irish history owes its essential impulses to Macpherson.

When some factions of the 1968 student movement hearkened back to Trotsky's permanent revolution and the Bolshevik idea of the cadre, they launched an unintentional parody; but this same movement helped to bring some buried traditions of the European left to light. Even in its more dubious forms, anachronism can be productive.

It would be reckless to claim this of its most transitory and trivial stages of decline, however, which have appeared in the victory march under the title of postmodernism. Will this costume ball of nostalgia come to an end in the foreseeable future? No one can say. In any case, the industrial-strength reprocessing of the past is a cheerless affair. "Retro" and "recycling" are names for strategies for cultural plundering and attrition. But there is no need to get overexcited about this ideological and artistic flea market. Commercial anachronism steers clear of anything truly significant. It would like to replace the leaping point with calculation. It is incapable of discoveries, because it lacks the preparation for conflict, for that "violation" which is the thing that makes the reciprocal relationship with earlier layers in the temporal structure productive in the first place. And so one could speculate that even anachronism has seen better days, when it threatens to become anachronistic itself.

Yet that would be getting ahead of ourselves—an attempt to foresee the unforeseeable, and like every other such attempt, doomed to failure. The unexpected remainder will not allow itself to be driven off under any circumstances. And here I will speak, without arrogance, but also without shame, of my own situation. For if there is an anachronistic figure par excellence, it is that of the poet.

Hardly any other phenomenon has been declared dead as often as this one. Any economist can prove effortlessly that this is a profession which, according to the laws of the market, should not even exist. And as for the media theorists, who have been enthusing for decades about the end of print culture and the death of literature—their number is legion, and their joy over simultaneity knows no bonds.

One of the most sensible of them, Jochen Hörisch, compares poetry to paper money. "Both are illusory, both are constructions, both operate in a morally dubious economy of currency and a universal exchange with nearly everything (money makes a product of everything, poetry makes a theme of everything), both are elements of the Gutenberg galaxy, and both will be anachronistic phenomena in the media age." But the terminator does not stop there. He continues with a virtuoso leap: "Or rather, the following prognosis [!] will apply: the future of the (literary) book will depend upon its anachronism—even as regards its external form. Communication will continue to belong in books in the future; information will be in the realm of electronic media."

Up until now the phenomenon of literature has simply blundered on in its own hopeless way, "out of harmony with the present," as the dictionary so beautifully put it. Heedless of profitability, it shows up in the most unexpected places, an imaginary raisin in the pastry dough, whose future path no one can predict.

The epigraph quotes Montaigne's *Essais* from the first chapter of the second and the second chapter of the third books; the titles are "On the inconstancy of our action" and "On Regret."

The famous passage from *Confessions* of Augustine come from Book 11, section 14. The definitions of "anachronism" can be found in *Meyers Enzyklopädischen Lexikon* and the *Oxford English Dictionary* (1971). The depiction of the baker's transformation primarily follows that of Ivar Ekeland's essay *Le Calcul, l'imprévu* (Paris, 1984). A German version appeared in 1985 in Munich under the title *Das Vorhersehbare und das Unvorhersehbare*. Another interpretation is given by Ilya Prigogine and Isabelle Stengers in *Order Out of Chaos: Man's New Dialogue with Nature* (New York, 1984). A seminal work is that of V. Arnold and A. Alvez, *Ergodic Problems of Classical Mechanics* (New York, 1968). Gonzague de Reynold is quoted by Christoph Keller in "Der Homo alpinus helveticus," from *Passage*, vol 19 (Zurich, 1995). Jochen Hörisch's brilliant book *Kopf and Zahl: Die Poesie des Geldes* appeared in 1996 in Frankfurt am Main.

My thanks to Klaus Meyer and Jan Riemer (Munich) for the pastry-dough diagrams.

1996

Part Two

4) MY FIFTY-YEAR EFFORT TO DISCOVER AMERICA

A Hapless German's Tale

WHEN I WAS YOUNG, any German lucky enough to travel abroad had to pass an informal test. How old, the silent question went, must he or she have been in 1933, and in 1945? People in Poland and Norway, in France and in Russia had good reasons of their own to wonder.

As to myself, I had the good fortune to be born in 1929, which means that I was sixteen at the end of World War II. To use a term coined by an American philosopher, this was a piece of "moral luck"; I was simply too young to qualify as a full-grown Nazi. Maybe this was the reason why the Military Government for Germany issued to me in 1947 a little green booklet called a "Temporary Travel Document in lieu of Passport for German Nationals." I proceeded to make as much use of it as possible.

My hard-won ersatz pass was not exactly a magic carpet. It was valid for travel only "if properly visaed," and there was the rub. To obtain a visa was a process too tortuous to go into here. Today's immigrants from the poorer parts of the world will know what I am talking about.

To what extent my earnest attempts at discovering America may be typical for my generation of Germans I cannot say. I shall try to describe them for what they are worth. Tracing the complicated history of German–American relations from 1945 to our days is, of course, beyond my scope. What I have to tell is a personal tale, no more, and if it has wider implications, it is not for me to sort them out. I shall try to encapsulate a long story in seven short episodes.

1

As a child, I knew next to nothing about America. It was for me a continent of pure fantasy, populated by cowboys and red Indians, perhaps with a few gangsters thrown in, though what these unshaven figures were up to was far from clear to me.

One of the salient facts of life in Nazi Germany was that you simply could not leave the place. To travel abroad was a privilege not available to ordinary people. In this respect, the Germany of the late 1930s was like the Soviet Union, a self-contained, claustrophobic space, which offered to my elders only one way of escape: invading and plundering their European neighbors.

I remember wondering whether America was real. It sounded like a figment, like something out of a children's book. Every now and then our vacuous newspapers tried to convince their readers that the United States was run by plutocrats. These were pictured with big cigars in their mouths and wearing top hats. It was not easy to believe that such people really existed. They looked like the equally implausible Jews whose caricatures appeared on the bulletin board of my elementary school. Nobody had ever seen anyone remotely resembling them in real life.

It is not true that children was easily won over by propaganda. They don't find it difficult to distinguish between fact and fiction. Whereas I had no doubts about our janitor or about the little bastard of a Hitler Youth leader who ordered me around, surely plutocrats, Jews, and red Indians belonged to the world of Grimm tales and horror stories.

When Hitler declared war on the United States, I was probably too busy passing a Latin translation test to take notice. Because of the war, my family had moved to a village in Bavaria. To go to school was a nuisance. Every day at five in the morning we had to take the train to a nearby town which boasted a *gymnasium*. In late 1944, the railroad tracks were bombed and all traffic was suspended. This meant that we had to walk about seven miles to school and back, a daily trip which before long became very boring.

On this road I had my first direct contact with America, an experience which settled any lingering doubt about its existence. On a bright autumn day, a fighter plane suddenly roared down on us. We were three fifteen-year-old kids and had very good reflexes, so we immediately took cover in the ditch on the side of the road. I remember clearly the little clouds of dust rising in front of me where the bullets hit the ground, and only a fraction of a second afterward the hammering of the machine gun. It was a near miss. When the plane had passed us, we looked up and saw it glitter in the sky. I think it was a Mustang. We even could distinguish the star on its wings and the pilot in his cockpit. In any case, the plane took a U-turn and came back at us, but since we did not offer a good target, it swept by without another volley. When it was gone, we leaped up and danced on the road. Strangely enough, it was an altogether exhilarating experience.

2

Half a year later I was called upon to defend Germany. I was handed a greenish uniform made of scratchy cellulose, a gun, and a bazooka. The Allies had long since crossed the Rhine. Together with a group of thirty other kids I was stationed at a trunk road about twenty miles from our village. We were supposed to save the Reich, which consisted of a vast heap of rubble, by shooting at the approaching American tanks. Under the circumstances, I did not see much point in pretending to be a hero. I prepared myself carefully, taking along a good topographic map and a hoard of civilian clothes which I tucked away at a few strategically chosen locations. It was a risky business, since there were a lot of people who had a mind to shoot you: on the one hand, the advancing Allied armies, and, on the other, our own officers who were eager to execute deserters.

The choice of the right moment was therefore decisive. As soon as I heard the first Sherman tank rumbling in the distance, I ducked and took to my heels. In a nearby forest I found my little cache, shed my uniform and became a civilian again. This was important, since I did not like the idea of spending a few months or years in a prisoner-of-war camp.

I walked the whole night, and when I arrived at my village early in the morning, I saw them coming: an endless host of armored vehicles, artillery, trucks, and jeeps. The men looked like visitors from outer space. They were well-fed, their khaki trousers were clean and neat, and their attitude was supremely insouciant. With a casual nod to the gaping peasants they jumped from their cars and proceeded to light a bonfire in the village square. Some of them were black giants, and they were chewing a substance unknown in our part of the world tasting of peppermint. As soon as they had settled down, round the fire, they began, to my utter astonishment, to read what looked to me like children's books. Overcome by curiosity, I began to talk to them in my rudimentary schoolboy's English. They laughed and handed me my first comic book.

It turned out that I was the only person in the village who had some slight command of the language, and within a week or so I was established as their more or less official interpreter. Only much later did I realize that they had acted against their regulations. On the very first day of occupation, they ignored military discipline and began to fraternize with the enemy.

Needless to say, I had a wonderful time. As long as I could remember, there had always been someone to boss me around, shouting orders: teachers, janitors, party bosses, and sergeants. Overnight, all these authorities had vanished into thin air. It was a huge relief. Of course, there was something called the Military Government, but this was an abstraction, an invisible entity far away in cities beyond our reach. All civilian road and rail traffic had ceased long ago. German newspapers did not exist. I was lucky, since I could glean fascinating bits of information from the pages of the army newsletters, a daily called *The Stars and Stripes*. It was clear that there existed an immense outside world unknown to me, and its name was America.

In due course, I made two other discoveries. One day, Captain McCann, our local commander, handed me a parcel the size and shape of a brick. It was wrapped in grease-proof paper, which gave no clue as to what it might contain. When I opened it, I found a tightly packed plethora of intriguing objects: first of all, a small can, to the bottom of which was attached an ingenious opener. Inside, I discovered an unfamiliar sort of shredded meat called Spam. Next came aluminum foil with a brown bitter powder in it which went by the equally mysterious name Nescafé. Furthermore, there were individually packed cubes of sugar, a bag of powdered milk, a supply of aspirin, a tin of sweet pineapple, matches, paper handkerchiefs, toilet paper, and, most intriguing of all, a rubber embedded in plastic and a tube of ointment, which upon close scrutiny turned out to be an antibiotic for the prevention and cure of venereal disease.

All these things were organized and put together in the most thoughtful manner. The whole contraption was called a C-ration. It contained everything a soldier far away from home might need, not excluding what in my eyes seemed to be extravagant luxuries. It was clear to me that a nation capable of such foresight was invincible.

My next surprise was even more overwhelming. Captain McCann had set up his headquarters in a large farmhouse at the end of the village. I used to hang around his office, and one day I noticed in a corner a huge box full of books. Most of them were oblong in shape, had garish covers showing half-naked women and bore the imprint *Overseas Edition.* Somebody on the other side of the Atlantic had thought of the intellectual needs of the G.I. and supplied the American Expeditionary Forces with a cornucopia of world literature, absolutely free of charge. Help yourself, said Captain McCann.

Starved for reading matter, I could hardly restrain myself. I came home loaded with paperbacks. My hoard was a wild mixture of thrillers and classics, pulp fiction and philosophy. I wallowed in Somerset Maugham and Hemingway, Louis Bromfield and Thoreau. I remember a fat gray volume put together by an earnest American academic called Louis Untermeyer. His anthology of *Modern American Poetry* opened vast vistas to my fertile mind. Someone in Washington must have decided that the troops were eager to read William Carlos Williams, T. S. Eliot, Marianne Moore, and Wallace Stevens, though Ezra Pound, I believe, was off limits for the army. I am not sure that the G.I.s shared these concerns, but the whole operation was a sign of generosity and yet another proof, if proof were needed, of American superiority.

At the bottom of the heap I even found a few books by German authors: *Arch of Triumph* by Erich Maria Remarque, a best-seller long since forgotten, *The Magic Mountain* by Thomas Mann, and *The Trial*, written by someone I had never heard of whose name was Franz Kafka. They all made for heady reading, even in English. After the long cultural blackout of Nazi Germany, world literature, shipped by the ton from the United States and handed out for free, was an unforgettable source of illumination in the bleak and depressing climate of postwar Germany.

3

After a few years, my country returned to an uneasy sort of normalcy. Reams of worthless old banknotes were traded in for a new currency printed in the USA. Empty shopwindows filled up, almost overnight, as if by miracle, with shoes, sausages, screwdrivers, and apples. In a frenzy of reconstruction, roofs were mended, streets cleared of rubble, railroad tracks repaired. At the same time, and with the same amazing speed, millions of Nazis disappeared from sight. Most of them had instantly turned into demure democrats, blithely pursuing their careers in government, business, education, law, and medicine. Nobody wanted to hear about what was politely called "Germany's darkest years."

Within a very short time, the western part of the country had become an American protectorate. True, there were also British and French troops around, but everybody knew that the true winner of the war was the United States. To consider America a "young nation" is a well-worn European cliché. In the event, the alleged adolescent became the guardian of a decrepit and worn-out Germany. The USA took on the difficult job of resocializing our part of the world. This was not, of course, an act of sheer benevolence. Germany's future was determined by the beginning Cold War. Never was a defeated nation offered more generous terms, and never were such terms less deserved.

Despite the Allies' feeble efforts at denazification, there was something murky about our recovery. Many Germans harbored a silent resentment about what they saw as a disaster rather than as a liberation. Amnesia was a common affliction, and the old authoritarian frame of mind was still very much in evidence.

In the event, many people of my generation hankered for America, a place where such hangups did not seem to exist. In our imagination, it was a paradise of jazz, civil liberties, and easygoing morals.

As a student at one of our antediluvian universities, I one day found in my mailbox a letter from Washington inviting me to a six-week tour of the United States. How I came to be a candidate for the Fulbright exchange program I cannot say, but it certainly felt like a passport to utopia. I was given an airplane ticket and a small allowance. The itinerary was up to me, but the Washington office offered to put me in touch with an institution I wished to visit.

Since I cold not afford a car, I decided to buy a Greyhound pass valid for travel throughout the US. I walked the clapboard settlements of the Mississippi Delta, talked to plasma physicists and movie producers, and spent a lot of time at forlorn bus depots and in motels resembling flophouses. The lack of money provided me with certain insights into the American class system. The Greyhound bus served a clientele of sailors without hire, demobilised G.I.s, prostitutes, and a variety of other losers.

I found everybody from government offices to the last tramp incredibly easy to talk to, forthcoming, and helpful. The only hitch was when I boarded a bus in Alabama and took a seat at the back. I was politely told by an old black lady that I had to sit in front. Later on, at the bus stop, I ended up on a bench with a sign that said FOR WHITES ONLY. In the end, I could make up my mind about the vast country which I had set out to discover. It seemed exotic beyond my wildest dreams. Very often I felt lost, like a person in a Hopper painting. The natives seemed gregarious enough, more so than most Europeans, and yet I was stuck by a pervasive aura of loneliness.

Another baffling aspect was the weird discrepancy between image and reality. At the time, Europe was still an underdeveloped region in terms of advertising and public relations. The promises made by ads and neon signs seemed to be wide of the mark. The most wretched fast food joint on the wrong side of the tracks would proudly proclaim that only here could you relish "Arthur's world famous meatballs." Similarly fantastic claims were made on behalf of shaving creams, motels, night spots, and even entire states. Nobody appeared to be bothered by the unbridgeable gap between promise and reality. It took me a lot of time and effort to learn the grammar of representation that prevailed in this outlandish civilization.

And when I finally came to Hollywood, another shock awaited me. I was given free tickets to a live television show. For a German student in 1953, this was a sensational attraction. I had never seen a standup comedian in action, and I daresay that most of his punch lines were lost on me. But what really filled me with apprehension were two signs which every now and then flashed their message to the audience, asking us to laugh or to applaud. Both of these instructions were dutifully followed. Even now, when this arrangement has become commonplace all over the civilized world, it remains a riddle I have never been able to solve.

And thus, when I returned home, envied by my fellow students, I had to confess that my first American venture had been a glorious failure—that I could admire this far-flung land of promise, worry about it, dream about it, but that to understand it was beyond me.

4

When the Soviets started a blockade of Berlin, the U.S. Air Force supplied our old capital with food and fuel and saved it from a communist takeover. The Marshall Plan gave rise to a seemingly endless business boom, which went down in pop history as the "economic miracle." If America had problems of its own, the Germans did not want to hear about them. We preferred to hang on to our fantasies, and saw Uncle Sam as a sort of Santa Claus. American films and American music conquered the market. In the early 1960s, rock and roll became the mainstay of youth culture, and the hippie movement began to sprout.

Our elders were not entirely happy with our cultural cargo cult. They muttered darkly about "Americanization." Old-world values and virtues were ritually invoked by priests, philosophers, and politicians. Behind the advance of Coca-Cola and blue jeans loomed the larger perils of free speech and insubordination.

We asked ourselves what was so venerable about our German traditions, and a convincing answer to this question was not at hand. The conservative discourse on the heritage of Humanism and Christianity looked like a thoroughly hypocritical maneuver, an obscene cover-up. Except for occasional philosemitic Sunday speeches, the Holocaust remained the most closely guarded taboo in Adenauer's Germany.

5

At long last, by the end of the 1960s, the confrontation with the past came to a head. The Federal Republic had, so to speak, reached its adolescence. Once more, America served as a model. The Free Speech Movement and the Students for a Democratic Society preceded and inspired our own version of '68. I shall not try to resume its vagaries. Suffice to say that it was overdue, and that, despite a record of confusion, vainglory, and sectarianism, it did us a lot of good. I would even claim that it made Germany inhabitable. It cleared the air, it put the Nazi crimes squarely on the agenda, and it did away with our residual habit of obedience.

This is not to deny that it had its loony side. No social movement of any scope can do without a touch of madness. One of the striking aspects of the student movement was the sudden collapse of the American dream. The same kids who adored Hollywood westerns and read Jack Kerouac were seen shouting anti-American slogans in front of the American embassy and throwing pudding bombs at Vice President Humphrey. It was, of course, the Vietnam War that brought about this reversal. It followed the classical mechanism of projection. You pin your highest hopes on an outside agent, and when you discover that he does not intend to fulfill your expectations, you blame him, and your disappointment turns into aggression.

We discovered, rather belatedly and with a little help from Marx and Engels, that capitalism was not very nice at heart, and that the United States was an imperialist power. Moments of rebellion are a rather rare occurrence in German history, and I was not willing to pass by this chance. I soon found myself up to my neck in the theatrical happenings of '68.

By a bizarre coincidence, and in the same year, I was offered another opportunity to discover America. A renowned university gave me a fellowship. The terms were exceedingly generous, and I could not resist the temptation. The small campus town where I ended up was very quiet, very genteel and far from the agitation of Berkeley or Columbia, which I had looked forward to. Opposition to the war in Vietnam was reduced to a polite whisper. I discovered that my predecessor at the house I was given had been writing speeches for President Johnson. I began to feel that I was floating in one of those tanks where you lose your sense of reality, and finally I bolted. I decided to go to Cuba instead, where I was offered a job. This was a scandalous thing to do and an affront to my amiable hosts.

Even then, it was clear to me that there was something faintly ridiculous about my act. I felt like a mouse telling the elephant that from now on I would avoid his company if he did not behave. The politics of gesture carry their own penalty.

Still, I cannot quite bring myself to regret this episode. I had failed in another attempt to discover America, but, on the other hand, the year I spent in Cuba gave me a very solid education in the realities of communism. I found it worthwhile indeed to rid myself of any illusions which may have been lingering in my mind.

6

It is often said that the Vietnam War was worse than a crime, that it was a mistake. I still prefer the first of these descriptions. But, in contrast to other mighty nations, the people of the United States themselves put an end to their government's aberration. In the end, and after grievous losses, American democracy had worked.

Meanwhile, on the other side of the Atlantic, West Germany had shown some signs of growing up. The need for American tutelage began to diminish, and a more normal relationship seemed in the offing. Still, when asked where our capital lay, we did not quite know what to answer. It was impossible to take Bonn seriously. In cultural terms, it was a hopeless backwater. In the end, everybody looked to New York for inspiration. In order to understand what was going on in the world, it was deemed essential to fly over at least once a year.

A new, more worldly crop of Germans had appeared on the scene. They did not idealize the United States any longer, nor did they suffer from the inferiority complex of their parents. The disillusionment of the 1960s had paid off. Naive idolatry and latent resentment had made place for a more balanced view of America.

It was perhaps a straw in the wind that in 1980 I founded a monthly review which was called *TransAtlantik*. I was fed up with German journalism, which I found boring and short of breath. I wanted to resurrect the lost art of the ambitious reportage, a genre in which American and British authors excelled. Fascinated by the work of Norman Mailer, Tom Wolfe, Norman Lewis, and Bruce Chatwin, I thought that the time was ripe for a German magazine emulating *The New Yorker*, *Harper's*, *The Atlantic*, with a pinch of *The Na-*

tion and the *New York Review of Books* thrown in for good measure. I was wrong. The magazine folded after a few years, but it won a following of writers who have carried on and set new standards in German journalism.

On the level of diplomacy, German–American relations seemed to thrive. In Bonn, at least, the friendship between our nations was much touted. Our politicians probably did not realize that there was a cultural misunderstanding at the base of their rhetoric. In Europe, and especially in Germany, friendship is a concept loaded with sentiment. Whereas in America a friend is someone you have met at a party and found agreeable enough to send him or her a Christmas card, Germans like to believe in a deeper emotional involvement. This is a bit too much to ask for in the field of foreign policy, where the best you may hope for is a working relationship. Small wonder then that in Washington not everybody was happy with German *Ostpolitik*, and that there was quite a row over the stationing of Pershing missiles on German territory. For a time, the Peace Movement even tried to revive the anti-American feelings of the 1960s, albeit without much success. When all was said and done, we had settled down to a very comfortable routine under the nuclear umbrella provided by the United States.

In the meantime, my trips to America had become more and more frequent. As ever, I was well received and grateful for the goodwill I was shown. But there was one thing that filled me with dread. During the 1980s, my friends had begun to worry about their address and about the price of champagne. They explained to me that as a professional you were doomed if you were reduced to living outside of certain severely circumscribed areas of Manhattan and the Hamptons. Apparently, New York was a party to which you were not invited if you belonged to the bridge and tunnel people.

The old days when money and celebrity were minor matters seemed gone forever.

Success had become an absolute must or even a moral obligation. This was not only sad, it was in the end very boring. Obviously, the class struggle had, like so many other things in America, been "personalized." In my piecemeal exploration of the unfathomable United States, another lesson had been brought home to me.

7

The next sea change began in 1989, with the collapse of the Soviet empire and the unification of Germany. Suddenly, the world had to cope without the precarious certainties of the Cold War.

The Federal Republic of Germany had, as it were, come of age, not without a certain reluctance. After a short bout of euphoria, the Germans realized that there were a few drawbacks to their bonanza. Not only were they faced with an economy ruined by the communists and with millions of new citizens deformed by two successive dictatorships; on top of that, they had to deal with another unfamiliar challenge. Gone were the days when you could duck in the shadow of your transatlantic guardian who saw to it that your oil supply was assured and that nobody threatened your security. From a grownup, the world expects that he shoulder his responsibilities. When the American army left Berlin, quite a few tears were shed. It was probably the only case in recorded history when people regretted the departure of an occupation force.

On the face of it, American culture held its sway. Every single fad or fashion originating in California, Texas, or New York was devoutly aped in Germany. Our media, our advertising, our management continued to speak their rather barbarous brand of airport English, much of it quite incomprehensible to the population at large. On a deeper level, however, one could sense a widening gap between Europe and the USA, a slow but inexorable displacement not visible to the naked eye, rather like the shift of tectonic plates in geological time.

The first symptoms made themselves felt in foreign policy. The American people and their representatives began to get fed up with the endless squabbles of the outside world, not only in Asia and Africa, but also in Europe. Why couldn't the French and the British, the Italians and Germans take care of the Yugoslavian maze? It was, after all, their own backyard. The United States had very obvious and pressing problems of their own. Why should they send their boys to all sorts of foreign places with unpronounceable names which the average citizen could not even find on the map? To be the only world power was not fun, and to police the entire globe was a nuisance. Let the bastards out there sort out their own mess! Let them fend for themselves! Let us get back to our own agenda and worry about our black people, our immigrants, our poor, our health and education systems. I must say that I cannot blame the American people for coming to such conclusions.

Nor were these sentiments purely a matter of foreign policy. I found that Americans had lost much of their interest in the outside world. Unless something very juicy happened, the networks could not be bothered with news from abroad. Foreign languages, never a strong side of American education, were on their way out.

Publishers lost interest in translation. Out of thirty bestsellers listed by the *New York Times*, twenty-nine are written by Americans, and the only odd man out is British. This is a record of ignorance not matched by any other nation.

Appearances to the contrary, the continental shift is to some extent reciprocal. It is true that American films, American music, and American technology continue to flood the world market. But at the same time, people overseas begin to revert to their own preoccupations. The old lure of America is not what it used to be. There is something jaded about the tourist or businessman who catches the transatlantic plane with a night out, a deal or a shopping spree in mind. It is as if we had seen it all on television. This noncommittal air on both sides, a familiarity bordering on indifference, is not, of course, specific to German-American relations. It has to be seen in a wider context, as a developing rift between America and the outside world, and this is why I shall leave it for more competent voices to analyze.

As for myself, wandering about the wilderness of south Los Angeles, getting lost in the shopping malls of Texas, admiring the manicured lawns of Princeton, I am just as bewildered as I was forty years ago when I first landed on these shores.

After so many exciting expeditions, I realize that I have failed to discover America. How could I make up my mind about it, torn as I am between shock and gratitude, bliss and frustration, dismay and surprise? Of all my lifelong failures, this is one which I would hate to do without.

1997

5) LAS CASAS

or, A Look Back into the Future

I

"THE INDIES [that is: the West Indian Islands and the coasts of Central and South America] were discovered in the year one thousand four hundred and ninety-two. In the following year a great many Spaniards went there with the intention of settling the land. Thus, forty-nine years have passed since the first settlers penetrated the land, the first so-claimed being the large and most happy isle called Hispaniola, which is six hundred leagues in circumference. Around it in all directions are many other islands, some very big, others very small, and all of them were, as we saw with our own eyes, densely populated with native peoples called Indians. This large island was perhaps the most densely populated place in the world. . . . And all the land so far discovered is a beehive of people; it is as though God had crowded into these lands the great majority of mankind.

"And of all the infinite universe of humanity, these people are the most guileless, the most devoid of wickedness and duplicity, the most obedient and faithful to their native masters and to the Spanish Christians whom they serve. They are by nature the most humble, patient, and peaceable, holding no grudges, free from embroilments, neither excitable nor quarrelsome. These people are the most devoid of rancors, hatreds, or desire for vengeance of any people in the world. And because they are so weak and complaisant, they are less able to endure heavy labor and soon die of no matter what malady. . . .

"Yet into this sheepfold, into this land of meek outcasts there came some Spaniards who immediately behaved like ravening beasts, wolves, tigers or lions that had been starved for many days. And Spaniards have behaved in no other way during the past forty years, down to the present time, for they are still acting like ravening beasts, killing, terrorizing, afflicting, torturing, and destroying the native peoples, doing all this with the strangest and most varied new methods of cruelty, never seen or heard of before. . . .

"We can estimate very surely and truthfully that in the forty years that have passed, with the infernal actions of the Christians, there have been unjustly slain more than twelve million men, women and children. In truth, I believe without trying to deceive myself that the number of the slain is more like fifteen million. . . .

"There reason for killing and destroying such an infinite number of souls is that the Christians have an ultimate aim, which is to acquire gold, and to swell themselves with riches in a very brief time and thus rise to a high estate disproportionate to their merits. It should be kept in mind that their insatiable greed and ambition, the greatest ever seen in the world, is the cause of their villainies. And also, those lands are so rich and felicitous, the native peoples so meek and patient, so easy to subject, and that our Spaniards have no more consideration for them than beasts. And I say this from my own knowledge of the acts I witnessed. But I should not say 'than beasts' for, thanks be to God, they have treated beasts with some respect; I should say instead like excrement on the public squares."

So begins the *Brief Account of the Devastation of the Indies*, which Fray Bartolomé de Las Casas wrote in 1543.

II

Whether what this book says is true, whether its author should be believed—this question has produced a quarrel that has been smoldering, burning, and flaming up for four hundred years. This quarrel has been waged by scholars, and their tracts and dissertations, their investigations and commentaries could fill an entire library. Even in our day a generation of specialists in Spain, Mexico, South America, and the United States is poring over the faded prints, letters, and manuscripts from the pen of the Dominican monk from Seville. Yet the quarrel about Las Casa is not an academic one: what is under dispute is genocide, committed on twenty million people.

Since such a state of affairs does not sit well with the preferred contemplative stance of historical writing without anger and prejudice, it is scarcely surprising that the colleagues from the monk's fraternity, the theologians, historians, and legal scholars have dropped all niceties in their choice of weapons. Where they lacked arguments they reached for rusty knives. They are, as we shall see, in use even today. The *Brief Account* had scarcely been published when the Court historian of Charles V, the famous Dr. Juan Ginés de Sepúlveda, produced a pamphlet *Against the premature, scandalous and heretical assertions which Fray Bartolomé de las Casas has made in his book about the conquest of the Indies, which he has had printed without permission of the authorities.* The very title heavy-handedly alludes to the censor and the Inquisition. Later Las Casas was called a traitor and a Lutheran. In 1562, the Council of the City of México petitioned the king that Las Casas's writings had caused such an uproar that they had had to convene a commission of legal scholars and theologians to draw up an expert opinion against this "impudent frater and his teachings"; the king ought to reprimand Las Casa publicly and prohibit his books. A few years later the viceroy of Perú wrote: "The books of this fanatic and malicious bishop endanger the Spanish rule in America." He too demanded a royal prohibition; he too commissioned a refutation: for the official historians the fight against Las Casas turned into a flourishing business. The assessor, a man by the name of Pedro Sarmiento de Gamboa, had the following to say: "The devil has made a cunning chess move by making this deluded churchman his tool." In 1659, the censor of the Inquisition office in Aragón ruled that "this book reports of very horrifying and cruel actions, incomparable in the history of other nations, and ascribes them to Spanish soldiers and colonizers whom the Spanish King sent forth. In my opinion such reports are an insult to Spain. They must therefore be suppressed." Thereupon the Holy Tribunal of Saragossa finally issued a prohibition of the book in 1660. Yet new editions kept appearing: in 1748 the Seville chamber of commerce had a Latin translation confiscated, and even in 1784 the Spanish ambassador to France demanded a confiscation of a reprint.

Since the seventeenth century Las Casas's opponents have developed an even more elegant method to extirpate him. The historian Juán Meléndez, a Dominican, simply declared at that time that the *Brief Account* was a forgery; "noted authorities," whom he asked, had informed him that the book was written by a Frenchman and had been translated into Spanish with a forged title, something which should surprise no one: as the Spanish enjoyed the greatest fame as proclaimers of truth, the forgers had no choice but to camouflage their lies in this manner. Even in 1910 a Spanish historian seriously maintained that the *Brief Account*, to the best of human judgment, was not by Las Casas.

The reputation of the accused was not notably improved by this astonishing acquittal. Recent historians who write in Spanish have characterized him in the following words: "mentally ill" (1927); "a pig-headed anarchist" (1930); "a preacher of Marxism" (1937); "a dangerous demagogue" (1944); "a leveler possessed by the devil" (1946); "delusionary in his conceptions, boundless and inopportune in his expression" (1947); and the most respected Spanish historian of the twentieth century, Ramón Menéndez Pidal, in 1963 in Madrid, at age ninety-three, published an extensive book, in which he sought to exorcise the spirit of Las Casas once and for all. An American, Lewis Hanke, who has devoted his life to the study of the *Conquista*, remarks about this work of exorcism:

> Don Ramón passionately denies that Las Casas was an honorable man. He calls him a megalomaniac paranoid. In his retrospective look at the conquista Don Ramón scarcely detects a single dead Indian through his colored glasses: instead he sees a scene of well-being and of cultural progress for which America has to thank the Spaniards.

Only the unparalleled success that the *Brief Account* has had makes these tenacious and furious polemics comprehensible. Las Casa wrote a great deal: large-scale chronicles, theological and legal disputations, petitions and tractates. To this day there is no complete edition of his works. The ones with the greatest scholarly significance were first published in 1877 and 1909. There are obvious reasons for their long submersion in darkness. The *Brief Account*, true to its title, is nothing but a concise synopsis of the investigations and experiences that Las Casas elaborates in greater detail elsewhere. It was meant for a single reader: his Catholic Majesty, Charles I of Spain, as Charles V, Emperor of the Holy Roman Empire. Yet the *Brief Account*'s appearance in book form, at a time when printing was just beginning to flourish, acquainted all of Europe with it. Its original publication in 1552 in Seville was followed by translations into all the important languages of the time: Paris (1579), London (1583), Amsterdam (1607), and Venice (1630) were the first foreign places of publication, followed by Barcelona, Brussels, Lyon, Frankfurt, and later by Philadelphia, New York, Havana, Buenos Aires, Lima, São Paulo, Mexico City, and Santiago de Chile.

The book's sensational effect provides an early example of the power of the press. The *Brief Account* reached one of its climaxes during the rivalry between Spain and England at the turn of the sixteenth century. A second wave of translations was brought on by the French Enlightenment. The third flood of reprints occurred between 1810 and 1830 in Latin America; at that time, the *Brief Account* won direct influence on the leaders of the wars of independence against the Spanish colonial power. Simón Bolívar valued Las Casas, and the fact that he himself was a descendant of the conquistadors did not prevent him from making the book serve his revolutionary intentions. Las Casas had to serve as the chief witness against the Spanish even during the Spanish–American War in 1899, which secured control over the Caribbean area and rule over the Philippines for the United States.

The *Brief Account* was not spared by the tumult of power-political interests. Time and again Spain's opponents used Las Casas, often in a pharisaical manner, and so it is not surprising that the Hispanic world to this day discusses the book from a perspective that seems foolish to us: namely, whether or not it "sullies" the honor of Spain. Las Casas has become the exponent of the so-called Black Legend, *leyenda negra*, as the Spanish historians with a terminological trick call every conception of the conquest of South America that does not sing the official song of praise: as though what disparages the "honor of Spain" had been seized, willy-nilly, out of the blue.

This whole polemic is antiquated and superfluous. Spain's honor does not interest us. The French enlightener Jean François Marmontel, in his work on the destruction of the Inca empire, referring to Las Casas, already stated in 1777 what there is to be said on this subject: "All nations have their robbers and fanatics, their times of barbarousness, their attacks of rabies." The question of national character is not on the agenda. The extermination of the European Jews by the Germans, the Stalinist purges, the destruction of Dresden and Nagasaki, the French terror in Algeria, the Americans in Southeast Asia have demonstrated even to the most obtuse that all peoples are capable of everything; and as the *Brief Account of the Devastation of the Indies* is published once more, in a new English translation, the last of the Indians in Brazil are being inexorably exterminated.

The historians of the nineteenth century tried tenaciously, at times desperately, to invalidate Las Casas, and not only out of chauvinism or cowardice, but because the events he describes would have destroyed their historical picture. They believed in the mission of Christianity or in the "values" of European civilization, and what transpired during their own time in the Congo, in Indonesia, in India and China they would have considered as impossible as the genocide Las Casas described.

We have no such doubts. The news we receive on TV each

day would suffice to disabuse us of them. The actuality of the book is monstrous, has a penetratingly contemporaneous smell to it. Of course, our way of reading it is not devoid of an element of deception. Every historical analogy is ambiguous: for whoever rejects this analogy, history becomes a pile of meaningless facts; for whoever accepts it at face value, leveling the specific differences, it becomes aimless repetition, and he draws the false conclusion that it has always been this way and the tacit consequence that, therefore, it will always remain so too. No, Las Casas was not our contemporary. His report treats colonialism in its earliest stage; that is, the stage of robbery pure and simple, of unconcealed plundering. The complicated system of exploitation of international raw materials was as yet unknown at his time. Trade relations did not play a role during the Spanish *Conquista*, nor the spread of a superior material civilization; no "development policy" of whatever kind served it as justification—only a veneer of Christianity that proposed to convert the heathen, inasmuch as they survived the Christians' arrival. In its primal state, colonialism could do without the fiction of partnership, of bilateral trade. It did not offer anything; it took what it found—slaves, gold, anything it pleased. Its investments were confined to the indispensable essentials of every colonial exploitation: to armed power, administration, and the fleet. For these reasons the Spanish conquerors could also ignore the dialectic of enslavement that Sartre describes in a few sentences:

> That is what is so annoying about slavery: if you tame a member of our species, you diminish his or her profitability; and as little as you provide him or her with, a human being as a workhorse is always going to cost more than he or she earns. That is why the colonial masters are forced to stop their breaking-in process halfway. The result: neither human being nor animal, but

> native. . . . Poor colonial masters: that constitutes his dilemma. He should really kill those whom he robs. But that is just what he cannot do, because he also has to exploit them. He cannot transform the massacre into genocide or the enslavement to the point of brutalization, and that is why he must necessarily lose control.

Such a dilemma occurs only when the colonialists set themselves long-term objectives, when they begin to calculate the profitability of their venture. Such a rational procedure of exploitation was unknown in the sixteenth century. The conquistadors did not know double-entry bookkeeping, not even the tally of the simplest statistics; the continent's depopulation did not trouble them.

Las Casas's opponents did not hesitate to make him responsible, as it were, for the irrationality of the genocide. There is no trusting his figures, it was and still is said; they betray a medieval relationship to arithmetic. South and Central America never held twelve, fifteen or twenty million inhabitants during the time of the conquest; as in the reports of the crusaders the word *million* simply means "many people." Such an approach has something repulsive about it from the very outset. It would like to prove Las Casas a liar but let the murderers go scot-free because they only killed eight, five, or three million Indians instead of twenty million. That is the way the *National Zeitung* protects the German fascists, claiming that not six million Jews were killed but at most five.

Aside from the moral insanity manifested by such sophistry, it is also factually wrong. Two American scholars who have investigated the demographic conditions in old Mexico in recent years reached the conclusion that in the thirty years between Cortez's landing and the writing of the *Brief Account* the population of Central Mexico dwindled from twenty-five to roughly six million. That means that the *Conquista* must have had nineteen million victims in Mexico alone; Las Casas names only four. Even if one takes into account viral illnesses, malaria, famine, and forced labor—that is, the indirect causes of the depopulation—one reaches the conclusion that Las Casas was probably rather too careful with his figures.

Let us leave these arithmetic examples aside. Las Casas spent more than forty years in the American colonies. What he reports are, in large part, observations and firsthand experiences. The witness's life testifies to their authenticity. Where his observations contradict the reports of other witnesses, the historical investigator must engage in lengthy comparisons. We are not engaged in anything of the kind. What is decisive for today's reader of the *Brief Account* are two criteria that academic investigators usually ignore; that is, first of all, the inner cohensiveness of the book, its eye for detail, its care in sketching the episode. Las Casas rarely spends much time with abstract theses, and he not only describes the most horrible cruelties, but also shows the grinding everyday life; he shows us, if the abbreviation be permitted, not only the torture instrument, but also the fight for the daily crust of bread.

A second, external criterion of Las Casas's credibility is the precision of his view of the structure of colonial rule. Since these structures still exist today his statements are verifiable. For this, one does not need to be a Hispanic scholar; a visit to South Africa will suffice.

If one tests the *Brief Account* from this perspective one notices, first of all, its author's economic acuity. The cleric Las Casas did not confine himself to theological observations; he analyzed the basic structure and exposed the technique of colonial exploitation, whose first step is the recruitment of forced labor. For this purpose there existed the so-called *encomienda* system. *Encomienda* means as much as "recommendation." A random number of Indians were distributed by the local commanders to the individual Spanish landowners and "recommended" to them for the reason that they required this protection for their prompt conversion. In reality, the status of these protégés was that of serfs: they were totally at the mercy of their new masters and received no wages or upkeep for the work that their protector (*encomendero*) asked them to do.

The economy of the colonializers concentrated on two forms of business that dominate the economy of many South American nations to this day: mining and plantations. But whereas the North America concerns now extract tin, copper, lead, and vanadium, the conquistadors were interested in one metal only: gold.

Contact with the motherland during the time of the *conquista* was expensive, time-consuming, and dangerous; exploitation of the overseas possessions thus had to confine itself to the most valuable commodities. That explains a further specialty of the colonializers: the pearl fishing in the Caribbean of which Las Casas provides an unforgettable description:

> The pearl fishers dive into the sea at a depth of five fathoms, and do this from sunrise to sunset, and remain for many minutes without breathing, tearing the oysters out of their rocky beds where the pearls are formed. . . . It is impossible to continue for long diving into the cold water and holding the breath for minutes at a time, repeating this hour after hour, day after day; the continual cold penetrates them, constricts the chest, and they die spitting blood, or weakened by diarrhea. The hair of these pearl divers, naturally black, is as if burnished by the saltpeter in the

> water, and hangs down their back making them look like sea wolves or monsters of another species.

That is not a hearsay report; only someone who has seen the burnished hair and the encrusted shoulders with his own eyes speaks like that. This description by Las Casas led, incidentally, to a royal prohibition of pearl fishing—one of the few, albeit short-lived, victories that fell the valiant bishop's way.

Another enterprise that Las Casas deals with could only develop when one region after the other had been depopulated: the slave trade. After the Indians had been cut down by the millions and tormented to death, the colonializers noted with astonishment and even with a certain regret that they were running out of labor power. At this moment the savage became a commodity and the deportations became a profitable business in which the military and officials, who formed primitive corporations, engaged on their own account.

> The colonized world is a divided world. The dividing line, the border is marked by barracks and police stations. The rightful and institutional interlocutor of the colonized, the spokesman of the colonial masters and the repressive regime is the cop or the soldier. . . . The agent of power employs the language of pure power. He does not conceal his sovereignty, he exhibits it. . . . The colonial master is an exhibitionist. His need for security makes him remind the colonized, with a loud voice: "I am master."

These sentences are from a modern phenomenology of colonial rule. Frantz Fanon developed it in the first chapter of his book *The Wretched of the Earth* (1961). Las Casas's observations, made four hundred years earlier, agree with them exactly. Even the manifestly senseless cruelties, even the conquistadors' terroristic arbitrariness had its psychological function in that it demonstratively cut the New World in two. Proof of the fact that the Indians were not human beings was provided by the Spaniards anew every day when they acted as if they were not dealing with human beings: "But I should not say 'than beasts' for, thanks be to God, they have treated beasts with some respect; I should say instead like excrement on the public squares."

(Referring to the concentration camps of the twentieth century, Hannah Arendt has written that, if one appealed to the healthy human understanding of those in power by pointing out to them the superfluousness of the gigantic apparatus of terror, directed against completely pliable human beings, they might answer if they wanted to state the truth: this apparatus only seems superfluous to you because it serves to make human beings superfluous.)

Yet the blind terror with which the colonial masters demonstrate who they are, and that the colonized are nothing, leads to a new dilemma. It assures the colonizers of their identity while simultaneously endangering their ideology. Once they become afraid of the colonized, their terror robs them of their justification, which they would not like to relinquish. For the colonial master not only wants to have power, he also wants to be in the right: he keeps asserting ad nauseam that he has a mission, that he serves God and the king, that he is spreading the Christian teachings and the values of civilization—in a word, that he basically has something higher in mind. He cannot do so without a good conscience. But this means that he must hide the terror that he practices so ostentatiously and must deny his own demonstration. Something peculiarly schizophrenic, an insane formalism, thus is attached to all colonial undertakings. Of this, too, the *Brief Account* provides an excellent example:

And because of the pernicious blindness that has always afflicted those who have ruled in the Indies, nothing was done to *incline* the Indians to embrace the one true Faith, they were rounded up and in large numbers *forced* to do so. Inasmuch as the conversion of the Indians to Christianity was stated to be the principal aim of the Spanish conquerors, they have dissimulated the fact that only with blood and fire have the Indians been brought to embrace the Faith and to swear obedience to the kings of Castile or by threats of being slain or taken into captivity. As if the Son of God who died for each one of them would have countenanced such a thing! For He commanded His Apostles: "Go ye to all the people" (*Euntes docete omnes gentes*). Christ Jesus would have made no such demands of these peaceable infidels who cultivate the soil of their native lands. Yet they are told they must embrace the Christian Faith immediately, without hearing any sermon preached and without any indoctrination. They are told to subject themselves to a King they have never heard of nor seen and are told this by the King's messengers who are such despicable and cruel tyrants that deprive them of their liberty, their possessions, their wives and children. This is not only absurd but worthy of scorn.

This wretch of a Governor thus gave such instructions in order to justify his and their presence in the Indies, they themselves being absurd, irrational, and unjust when he sent the thieves under his command to attack and rob a settlement of Indians where he had heard there was a store of gold, telling them to go at night when the inhabitants were securely in their houses and that, when half a league away from the settlement, they should read in a loud voice his order: "Caciques and Indians of this land, hark ye! We notify you that there is but one God and one Pope and one King of Castile who is the lord of these lands. Give heed and show obedience!" Etc., etc. "And if not, be warned that we will wage war against you and will slay you or take you into captivity." Etc., etc.

The sentence that not the murderer but the victim is guilty becomes the dominant maxim under colonial rule. The "native" is the potential criminal per se who must be held in check, a traitor who threatens the order of the state: "Those who did not rush forth at once," Las Casas says, "to entrust themselves into the hands of such ruthless, gruesome and beastial men were called rebels and insurgents who wanted to escape the service of His Majesty."

But this guilty verdict is the very thing that helps the colonized to perceive their situation. For it leads to its own fulfillment: fiction becomes reality, the raped resort to violence. Las Casas describes several instances where it came to armed actions of resistance, even to small guerrilla wars. He calls the Indian attacks, where "a considerable number of Christians" lost their lives, a "just and holy war" whose "justifiable causes will be acknowledged by every man who loves justice and reason." Without hesitating, in three sweeping sentences that have been left unscarred by the centuries, Las Casas thinks his thoughts to their conclusion:

> And those wretches, those Spaniards, blinded by greed, think they have the God-given right to perpetrate all these cruelties and cannot see that the Indians have cause, have abundant causes, to attack them and by force of arms if they had weapons, to throw them out of their lands, this under all the laws, natural, human, and divine. And they cannot see the injustice of their acts, the iniquity of the injuries and inexpiable sins they have committed against the Indians, and they renew their wars, thinking and saying that the victories they have had against the Indians, laying waste the lands, have all been approved by God and they praise Him, like the thieves of whom the prophet Zechariah speaks: "Feed the flock of the slaughter; whose possessors slay them, and hold themselves not guilty: and they that sell them say, Blessed be the Lord; for I am rich."

The book that Las Casas left behind is a scandal. In its original sense the word *scandal* means "trap." The scholars who warn us of him have entangled themselves in that old *skandalon.* They do not sense that their quarrel is only a distant echo of a huge conflict. The tempest in the teapot of their profession points to other tempests. The ruffle in the historical consciousness indicates enormous tremors in historical reality. The process that began with the *Conquista* is not yet over. It continues in South America, Africa, and Asia. It does not behoove us to speak the verdict about the monk from Seville. Perhaps he has spoken ours.

III

Don Bartolomé de Las Casas was born in 1474 as the son of an aristocrat. The family came from the Limousin region and achieved respected and prosperous status in Andalusia. In 1492, when Columbus was venturing on his first trip to the West, Las Casas was taking up theological and legal studies at the University of Salamanca. His father, Don Francisco, was one of the first Europeans to see the new continent. The name Las Casas appears in the register of the *Santa Maria*. But we have little information about the father's activities. Not even his arrival in America is certain; some historians even claim that he only took part of Columbus' second journey. In any event, Don Francisco had already returned to Seville in 1497. He left no permanent traces in the history of the *Conquista*. His son must have followed him in the last years of the fifteenth century. His presence in Hispaniola is confirmed as of 1502. In 1511, he was elected to the priesthood in Santo Domingo. Evidently Don Bartolomé began to take interest in the Indian culture almost at once. There is testimony that he was a much-sought-after interpreter. During his life he learned more than a dozen Indian dialects. Besides,for fifteen years he behaved no differently than the other colonizers. He made the acquaintance of the leading people of the *Conquista*: Cortez,

Pizarro, Alvarado, Pedrarias, and Columbus the Younger. In 1512 he went with Diego Velásquez and Pánfilo de Narváez to Cuba. The intention of this expedition was to "pacify," that is to subjugate, the island completely. As Las Casas himself reports in his *History of the Indies*, he cared "more about his possessions and his mines than about the Christian teachings, for he was just as blind as the secular settlers."

It is possible to give the precise data on which he began his life work. At Pentecost 1514, aged forty, Las Casas was to give a sermon at the newly founded Ciudad de Espíritu Santo.

> While preparing for this sermon I began to think about several principles of Holy Scripture. I came upon a place in the book Sirach, chapter 34, where it says: "The poor man has nothing but a little bread; whoever deprives him of it is a murderer. Whoever does not give the worker his wages is a bloodhound. . . ." I thought about the misery and slavery in which the native people are living here. . . . And the more I thought about it the more convinced I was that everything we had done to the Indians so far was nothing but tyranny and barbarism. . . . And as much as I studied in every book I read, no matter whether it was in Spanish or in Latin, I came on more and new reasons and authentic teachings which spoke for the right of those Indian people and against the robberies, misdeeds and injustices we had committed.

This discovery, the second discovery of the New World, a world that has not been surveyed to this day, occupied Las Casas to the end of his life. This has nothing to do with religious enlightenment. Las Casas carefully insisted that this insight was accessible to everyone; he insisted on its rationality and with shining intelligence drew from it all theoretical and practical consequences.

First of all, he renounced all the possessions and slaves that had been assigned to him and proceeded to interfere in the administrative practice of the *Conquista*. The first objective of his attack was the terrorist methods of its justice. Soon occurred the first conflict between the frater and the commanders of the "pacification" of Cuba. Las Casas intervened with the Governor, appealed for mercy and wrote petitions, frequently in vain. The conflict developed a logic of its own. The monk reached the conclusion that the executions could not be fought separately from the system as a whole, which depends on the executions to maintain itself. In the spring of 1515 he therefore looked up the royal *general repartidor* for the Indian lands, the person who represented the system of forced labor, and revealed to him that his activity "was derisive of all Godly and human laws." Simultaneously, Las Casas turned with petitions, assessments, and complaints to the Spanish court.

The official is supposed to have listened to the unknown cleric without moving a muscle in his face; yet with this audience there began the unpleasantness that was to accompany Las Casas for the rest of his life. His letters got lost, his income did not arrive, and his attempts to get ship's passage met with the greatest difficulties. For Las Casas had decided to go to Madrid, to reach the king and effect the enactment of laws that would eliminate the whole system of slavery. This project is characteristic of Las Casas. His contemporaries thought him mad. Yet the mixture of boldness and naiveté with which he went to work was perhaps one of his greatest assets. Time and again it protected Las Casas and took his opponents by surprise. Besides, his strategy was entirely consistent. There was no authority in the colonies on whose support he could count: clerics and laymen, officials and private persons—all were participants in that firm whose earnings were threatened by Don Bartolomé's ideas.

* * *

In the summer of 1515 Las Casas began the first of fourteen journeys he undertook to protect the inhabitants of the West Indies from being exterminated. He reached King Ferdinand V, via his confessor, and before him made a thorough report of the conditions in America. There is no account of this audience, but the king was apparently sufficiently moved to convene a commission to investigate the "Indian question." Las Casas was asked to appear in Seville; his testimony made the commission recommend to the king that he should settle the matter legally. It is questionable whether Don Bartolomé at that time already knew the rules of the game that he had entered and that, always with new subterfuges, was to be protracted over a period of fifty years. He presumably did not know that the members, two bishops and one official, had a material interest in the exploitation of the West Indies: they received considerable income from that source. When the King died a few months after the audience, the commission dissolved itself. There was no further mention of the new laws. An intervention with the new monarch looked hopeless—Charles V, who was sixteen at the time, did not live in Spain. Las Casas now turned to the Grand Inquisitor, who was the king's representative. Ximenes made the Dominician "*Defensor universal de los Indios*," the adviser to all royal authorities on the Indian question and reporter to a new commission that was to accompany him to the Indies. There were new maneuvers, bribery attempts, denunciations, and intrigues; new trips, subpoenas, reports, delays, obstacles, open and concealed sabotage. In 1520, Las Casas finally achieved an audience with Charles V.

There occurred a lively interchange about which we are informed in detail. In the conversation, which formally resembled the "hearing" of our days, there participated the chancellor of the Spanish crown, several members of the Indian council, a representative of the commission of 1516, as well as the general notary of the Indian territories, a certain Conchillos, who represented the interests of the slave trade. The vehement dispute ended with the general notary offering his resignation to the king, which was accepted. Las Casas left with the title of court chaplain. The king reached the following decision: the procedure of the conquistadors in the Indian lands had been illegal; the Indian council should work out a plan by which the American possessions could be governed "without the force of weapons."

The man who accomplished all this at the imperial court was no longer a newcomer but an experienced politician, familiar with the way in which those who governed thought. Las Casas had not lost his uninhibitedness and he was less than ever prepared for compromises; yet surprisingly quickly he had developed into a tactician of great style. A few places in the *Brief Account* allow us to reconstruct his line of argument before the king. He proceeded in every respect from the assumption that the king knew nothing of the crimes being committed in his name.

> Your Majesty will find out that there are no Christians in these lands; instead, there are demons. There are neither servants of God nor of the King. Because, in truth, the great obstacle to my being able to bring the Indians from war-making to a peaceful way of life, and to bringing the knowledge of God to those Indians who are peaceful is the harsh and cruel treatment of these Indians by the Spanish Christians. For which scabrous and bitter reason no word can be more hateful to those Indians than the word Christian which they render in their language as *Yares*, meaning Demons. And without a doubt they are right, because the actions of these Governors are neither Christian nor humane but are actions of the devil.

Such sentences acquit the king of all complicity; but they are that much more dangerous for his representatives. Their ambiguity appears as soon as Las Casas turns to the question of how the booty is to be divided.

> Our King and Master has been deceived by certain highly pernicious and deceitful machinations; just as there have been continual efforts to hide the truth from Him that the Spaniards in the Indies are transgressing in the most terrible manner against God and Man and against His Majesty's royal honor.

Of course, Las Casas was completely aware that the Spanish crown was totally dependent on the income from the colonies. One year before the audience the Augsburg business firm Welser had financed the election of Charles V, and his dependency on the banks was notorious everywhere in Europe. Las Casas also turned this situation to his advantage. He charged that the conquistadors' violent behavior had cost the king hundreds of thousands of crowns year after year; their conduct deprived the state treasury and only enriched the local governors. This line of argument finally amounts to a demand for centralization and refinement of colonial exploitation, yet it certainly must have made more of an impression on Charles V than all the theological and legal arguments that Las Casas brought to bear.

Besides, Las Casas himself fell victim to the tactical ingenuity that he manifested in his 1520 audience. At that time he is supposed to have pointed out the delicate constitution of the Indians, and have said that the inhabitants of Africa were far better suited for the toil of the mine and plantation work. This suggestion was taken up, and in the course of the following 350 years between fifteen and twenty million people were dragged off and sold as slaves to America. The slave trade, one of the biggest business deals in the history of the world, invoked the words Las Casas had uttered in 1520 and called him its patron. He did not defend himself, but in his *Historia general de las Indias* one finds the lapidary sentence:

> The priest Las Casas was the first to suggest that one should introduce Africans to the West Indies. He did not know what he was doing. When he heard that the Portuguese were catching people in Africa against all laws and made them into slaves he bitterly regretted his words . . . the right of the Blacks is the same as that of the Indians.

Las Casas had found the support of the king. But the king was remote. The laws got stuck. Little changed in the practice of American colonialization. In 1523, Don Bartolomé entered a Dominican monastery in Hispaniola where he remained for nearly ten years. During this time he laid the theoretical foundation for his future actions. His major scholarly works were begun and conceived at that time: first the *Apologetic History of the Indies*, then the source book, the *Historia general de las Indias.* Though they may find some fault with Las Casas's methods, these works are invaluable for the modern historian of the *Conquista.* Their author was gifted with the instinct and sagacity of the true historian. He systematically collected manuscripts, letters, and official documents that referred to the conquest of America. The world is indebted to him, for example, for the knowledge of Columbus's ships' diaries—a transcript in his archives preserved them. However, Las Casas did not confine himself to the role of a chronicler. His understanding of the Indian cultures helped him to gain anthropological insights that were completely alien to his contemporaries. He supported the opinion that the American cultures could not be measured by European standards, that one should understand them out of their own prerequisites. He was probably the first to compare the Mayan temples in Yucatan to the pyramids. He felt that the Spanish had no reason whatsoever to feel superior to the Indians; he preferred them in many respects to his own countrymen. Such insights announce, two hundred years before Vico, the dawning of a historical consciousness. Las Casas understood human culture as an evolutionary process, and he understood that civilization is not a singular but a plural: he discovered the discontemporaneity of historical developments and the relativity of the European position. With such a historical understanding he stands, as far as I can tell, quite alone in the sixteenth century. To the governments of the West, judging by their actions, such an understanding has remained alien to this day.

In the 1530s, Las Casas resumed the political fight. He first visited Venezuela, Peru, New Granada, Darién, and Guatemala. There was another fracas in Nicaragua in 1539. One of the Dominican's sermons provoked the soldiers of a Spanish expeditionary corps to desert. The expedition ended with a defeat of the depleted troops whose commander denounced Las Casas in Madrid for treason. Again he had to make the trip to Spain, which at that time took from eight to sixteen weeks, so as to defend himself. It was at this time that he wrote the *Brief Account*, had himself consecrated bishop, and finally effected a comprehensive legal regulation of the Indian question. The new laws—*Las Nuevas Leyes de las Indias*—were announced in Seville in 1542. They prohibited the viceroys and governors, all royal officials and soldiers, the clerics and monasteries, and all public institutions from taking Indians into their service by way of the *encomienda*. All Indians who were subject to his law or those who had been "recommended" without royal decree were considered free. The law awarded every native worker an appropriate wage. Pearl fishing was prohibited. The new laws end with the sentence: "The inhabitants of the Indian Lands are to be treated in every respect as free subjects of the crown of Castile: for there exists no difference between the latter and the former."

The new laws immediately encountered bitter and organized resistance in the Spanish colonies in America. The entrepreneurs openly declared that they were dependent on the slave economy. The judges for the most part sided with the local interests; but even when they were not bribed it proved impossible for them to assert the new laws against the will of the military and civil administration. After four years the attempt by the "protector of all the Indians" to secure their rights legislatively broke down once and for all. Under pressure from the American interests, Charles V revoked the laws on 20 November 1545.

Las Casas, already an old man, must have realized that his fight could not be won politically. However, he did not think of resigning. He withdrew to a terrain where the pressure group of plantation owners could not attack him. This was the area of everyday theological practice. As bishop of Chiapas in Mexico, he issued a text with the following title: *Confessional: that is, Aid to all confessors who have to give the sacrament to the Spanish gentlemen in the Indian lands.* This penitential sets forth the condition under which a conquistador, a plantation or mine owner, a slave or weapon dealer can receive absolution. Las Casas demanded as prerequisite a notarized protocol in which the penitent had to obligate himself to complete indemnification—in legally binding form. Since such documents were usually drawn up at the deathbed, this amounted to a creation of testaments in favor of the Indians. The *Aid* determined down to the smallest detail how the dying person's possessions were to be disposed of, and how the inheritance was to be legally handled. The effect of the text was sensational. Las Casas had found a stronger ally than the king: the Spaniard's fear of hell. The advice he gave to the confessors meant that everyone who refused to fulfill the conditions would be excommunicated. Of course, Las Casas's penitential was effective in only a few dioceses. After a few years the horror of the faithful subsided and the penitential fell into disuse. Still, it earned its author a new denunciation for high treason and insult to the crown; the penitential could have the effect, so the accusation claimed, of undermining royal sovereignty in the West Indies. Once again Las Casas had to follow a subpoena to Madrid. He left America in the summer of 1547, never to return.

Las Casas was almost eighty years old. The proceeding against him petered out. He had himself divested of his bishop's office. In the decade left in his life he continued his anthropological and legal research and published the first edition of his works. Everything he thought and wrote focused on the problem of colonialism. He was to have one last great public appearance before the political and academic world in 1550. This was the famous disputation of Valladolid. The man whom Las Casas confronted there was the leading ideologist of the *Conquista:* Juan Ginés de Sepúlveda. The conflict was conducted very sharply by both sides. There exists a record of this conversation, whose florid title points to the heart of the dispute: *Disputation or controversy between the bishop Fray Don Bartolomé de Las Casas, formerly head pastor of the royal city of Chiapas, which lies in the Indies and belongs to New Spain; and Dr. Ginés de Sepúlveda, the court chronicler of our imperial majesty; about whether, as the Doctor claims, the conquest of the Indian lands and the war against the Indians is justified; or whether, as the Bishop counters and proclaims, the war is tyrannical, unjust and illegal; which question was probed in the presence of many theological and legal scholars at an assembly which was convened by the wish and will of his majesty in Valladolid in 1550.*

The disputation ended with a complete defeat for Sepúlveda, who withdrew from his courtly office and whose book *About the Just War Against the Indians* fell victim to the Inquisition. Like all of Las Casas's victories, this, too, was a Pyrrhic one. The theory of the *Conquista* had been heavily damaged, but nothing changed in the condition of the Indians.

Las Casas died in the summer of 1566 in Madrid. On his desk was found his last manuscript: *About the Sixteen Remedies Against the Plague Which Has Exterminated the Indians.* "The death candle in his hand," it says in a contemporary report, "and prepared to depart this world, he begged his friends to continue the defense of the Indians. He was sad that he had been able to achieve so little for them, yet was convinced that in everything he had done he had done right."

There is no monument in Spain to remind you of Las Casas, and no one knows where he is buried.

Bartolomé de las Casas was not a radical. He did not preach revolution. His loyalty to the Church and to the crown are undisputed. He fought for the equal rights of the Indians as subjects of an authority he acknowledged. A radical transformation of the social order was as unthinkable for him as for his contemporaries; he wanted to bring the one that existed to the point where it would live up to its own ideology. Every social order contains a utopia with which it decorates itself and that it simultaneously distorts. Las Casas did not guess that this promise, which was also contrary to the idea of the state of his time, can only be fulfilled at the price of revolution, partially, occasionally, as long and insofar as a new form of domination does not encapsulate and negate it again.

Yet utopian thoughts were not alien to Las Casas. He was the contemporary of Thomas More and of Machiavelli, of Rabelais and of Giovanni Botero. In 1521, he tried nothing less than the founding of his own Nova Atlantis. The undertaking shows the unity of theory and practice that characterizes all his work. It ended catastrophically.

At his audience with Charles V, Las Casas suggested to the emperor, as proof that his principles withstood the test of practice, to found a model colony of "the plough and the word." The emperor decreed the district of Cumaná in Venezuela to him with the proviso that "no Spanish subject may enter this territory with arms." Las Casas recruited a group of farmers, outfitted an unarmed expedition, and started to build his colony. Attacks by Spanish soldiers and by slave dealers on the peaceful territory, uprisings by embittered Indians, whiskey smuggling, and acts of violence destroyed the colony in a short time. None of the defeats he suffered hurt Las Casas more deeply than this loss.

The proof of the experiment has not been exhausted to this day. There is no peaceful colonialism. Colonial rule cannot be founded on the plough and the word, but only on the sword and the fire. Every "alliance for progress" needs its "gorillas," every "peaceful penetration" is dependent on its bomber commando, and every "reasonable reformer" such as General Lansdale finds his Marshal Ky.

Bartolomé de Las Casas was not a reformer. The new colonialism that today rules the poor world cannot invoke his name. In the decisive question of force, Las Casas never wavered; the subjugated people lead, in his words, "a just struggle, the lawful basis of which will be acknowledged by every reasonable and justice-loving man." The regime of the wealthy over the poor, which Las Casas was the first to describe, has not ended. The *Brief Account* is a look back into our own future.

1966

6) RELUCTANT EUROCENTRISM

A Political Picture Puzzle

THE INTELLECTUAL WORLD has its own deadly sins, which are not to be found in the catechism. As if they didn't have their hands full with envy and gluttony, pride, and fascination, the intellectuals are constantly inventing (and trespassing against) new prohibitions. Venerable and familiar names, like those listed in the confessional—sloth, avarice, pride—are out of the question as sins for the intelligentsia; they lack the high-quality scientific cachet, the watermark of abstraction.

Nor can the deviations of consciousness put in a claim for consecration by eternity. A wrathful god who would separate the white from the black sheep is not in sight, and the world spirit has fallen silent too. Rather, it's the watchdogs of whatever doctrine is dominant, if not indeed of fashion, who take care that the villain is exposed and the upright man is rewarded. So whoever sins intellectually by no means risks eternal damnation. At worst he is reviled for a while, pulled apart by critics, or completely ignored. A few years or decades pass, a new register of sins is agreed upon, and the formerly depraved deviationist is rehabilitated. Anticommunism, for example, an aberration which was considered unforgivable among enlightened people for decades, is today altogether socially acceptable again, indeed it is almost de rigueur.

It's quite a different matter, however, with the cardinal

intellectual sin of the 1970s, a mode of thought which bears the curious name Eurocentrism; its reprehensibility, I believe, remains unquestioned even today.

The Europeans noticed quite early on that they are not alone in this world; and they turned this circumstance to their advantage quite early on. The history of our "discoveries" consisted, as we know, of colonizing the inhabitants of other continents, and that meant conquering and robbing them.

Ethnology, a new science of humanity, owes its development to this bloody process. Its Anglo-Saxon representatives have introduced the ambitious name "anthropology" for their subject, a variation that, for lack of specialist knowledge, I would rather leave unexamined. After the seafarers and the soldiers, the adventures and the missionaries, the planters and the engineers, the traveling scholars also fanned out in their turn, to discover what kind of people were to be converted and robbed, civilized and exterminated, out there in the remotest regions of the earth.

The more intelligent among the anthropologists soon noticed that their researchers were leading them into an epistemological and moral labyrinth. Because it was precisely what interested them most, the otherness of what used to be called the primitive peoples, the savages, the barbarians, the colored races, which remained inaccessible, and not only because the latter received them with a mistrust that was all too justified.

Yet the real hindrance to research was the researcher himself, together with his discipline. It was this, like everything else that the ethnologist brought with him—his gaze, his standards, his prejudices, his language—which placed itself between him and what he wanted to investigate, and so he ran the risk of bringing home only dead facts and living errors. His arrival alone was already a considerable invasion of the societies he wanted to observe, an interference factor of incalculable magnitude.

It is not surprising therefore, that (as the ethnologist Fritz Kramer has shown in a brilliant book) the booty of anthropological research consists largely of European fancies. It's our own reflection that perpetually appears on the projection screen of science; only we have no desire to recognize ourselves in it.

Ways of escaping ethnology's dilemma are few and risky. Of course, it is possible to postulate the equality of all human societies and to raise the demand that every community must be described and judged on the basis of its own conditions. But that is easier said than done. A consistent relativism assumes an observer who would be in a position to leave his own cultural baggage at home. Such a scientist would not only have to be a master of brainwashing, he would also have to be capable of using it on himself. Only then would he, as an ethnologist, be completely free of his "European" prejudices—but along with them of his science as well.

Another way of solving the dilemma—it could be called the existential one—is to gamble one's own identity. The researcher becomes a kind of renegade. He joins his Melanesians, Nahuas, Malagasies in the bush. *He goes native:* that's what in their day the English colonial rulers called the irregular, unscientific form of such a change of identity. In anthropology, a mild version of this method is described as "participant observation." The stranger adapts to the way of life he meets with, he tries to penetrate the mentality of the peoples with whom he is staying, by transforming himself into a Melanesian, Nahua, Malagasy.

It is evident that such experiments do not spirit away the original dilemma. They lead, rather, into an extensive maze of ambiguities. Because the researcher's transformation is an experiment with a time limit, an as-if which once again divides him from his hosts. His ulterior motive remains intact. The anthropologist becomes an actor, a ventriloquist, or a spy.

These are roles that a respectable academic finds difficult. Anthropology as a shell-game of culture and identity: not all researchers would be prepared to come to terms with such a definition. A minority sought and found a way out of the dilemma in the politicization of their discipline. They took the side of the oppressed and threatened peoples who were the object of their work. Some of these radical renegades saw the civilization from which they came as the principal enemy of humanity. In accordance with the maxim "the last shall be the first," they believed in the future of the "savages" and demonstrated their solidarity with them. And it was they who coined the term Eurocentrism and turned it polemically against their academic colleagues who preferred to remain what they were: professors in Uppsala and Göttingen, in Louvain, Cambridge, and Paris.

All in all an esoteric business, one of those theoretical bones on which a small band of specialists gnaws in quiet and with some pleasure. So it might appear, and so indeed it was, until about twenty years ago. In the short period of time which has passed since then, the problem of Eurocentrism has irreversibly established itself in our consciousness—yes, one can say that in its most general and trivial form it has become a platitude.

The historical reasons are obvious. The collapse of European colonial rule in its traditional form, the liberation movements in Asia, Africa, and Latin America and the political, economic, and ideological consequences of this global process have fundamentally altered our picture of the world.

We have learned that we are in the minority, and that those others, the majority, are not hanging around somewhere on the periphery of the inhabited world as passive objects of our economic interests and our scientific curiosity. Such knowledge is not gained voluntarily; it only establishes itself when there is no other possibility.

Only thirty years ago Europeans and North Americans could still ignore the most enormous events without much effort; the Chinese Civil War, the colonial massacres in Indonesia and Madagascar were only hazily noticed. That only changed with the Algerian War, the Cuban revolution, the conflict in the Near East, and the wars in Indochina. The brightly colored scenes from the cigarette card album, the wax figures in the ethnological museum came to life, they turned up in person in the living room. The TV screen teemed with evidence. A problem that until then a couple of anthropologists had discussed in their tent or in a seminar, became the common property of primary school teachers and journalists, of social workers and parish priests.

Really understanding what was now on the agenda of history was another matter. That is obvious even from the attempts to give the state of affairs a name. The crudest terms were good enough to indicate the breach that had opened up before our eyes: over here the developed, over there the underdeveloped countries, over here the poor, over there the rich countries; and the confrontation between them was sometimes called the "international class struggle," and sometimes, in the euphemistic vocabulary of Social Democracy, the "North–South conflict." In a futile effort to label an explosion, the majority of the others in Asia, Africa, and Latin America were given the name "the Third World."

That this was not a concept but a portmanteau, a semantic

all-purpose term, became clear in the 1970s at the latest, when the oil-producing countries became the moguls of the world economy while in Africa and Indochina whole countries more or less starved.

Has there ever been a European who seriously believed that the yellow races were yellow? Did you really think that the Savages were savage, the Coloreds colored, the Primitives primitive? Did you perhaps think that the explosion of the world could be numbered one, two, and three? What can China and Niugini have in common, for example? If they have a common denominator at all, then it can only be defined negatively—and that is from our perspective: as lack. These people were missing something, whether it was history or development, a god or a state. And with that we arrived at Eurocentrism again.

Wolfgang B. from Nördlingen, for example, has had himself driven to the top of Victoria Peak even though it's late afternoon. He looks toward China over the glittering skyscrapers, the harbor and the bay and he has to admit the panorama is unique. He's a model-builder by profession, one of the best model-builders in the world probably, en route to Guangzhou, formerly Canton. He's going to construct a complex industrial plant for the trade fair on a scale of 1:30, a toy that doesn't reveal at first glance that the cost is going to run into billions.

Wolfgang B. is an unprejudiced man, he has read books, Edgar Snow, a biography of Mao, a report from a Chinese village. He is looking forward to China, and as far as Hong Kong is concerned, two days' holiday have been enough for him to notice some flaws in the weave of his paradise. He has never studied sociology; quotes from Engels don't flow from his lips on his walks through Kowloon. Instead, he has the habit—simply because of his job—of looking very carefully at what he sees; so, too, at the slums of Hong Kong, the fragile boats of the refugees, the overcrowded blocks of flats, the prostitution, the traffic chaos.

He notices that an omnipresent mafia controls the street-traders, the nightlife and the smuggling; that the salesgirls, the waiters, the employees in the travel agencies play the stock exchange, a kind of Chinese roulette with forward merchandise option deals and goldmine shares; that the Hong Kong police are exceptionally corrupt; and that real-estate speculation has reached terroristic dimensions. Hong Kong is the most beautiful of capitalism's Asiatic dependencies. But the neat promenades, the extravagantly luxuriant parks, the faded dignity of the Hong Kong Club don't delude model-builder Wolfgang B. as to its wolflike character. Only he would express himself a little more succinctly; after all, he isn't an assistant professor.

Fourteen days later, the job in the People's Republic has been concluded, the model completed and handed over to the prospective Chinese buyers, Wolfgang B. begins the return journey. He sits in the air-conditioned express train that links Guangzhou with Hong Kong and feels surprised. He's surprised that he's looking forward to Hong Kong, that he can hardly wait to step out of the train. He'll take a quite ordinary taxi, not the big limousine from the ministry as in Guangzhou. No one will brief him, look after him, patronize him, supervise and instruct him. He will sleep alone in a room without official permission, or not sleep alone in a room, and eat and drink when and where and what he wants. He won't buy himself a diamond-studded watch, neither does he need a Rolls-Royce; but a newspaper in which news is to be found wouldn't be bad, a little naturalness wouldn't be bad. Wolfgang B. thinks of Guangzhou with its crumbling façades, its black-market traders, its sad old men. At the border he leaves a sigh. He can't slip out of his skin.

Eurocentrism—is that model-builder Wolfgang B.'s sin, or is he only suffering from homesickness, a longing that as we well know, does not only draw on the good, true and beautiful things but attaches itself with particular stubbornness to the shabby, the questionable and the defective?

But why then does Wolfgang B., a native Swabian, feel at home in Hong Kong?

If it was only that! But I sat on the same train, and I was told that in the river which forms the border and which the train crosses, the floating bodies of the drowned are found again and again; others have themselves nailed up in containers in order to get over the border to Hong Kong, a dangerous method because it's possible to suffocate in the attempt. These unfortunates, too, are envoys of the overwhelming majority, just as much as those Chinese who legally, for whatever reason, travel from one world to another on the Guangzhou–Hong Kong express and stock up from the hostess with American soft drinks, French *petits fours*, and English cigarettes.

It's the commodities that tell the truth; the cassette recorders in the souks of Damascus, the Seiko watches in the shopwindows of Peking, the jeans and the sunglasses, the whiskeys, the perfumes and the cars. Above all the cars. No victorious liberation front, no starving tropical country, no pedagogic dictatorship, no matter how puritanical, gets by without them. Electrically controlled sliding windows, air conditioning, tinted and bulletproof glass, stereo, automatic locking devices—all inclusive.

This frenetic desire to imitate is a worldwide phenomenon whose implications no one has yet thought through to the end. Its effects are like those of a natural force, they are as irresistible and as little responsible to the control of reason as an avalanche. There has certainly been no shortage of attempts to analyze rationally the needs of poor and underdeveloped countries. Again and again intermediate technologies were proposed in order to relate the structures of traditional societies to the demands of industrialization.

After years of work, the engineers of a European car company developed a vehicle adapted to the conditions of poor tropical countries. Built on a simple modular principle, it didn't need any care, was economical, easy to repair and handle; it was also cheap, since all unnecessary accessories were missing. This car never went into production, since the countries concerned firmly refused to drive cheaper cars than the French or the Americans.

This confidence, or rather this lack of confidence, is not only to be observed in the drawing board states of Central Africa; even great nations with a great past are not free from it. In China a luxury limousine is still being manufactured today which matches in every detail a Russian vehicle from the 1950s, which in its turn is copied from a 1940s American Packard. This copy of a copy moreover bears the name "Red Flag."

On its sky-blue cover the Shanghai telephone directory shows happy people gazing at a sky that is pierced by television towers, rockets, and satellites. The text is interspersed with black and white advertisements and colored plates in which European-looking models display European women's fashions. The pieces of furniture are exact copies of those splay-legged side-tables, dressing tables and wardrobes we remember from the Adenauer era. The whole book is a slim version of the Neckermann mail-order catalogue of 1957.

Now, I haven't the least wish to poke fun at this evidence

of Chinese modernization policy. It's much too depressing for that. What makes one's heart sink is not the fact that the population of a poor country is insisting gently but with elementary force on an improvement in its living standards, but the path of compulsive imitation it adopts in doing so. It seems as if every mistake, every whim, every folly of the West has to be repeated, as if no deformation, no wrong turning can be left out.

Every chair, every bottle of lemonade, is a slavish imitation of a foreign model, as if it would be unthinkable to invent something of one's own, even if only a new reading lamp or radio cabinet. It's inevitable that the copy is inferior to the original. It's not only the shortage of materials and the industrial shortcomings that ensure that this is so; rather, it's in the nature of the process itself, that the out-of-date, the stale, and the shabby triumphs whenever a society puts up with living at second hand.

But, you will object, a society doesn't consist of commodities. Let the Chinese and the Peruvians, the Congolese and the Pakistanis make themselves comfortable however they like; the main thing is that they manage to get hold of the most essential things of all that a human being needs in order to live, a pair of shoes, a bowl of food, a doctor who can bind their wounds. No one can dispute that. But the commodities propagate something beyond their immediate consumption. At just that point at which each person has his shoes, his bowl, his surgeon—and this goal has been achieved in China—they prophesy the future victory of a single culture. But this culture is not Chinese.

Or do you think it doesn't make any difference whether someone carries out calculations with an abacus or with a computer? What happened to *us* at that moment when we sat down behind a steering wheel for the first time, alone, in our own car? Our tools, machines, and products have altered us beyond recognition. Our idiotic architecture, our supermarkets, our three-room apartments, our cosmetics, our television programs which are spreading across the whole world are only individual elements of an evidently irresistible totality.

We've experienced more than one fiasco with "the iron laws of history," but a person who watches television is very different from someone who listens to stories. A Marxist thesis, which no one has yet refuted, says that the unfettered productive forces of capitalist industry make short shrift of every recalcitrant legacy, every autonomous "superstructure." They are the bulldozer of world history, which clears away everything that blocks its way and levels every traditional culture.

And the commodities, appliances, and machines are only the most visible part of what the "developing countries" import. We supply them with weapons and toxins, techniques of government, and propaganda. Even the symbols of their sovereignty are slavish imitations of what they believe they have liberated themselves from through bloody struggles; the idea of the nation, the slogans of the revolution, the concept of the party, the emblems of statehood from national anthem to constitution, from flag to protocol.

Khomeini owes his victory to the cassettes of the Philips company, Amin commanded his gang of murderers in finery that was nothing more than a grotesque imitation of a British general's uniform. Gadhafi equipped his killers with the technical know-how of the West German Federal CID, and Soviet advisers call the tune in the corridors of the interior ministries of Cuba and Mozambique. Among the "West's" inventions that are eagerly copied throughout the world are not only aftershave and the deep-freeze, but also the electric shock and the concentration camp. The *idée fixe* of progress is increasingly being questioned by Europeans and North Americans; it dominates unchallenged only in the "developing countries" of Asia, Africa, and Latin America. The true Eurocentrics are the others.

It is probably fair to say that there is a lot of cant in Western anti-imperialist discourse. There is, by now, a long tradition of self-criticism in our part of the world, particularly on the Left. Ever since the beginning of the twentieth century, it has been commonplace to complain about the decadence of Western civilization, a thesis that has strong roots in conservative thought. Marxist theory has emphasised the economic exploitation of colonial and ex-colonial societies, but simplistic preachers have long since reduced serious analysis to a sort of zero-sum game, arguing that industrial societies live by pilfering the Third World: "*We* are rich because they are poor." In the course of time, the myth of the Noble Savage has been resurrected in the shape of *tiers-mondisme.* The polemic against "consumerism" has been a mainstay of the opposition ever since the 1960s. Inevitably, idealist notions engender a rhetoric rich in banality and bad faith. An opposition based on them may be subjectively well meant, but sooner or later it is bound to founder, because there is no mediation between its "convictions" and the social reality it seeks to transform. The result is, even from a strictly moral point of view, painfully ambiguous: the Left is just as Eurocentric as the rest of us. Its only distinction is a bad conscience, reluctant Eurocentrism.

Others, however, and perhaps they are the best among us, take a different decision. I'm not thinking about the drilling engineers in their air-conditioned ghettos, or the businessmen in their private jets, or the mercenaries, policemen, and marines, but about the doctors on the Cambodian border and the agronomists in the Sahel; about people who have given up their three-room apartments in Wuppertal or St. Louis in order to train mechanics somewhere in the bush or to sink wells in the desert.

The readiness to render spontaneous, altruistic aid appears so strange under prevailing conditions that one responds with perplexity to such nonconformists. Some admire them, others call them, with a certain dubious respect, idealists. Yet others shake their heads or even believe them to be unsuspecting tools of some imperialist plot.

That is always unjust and usually wrong. Nevertheless, it is still necessary to inquire about the inner motives and the meaning of that solidarity with the "Third World" that stirs here and there in the industrial countries of the West. Official development aid doesn't need to concern us any further; its political and economic goals are not secret after all. It is a matter of spheres of influence, raw materials, export interests. The development policies of every industrial power East or West are the continuation of colonial policies by other means.

Anyone, on the other hand, who risks his life as a doctor in order to dress the wounds of rebels or refugees in some African civil war has something else in mind; and something of this larger interest is also to be found among those who have stayed at home, working on obscure committees to raise money for imprisoned trade unionists in Bolivia. The self-deceptions to which such a commitment can lead are well known, and it's also no secret that the ritual playing of Chilean protest songs in Berlin bars had no noticeable influence on the bloody course of events in that country.

But independently of that, of how seriously or halfheartedly, of how effectively or how ineffectively the helpers of the "Third World" may go to work, they are agreed on one point, and this point is the decisive one: they all identify themselves with a cause that is not their own. In this respect, they are the successors of those ethnologists who understood themselves as cultural renegades. The Dane who makes the problems of the Eskimos his own, the student from Massachusetts who organizes a lobby for the Brazilian Indians—all these people want to help not only others but themselves too, and that is completely legitimate.

One could perhaps call what they are looking for among those distant peoples the utopian minimum. The stubborn hope they place in the future of the "Third World" corresponds to their scratching critique of the society that produced them, which has consumed any utopian surplus. The ideological shreds of Marxism or religion in which some of them clothe their search cannot conceal the fact that the goal of this search is to find the "completely other."

But what if this "completely other" doesn't exist? These peoples, proud of their own traditions, unhampered by "consumerism," less decadent and ruined, but older, purer, less corruptible than we are, pursuing their own project despite sacrifices and hardships—perhaps they only exist in the imagination of those who are looking for them?

And does this search not also have a disagreeable side? Does it not reproduce the old dilemma of the anthropologist, forever confronted by his own ghosts in the stranger's mirror? Is the "Third World" in the end nothing more than a projection?

At any rate, there's something odd about the enthusiasm with which many visitors from the industrialized world regard the Spartan features of some "liberation movements."

Someone who, having flown four thousand miles, enthuses about the unique dignity of the rice farmers cultivating their fields with their bare hands standing knee deep in the mud, deserves to have his behavior called moral cretinism rather than solidarity. And what about the iron social control, the sexual repression, the dull-witted formalism, the bureaucratic despotism that weighs upon large parts of the underdeveloped world? We can't judge that from our position, these are transitional phenomena, the people there have different needs. . . . Admittedly that wouldn't be right for us, but in their circumstances . . . And so on.

Is that not the most naked racism masked as sympathy? Is it asking too much for an American in Angola, a Swede in China, a German in Cuba, to say to himself, at least once a day, as an experiment: These people are just like us? And that means that they not only want schools and hospitals, canteens and barracks, they want to choose their profession just like us. They want to love one another. They want to have the choice. They want to have freedom of movement. They want to think for themselves and make decisions for themselves. And apart from that they want machines instead of flails, cars instead of handcarts, refrigerators, holiday trips, telephones, three-room apartments. Just like us.

Poor Pasolini resisted this truth to the point of self-destruction. His utopia of the "Third World" didn't flinch from any conclusion. It didn't just put up with poverty; it elevated it into a virtue. To this moralist, underdevelopment appeared as paradise lost; a paradise that was cruel and hard but also humane. He found this "Third World" in his own country, in the backward regions of Italy, and he watched as it was gradually destroyed by industrial progress. Disappointment over this loss put Pasolini in a rage that was as clear-headed as it was reckless. In the end he reviled the very people he wanted to protect from this crime: his countrymen who were fleeing the chronic underdevelopment of the south to look for a better life. And for them that meant looking for the world which promised them cars, television, and three-room apartments, and which in the eyes of Pasolini, who was murdered in his own sports car, was corrupt and the devil's work.

Since the abandonment of the last alternative project of history, that of Mao Zedong, only one future seems still to be left. The peoples of Asia, Africa, and Latin America have fallen under the spell of a universal cargo cult: everything new, whether for good or ill, comes from the industrial countries, and everything old must be sacrificed to the new.

But the massive approval our civilization receives does not fill us with triumph. On the contrary, it disappoints us, irritates us, makes us uneasy. We have no desire to be number one. We long ago got out of the habit of regarding Europe as the navel of the world, and we find the idea that the future of the human race could resemble a migration of lemmings led by us altogether depressing.

There are several reasons, subjective and objective, good and bad, why we don't like to be confronted by the Eurocentrism of the underdeveloped. It is not an uplifting thought to be flag-bearers of a civilization whose catastrophic potential becomes more obvious year by year. It has never been the case before in history that humanity has staked everything on a single card. To a certain extent, it lived scattered in a great number of autonomous cultures, each one pursuing its own project. Looked at in that way, the Tower of Babel had its positive side: far from coming to terms with one another, a multiplicity of societies evolved, inventing specific solutions for their own survival. With the industrial revolution this diversity began to disappear. Its last remnants are being liquidated before our eyes. That's not only sad, it's very dangerous; because the more homogeneous a population is, the more susceptible it is to catastrophes and the gloomier are its prospects for the future.

Besides, it's as good as certain that our able successors in the poorer countries are backing the wrong horse. A simple computer projection of their needs and of the resources that would be required to generalize the material standards of the Western industrial countries demonstrates the hopelessness of such an undertaking. Three billion cars, 400 million tons of meat, 40 million gigawatt hours of electricity, 12 billion tons of oil per annum. The planet that is our home can't provide all that. The consequences of unchanged targets are wars of distribution, extortion, vast conflicts. The "Third World's" enthusiastic willingness to learn does not only worry us for noble reasons. The closer industrial progress gets to the ecological limits of capacity, the more our civilization resembles a zero-sum game: one player's gain is another's loss.

Yet the existence of the others with projects that weren't ours, the existence of fundamentally different cultures somewhere out there in the jungle, in the taiga, in the desert, was also a psychological comfort to the "civilized" of the earth. These distant neighbors meant a relief from the strain. They allowed us to dream of another, lost life. Whenever the price we had to pay for progress was hurting us, we thought of the others, savages, blacks, bedouins, orientals, nomads, Eskimos, hunters, Malays, inhabitants of mythical islands; the naive patchwork of a colorful humanity, that was different from us, and with whom our disappointed hopes found an ambiguous refuge. We imposed upon the others what our own industrialized existence denied us, desires, promised lands, utopias. The method of projection is deeply rooted in the European tradition. I even believe that the internationalism of the Left in Europe and North America derives for the greatest part from such sources. So the revolutionary hope that has come to nothing is transferred further and further into the distanced, first to Russia and Central Asia, then to China and to the so-called Third World.

It is time to take leave of such dreams. It was always an illusion that liberation could be delegated to the faraway others; today this self-deception has become a threadbare evasion. An exotic alternative to industrial civilization no longer exists. We are encircled and besieged by our own limitations.

Their worries are different from ours. How does a poor country achieve primary accumulation? How can an unstable nation be consolidated? How can steel production be increased? How can agriculture be mechanized? These are questions that were on the agenda in Europe and North America a hundred years ago. It is part of the fateful inheritance of the underdeveloped countries that they are unable to set themselves any historically new problems. That is a consequence of their situation and not, as the incorrigible racists among us imagine, of some kind of original inferiority. (A parenthesis for idiots of this kind, who, it is to be feared, will never die out: take a look at the Chinese physicists in Princeton, the Indian biochemists in Berkeley, the Iranian surgeons in Holland. And who built glittering Hong Kong? The 2 percent who are white, and live there more tolerated than determining, or the 98 percent who are Chinese? It is all simply and solely a question of social context. So much for the obvious. Close parenthesis.)

It is the West that remains, spreading out in every direction. The new problems are being posed here, and here alone, and here alone are to be found, sparingly enough, the new solutions. Not too much has occurred to us in recent decades: apart from birth control, ecology, feminism, they have been, above all, technological tricks—microcomputers, means of communication, and decisive steps in basic research, principally in molecular biology.

But perhaps, behind our backs as it were, something else has happened that would be much more momentous. Perhaps that savage, distant, brightly colored diversity which was external to our civilization has immigrated into its centers. The increasing dangerousness of everyday life in the great cities of the West would be one indication of that. The more the exotic is eliminated worldwide, and the more traditional diversity is made to conform, the more the industrial societies become a patchwork internally. Not only the United States, but also France, Sweden, West Germany are melting pots today, multiracial states. Ethnic minorities, subcultures, political and religious sects establish themselves in the metropoles. This unpredictable confusion is not only a result of immigration from outside, its roots lie in the same historic continent that gave birth to industrial growth.

The vitality of the West derives, in the end, from the negativity of European thinking, its eternal dissatisfaction, its voracious unrest, its *lack*. Doubt, self-criticism, self-hate, even, are its more important productive forces. It's our strength that we can't accept ourselves and what we have produced. That's why we regard Eurocentrism as a sin of consciousness. Western civilization lives from whatever calls it into question, whether it's barbarians or anarchists, red Indians, or Bolsheviks. And if a cultural other is no longer available, then we just produce our own savages:

technological freaks, political freaks, psychic freaks, cultural freaks, moral freaks, religious freaks. Confusion, unrest, ungovernability are our only chance. Disunity makes us strong.

From now on we have to rely on our own resources. No Tahiti is in sight, no Sierra Maestre, no Sioux and no Long March. Should there be such a thing as a saving idea, then we'll have to discover it for ourselves.

1980

7) EUROPE IN RUINS

A few days before I left Luanda, I was taken by American friends to dine in a black-market restaurant. We ate at outside tables in a little enclosure on the street. The clientele all looked more or less as if they were black-market profiteers themselves. We were sitting right next to the rail that fenced us in from the street, and I had my back to this, so that, absorbed in conversation, I did not notice at first that a crowd had gathered behind us and people were reaching in to grab things from our plates. But the management soon sent out a bouncer, who knocked down an old woman with a blow on the head, and drove back the mob, mostly women and children, some of whom disappeared, while others, keeping their distance, stood dumbly and stared at the diners.

Here in Beirut, refugees are lying on all the steps, and one has the impression that they would not look up even were a miracle to take place in the middle of the square, so certain are they that none will happen. One could tell them that some country beyond the Lebanon was prepared to accept them, and they would gather up their boxes, without really believing. Their life is unreal, a waiting without expectation, and they no longer cling to it: rather, life clings to them, ghostlike, an unseen beast that grows hungry and drags them through the ruined railway stations, day and night, in sunshine and in rain; it breathes in the sleeping children as they lie on the rubble, their hands between bony arms, curled up like embryos in the womb, as if longing to return there.

The war in El Salvador has gone on for years now, with no sign of peace in sight. Time and again it has seemed that the govern-

> ment has gained a decisive victory; but the guerrillas always crop up again, not much weaker than before. A point to be kept in mind vividly is that the leadership had roughly eight thousand troops when the war was started; today, though the losses in killed and captured have been considerable, they number more than twenty thousand.
>
> Unsettling about this place in the North of Sri Lanka is not that one fears being molested—at any rate not during the day—but, rather, because of the sure knowledge that people of one's own sort, if suddenly faced with living this kind of life, would go under within three days. One feels very keenly that even a life like this has its own laws, and it would take years to learn them. A truck full of policemen: at once they scatter, some stand still and grin, while I look on and have no idea what is happening. Four boys and three girls are loaded into the truck, where they squat down among others who have already been picked up elsewhere. Indifferent, impenetrable. The police have helmets and automatics, therefore authority, but no knowledge. The newspapers carry a daily column of street attacks, sometimes naked corpses are discovered, and the murderers come as a rule from the other side. Whole districts without a single light. A landscape of brick hills, beneath them the buried, above them the twinkling stars; nothing stirs there but rats.

Reports from the Third World, the kind we read every morning over breakfast. The place names are false, however. The locations involved are not Luanda and Beirut, El Salvador an Trincomalee; they are Rome and Frankfurt-am-Main, Athens and Berlin. Only forty-five years separate us from conditions we have become accustomed to thinking of as African, Asian, or Latin American.

At the end of World War II, Europe was a pile of ruins, not only in a physical sense; it also seemed bankrupt in political and moral terms. It was not only the defeated Germans for whom the situation seemed hopeless. When Edmund Wilson came to London in July 1945, he found the English in a state of collective depression. The mood of the city reminded him of the cheerlessness of Moscow: "How empty, how sickish, how senseless everything suddenly seems the moment the war is over! We are left flat with the impoverished and humiliating life that the drive against the enemy kept our minds off. Where our efforts have all gone toward destruction, we have been able to build nothing at home to fall back on amidst our own ruin."[1]

No one dared believe that the devastated continent could still have a future at all. As far as Europe was concerned, it seemed as if its history had come to an end with an overwhelming act of self-destruction, which the Germans had initiated and completed with savage energy: "This is what exists," noted Max Frisch in the spring of 1946, "the grass growing in the houses, the dandelions in the churches, and suddenly one can imagine how it might all continue to grow, how a forest might creep over our cities, slowly, inexorably, thriving unaided by human hands, a silence of thistles and moss, an earth without history, only the twittering of birds, spring, summer and autumn, the breathing of years, which there is no one to count any more."

If, in the 1940s, someone had told the cave-dwellers of Dresden or Warsaw what life in 1990 would be like, they would have thought him crazy. But for people today, their own past has become just as unimaginable. They have long repressed and forgotten it, and those who are younger lack the imagination as well as the knowledge to make a picture of those distant times. It grows increasingly difficult, year by year, to imagine the condition of our continent at the end of World War II. The storytellers, apart from Heinrich Böll, Primo Levi, Hans Werner Richter, Louis-Ferdinand Céline and Curzio Malaparte and a few others, capitulated before the subject; the so-called *Trümmerliteratur*—literature of the ruins—hardly delivered what it promised.

Old newsreels show monotonous pictures of destruction, the narration consists of hollow phrases; the films provide no indication of the inner state of the men and women passing through the devastated cities. The memoir literature that came later lacks authority, in part because the authors are often prone to self-justification and self-accusation. But another objection weighs more heavily, one that does not cast doubt on their integrity, but on their perspective. In looking back, they lose the very thing that should matter most: the coincidence of the observer with what he is looking at. The best sources tend to be the eyewitness accounts of contemporaries.

Studying eyewitness reports is, however, an odd experience. A peculiarity of the postwar period is a strange ignorance, a narrowing of horizons, that is unavoidable under extreme living conditions. At best it is a straightforward lack of knowledge of the world, which is easily explained by the years of isolation. John Gunther writes of a young soldier in Warsaw, with whom he entered into conversation on a summer evening in 1948: "There was no nonsense about him. He knew exactly what Poland had suffered and what he himself had suffered. His ignorance of the outside world was, however, considerable. He had never met an American before. He wanted to know if New York had been made *kaputt* by the war like Warsaw."

Elsewhere the Americans were looked at as though they were men from mars, and everything they brought with them was treated with a reverence reminiscent of the cargo cults of Polynesia. During these years, Europeans displayed attitudes akin to those found in the Third World. Someone who is only thinking of the next meal, who is forced to nail together a roof over his own head, will usually lack the desire and energy to make himself aware and well informed. On top of that, there was the absence of freedom of movement. Millions were on the move, but only to save their skins. Travel, in the usual sense of the word, was not possible.

The poverty of sources is not, however, due to external causes alone. In the first years after the war, the long-term consequences of the fascist dictatorships were becoming evident everywhere. That was true above all in Germany, but could also be observed elsewhere (there were collaborators in every occupied country). And this is exactly why those directly involved make the worst witnesses. Europeans took shelter behind a collective amnesia. Reality was not just ignored, it was flatly denied. With a mixture of lethargy, defiance, and self-pity, they regressed to a kind of second childhood. Anyone meeting this syndrome for the first time was astonished; it seemed to be a form of moral insanity. When she visited the Rhineland in April 1945, the American journalist Martha Gellhorn was incensed, indeed staggered, by the statements of the Germans she met:

> No one is a Nazi. No one ever was. There may have been some Nazis in the next village, and as a matter of fact, that town about twenty kilometres away was a veritable hotbed of Nazism. To tell you the truth, confidentially, there were a lot of Communists here. We were always known as very Red. Oh, the Jews? Well, there weren't really many Jews in this neighbourhood. Two, maybe six. They were taken away. I hid a Jew for six weeks. I hid a Jew for eight weeks. (I hid a Jew, he hid a Jew, all God's chillun hid Jews.) We have nothing against the Jews; we always got on well with them. We have had enough of this government. Ah, how we have suffered. The bombs. We lived in the cellars for weeks. We welcome the Americans. We do not fear them; we

have no reason to fear. We have done nothing wrong; we are not Nazis.

It should,we feel, be set to music. Then the Germans could sing this refrain and that would make it even better. They all talk like this. One asks oneself how the detested Nazi government, to which no one paid allegiance, managed to carry on this way for five and a half years. Obviously not a man, woman or child in Germany ever approved of the war for a minute, according to them. We stand around looking blank and contemptuous and listen to this story without friendliness and certainly without respect. To see a whole nation passing the buck is not an enlightening spectacle.

More than two years later, another observer from abroad, the journalist Janet Flanner, came to similar conclusions:

The new Germany is bitter against everyone else on earth, and curiously self-satisfied. Bursting with complaints of her hunger, lost homes, and other sufferings, she considers without interest or compassion the pains and losses she imposed on others, and she expects and takes, usually with carping rather than thanks, charity from those nations she tried to destroy. . . . The significant Berlin catch-all phrase is: "That was the war, but this is the peace." This cryptic remark means, in free translation, that the people feel no responsibility for the war, which they regard as an act of history, and that they consider the troubles and confusions of the peace the Allies' fault. People here never mention Hitler's name any more. They just say darkly "*Früher war es besser*" (things were better before), meaning under Hitler. Only a few Germans seem to remember that, beginning with the occupations of 1940, some of them had the sense to launch the slogan "Enjoy the war. The peace will be terrible." It is.

So much for the state of consciousness of the Germans. Other Europeans were no less deluded. John Gunther reports: "I asked one responsible Greek politician what the solution was, if any, and he replied in one word, 'War.' Indeed many conservative Greeks feel that nothing but outright war between the United States and the Soviet Union can rescue them; they actively want a war, horrible as this may seem, and make no bones about it. I asked my friend, 'But do you think there is going to be a war?' He answered, 'Europe is in anarchy. One hundred million people are slaves. We *have* to have war. There *must* be a war, or we will lose everything.' "

Anyone who now turns to published opinion in the hope of gaining a clearer picture of the situation in postwar Europe, faces further disappointment. It is virtually impossible to find sober verdicts, intelligent analyses, and convincing reportage in the newspaper and magazine columns of the years 1945 to 1948. That is not solely due to the restrictions imposed by the occupying powers. The state of mind of the journalists, their internal self-censorship is of much greater consequence. The Germans distinguished themselves in this respect, too. Instead of coolly bearing witness to the facts, the intellectuals by and large took flight into abstractions. One searches in vain for the great reportage. What one finds, besides philosophical generalizations on the theme of collective guilt, are endless invocations of the Western tradition. Curious how much talk there is of Goethe, of humanism, the forgetfulness of being and the "idea of freedom." One gets the impression that this faded idealism is only another form of unconsciousness. Evidently, it was not only the physical surroundings that were devastated, but the powers of observation as well. The whole of Europe had, as it were, "been knocked on the head."

For all of these reasons, little reliance can be placed on the testimony of those directly affected. Anyone who wants to get a reasonably accurate picture of conditions immediately after the war has to turn to other sources. There can be little doubt that our most trustworthy source is the gaze of the *outsider*. The most acute reports were provided by those authors who followed the victorious Allied armies. Among them stand out the best reporters of America, journalists such as Janet Flanner and Martha Gellhorn, and writers like Edmund Wilson, who did not think themselves too good to work for the press. They are all part of the great Anglo-Saxon tradition of literary reportage—continental Europeans have, until now, failed to produce anything to equal it. Other valuable sources were the product of chance, like the confidential reports of an American editor who worked for the US secret service, or the notes of émigrés who made the attempt to return to the Old World. Later, authors from countries the war had spared, such as the Swiss Max Frisch and the Swedish novelist Stig Dagerman, also made contributions.

They each came from a world that was similar to ours: orderly, normal, characterized by the thousand and one things we take for granted in a functioning civil society. The sense of shock engendered by the European disaster they confronted was all the greater. They could hardly believe their eyes in the face of the brutal, eccentric, terrifying, and moving scenes they experienced in Paris and Naples, in the villages of Crete and the catacombs of Warsaw. It is the stranger's gaze that is able to make us comprehend what was happening in Europe then; for it does not rely on restrictive ideological analysis but on the telling physical detail. While the leading articles and polemics of the period have a strange mustiness about them, these eyewitness reports remain fresh.

The specialists in perception are at their best when they generalize least, when they do not censor the fantastic contradictions of the chaotic world they have entered, but leave them as they are. Max Frisch concludes his notes on Berlin quoted at the beginning with a laconic remark that silences all discussion of the state of civilization: "A landscape of brick hills, beneath them the buried, above them the twinkling stars; nothing stirs there but rats.—Evening at the theatre: *Iphigenia.*"

An altogether startling degree of foresight emerges from the texts of these outsiders. In the capitals of the victorious powers at the time, whole planning commissions of politicians, economists, and social scientists were at work, with the aim of writing reports on future developments in Europe. It is astonishing to discover that the accounts of the best journalists, who roamed the continent quiet independently and relied only on their eyes and ears, are far superior to the analyses of these experts. A good example is Martha Gellhorn's reportage of July 1944, a time when not a soul in Washington was thinking about the Cold War. In a village on the Adriatic, in the middle of an artillery duel, Gellhorn got into conversation with soldiers of a Polish unit fighting against the Germans:

> They had come a long way from Poland. They call themselves the Carpathian Lancers because most of them escaped from Poland over the Carpathian mountains. They had been gone from their country for almost five years. For three and a half years this cavalry regiment, which was formed in Syria, fought in the Middle East and the Western Desert. Last January they returned to their own continent of Europe, via Italy, and it was the Polish Corps, with this armoured regiment fighting in it as infantry, that finally took Cassino in May. In June they started their great drive up the Adriatic, and the prize, Ancona—which this regiment had entered first—lay behind us.
>
> It is a long road home to Poland, to the great Carpathian mountains, and every mile of road has been bought most bravely. But now they do not know what they are going home to.

They fight an enemy in front of them and fight him superbly. And with their whole hearts they fear an ally, who is already in their homeland. For they do not believe that Russia will relinquish their country after the war; they fear that they are to be sacrificed in this peace, as Czechoslovakia was in 1938. It must be remembered that almost every one of these men, irrespective of rank, class or economic condition, has spent time in either a German or a Russian prison during this war. It must be remembered that for five years they have had no news from their families, many of whom are still prisoners in Russia or Germany. It must be remembered that these Poles have only twenty-one years of national freedom behind them, and a long aching memory of foreign rule.

So we talked of Russia and I tried to tell them that their fears must be wrong or there would be no peace in the world. That Russia must be as great in peace as she has been in war, and that the world must honour the valour and suffering of the Poles by giving them freedom to rebuild and better their homeland. I tried to say I could not believe that this war, which is fought to maintain the rights of man, will end by ignoring the rights of Poles. But I am not a Pole; I belong to a large free country and I speak with the optimism of those who are forever safe. And I remember the tall, gentle twenty-two-year-old soldier who drove me in a Jeep one day, and how quietly he explained that his father had died of hunger in a German prison camp, and his mother and sister had been silent for four years in a labour camp in Russia, and his brother was missing, and he had no profession because he had entered the army when he was seventeen and so had had no time to learn anything. Remembering this boy, and all the others I knew, with their appalling stories of hardship and homelessness, it seemed to me that no American had the right to talk to the Poles, since we had never even brushed such suffering ourselves.

The editors of *Collier's* magazine, for which Martha Gellhorn was working, refused to publish this report, because the Poles' prophetic remarks about the Soviet Union, the United States' most important ally, did not suit them.

What makes the work of these reporters so illuminating is not that they lay claim to a higher objectivity, but the reverse, that they hold on to their radically subjective viewpoint, even when—especially when—they put themselves in the wrong. Among the costs of immediacy is that one is infected by one's surroundings and cannot stand above them. The sore points in the context of the postwar years emerge all the more clearly: the frictions between English and Americans, the fury of the victors at the grandiose impudence of the Italians, above all the hatred of the Germans, which in some observers turns to disgust and a desire for revenge. Whoever had behaved like the Germans and whoever continued to behave like them—that is, without any remorse—could not expect *fairness*; almost all representatives of the victorious nations were convinced of that, and it is by no means superfluous to be reminded of the extreme expressions of feeling during those years.

It is not surprising that the observers from neutral countries are more sophisticated in their judgments. Not that one could accuse them of particular sympathies for the Germans; but they are more able than the victors to recognize the ambiguities of their own role. After a visit to Germany in autumn 1946, the Swede Stig Dagerman wrote:

> If any commentary is to be risked on the mood of bitterness towards the Allies, mixed with self-contempt, with apathy, with comparisons to the disadvantage of the present—all of which were certain to strike the visitor that gloomy autumn—it is necessary to keep in mind a whole series of particular occurrences and physical conditions. It is important to remember that statements implying dissatisfaction with, or even distrust of, the goodwill of the victorious democracies were made not in an airless room or on a theatrical stage echoing with ideological repartee, but in all too palpable cellars in Essen, Hamburg or Frankfurt-am-Main. Our autumn picture of the family in the

> waterlogged cellar also contains a journalist who, carefully balancing on planks set across the water, interviews the family on their views of the newly constituted democracy in their country, asks them about their hopes and illusions, and, above all, asks if the family was better off under Hitler. The answer that the visitor then receives has this result: stooping with rage, nausea and contempt, the journalist scrambles hastily backwards out of the stinking room, jumps into his hired English car or American Jeep, and half an hour later over a drink or a good glass of real German beer, in the bar of the press hotel composes a report on the subject 'Nazism is alive in Germany.'

Fifty years after the catastrophe, Europe understands itself more than ever as a common project, yet it is far from achieving a comprehensive analysis of its beginnings in the years immediately following World War II. The memory of the period is incomplete and provincial, insofar as it has not entirely given way to repression or nostalgia. That is not only because people were busy with their own survival and hardly bothered with what was happening next door; it is also because now they are reluctant to talk about the skeletons in the closet. We prefer to address the glowing future of the European Community or the opening up of Eastern Europe, rather than to think about those unpleasant times when no one would have put a brass farthing on a rebirth of our continent. A somewhat fatal strategy, for in retrospect it appears that during the years 1944–48, without the protagonists suspecting it, the seeds were sown not only of future successes but also of future conflicts.

A high-explosive bomb is a high-explosive bomb, a hunger swelling does not distinguish between black and white, just and unjust; but neither the destructive power of the air forces nor the postwar misery was capable of homogenizing Europe and extinguishing its differences. These differences were not visible in the burnt earth, but had hibernated in people's heads. The European societies were like cities that had been destroyed, but for which detailed construction diagrams and land registers had been preserved; their invisible circuit and critical path diagrams and network plans had survived the destruction, and in all their variety. Differences in traditions, capacities, mentalities reemerged. Attempts at resuscitation were correspondingly diverse.

As Norman Lewis wrote in his Naples reportage of 1944:

> It is astonishing to witness the struggles of this city so shattered, so starved, so deprived of all those things that justify a city's existence, to adapt itself to a collapse into conditions which must resemble life in the Dark Ages. People camp out like Bedouins in deserts of brick. There is little food, little water, no salt, no soap. A lot of Neapolitans have lost their possessions, including most of their clothing, in the bombings, and I have seen some strange combinations of garments about the streets, including a man in an old dinner-jacket, knickerbockers and army boots, and several women in lacy confections that might have been made up from curtains. There are no cars but carts by the hundred, and a few antique coaches such as barouches and phaetons drawn by lean horses. Today at Posilippo I stopped to watch the methodical dismemberment of a stranded German half-track by a number of youths who were streaming away from it like leaf-cutter ants, carrying pieces of metal in all shapes and sizes. Fifty yards away a well-dressed lady with a feather in her hat squatted to milk a goat. At the water's edge below, two fishermen had roped together several doors salvaged from the ruins, piled their gear on these and were about to go fishing. Inexplicably no boats are allowed out, but nothing is said in the proclamation about rafts. Everyone improvises and adapts.

The attitudes that Lewis describes have remained characteristic of the population of southern Italy up to the present day: an ingenuity which knows how to take advantage of every opening, a parasitism of quite heroic energy and an untiring readiness to exploit a hostile world. At about the same time, the priorities of the French were quite different. In February 1945, Janet Flanner wrote:

> The brightest news here is the infinite resilience of the French as human beings. Parisians are politer and more patient in their troubles than they were in their prosperity. Though they have no soap that lathers, both men and women smell civilized when you encounter them in the Métro, which everybody rides in, there being no buses or taxis. Everything here is a substitute for something else. The women who are not neat, thin and frayed look neat, thin and chic clattering along in their platform shoes of wood—substitute for shoe leather—which sound like horses' hoofs. Their broad-shouldered, slightly shabby coats of sheepskin—substitute for wool cloth which the Nazis preferred for themselves—were bought on the black market three winters ago. The Paris *midinettes*, for whom, because of their changeless gaiety, there is really no substitute on earth . . . still wear their home-made, fantastically high, upholstered Charles X turbans. Men's trousers are shabby, since they are not something that can be run up at home. The young intellectuals of both sexes go about in ski clothes. This is what the resistance wore when it was fighting and freezing outdoors in the *maquis*, and it has set the Sorbonne undergraduate style.
>
> The more serious normalities of traditional Paris life go on in readjusted form. Candy shops display invitations to come in and register for your sugar almonds, the conventional sweet for French baptisms, but you must have a doctor's certificate swearing that you and your wife are really expecting. Giddy, young wedding parties that can afford the price pack off to the wedding luncheon two by two in *vélo-taxis*, bicycle-barouches which are hired for hundreds of francs an hour. The other evening your correspondent saw a more modest bridal couple starting off on their life journey together in the Métro. They stood apart from everyone else on the Odéon platform, the groom in his rented *smoking* and with a *boutonnière*, the bride all in white—that is,a white raincoat, white rubber boots, white sweater and skirt, white turban, and a large, old-fashioned white nosegay. They

> were holding hands. American soldiers across the tracks shouted good wishes to them.

Of course, such descriptions also express the prejudices and *idées reçues* of the particular observer. But such an interpretation misses the point. That is especially clear from the following report by John Gunther. It flies in the face of just about every cliché about the Poles.

> This concentrated tornado of pure useless horror turned Warsaw into Pompeii. I heard a serious-minded Pole say, 'Perhaps a few cats may have been alive, but certainly not a dog.' After liberation early in 1945 the Polish government took the heroic decision to rebuild.
>
> Every Pole I met was almost violent with hope. 'See that?' A cabinet minister pointed to something that looked like a smashed gully. 'In twenty years that will be our Champs Elysées.'
>
> Particularly impressive is [the work of rebuilding] in the Old City, which is almost as complete a ruin as the ghetto. A patch of ravaged brick is all that remains of the Angelski Hotel where Napoleon stayed. The old bricks are used in the new structures, which gives a crazy patchwork effect. Hundreds of houses are only half rebuilt; as soon as a single room is habitable, people move in. I never saw anything more striking than the way a few pieces of timber shore up a shattered heap of stone or brick, so that a kind of perch-like room or nest is made available to a family, high over crumbling ruins. One end of a small building may be a pile of dust; at the other end you will see curtains in the windows.
>
> Much of this furious reconstruction is done by voluntary labour; most, moreover, is done by human hand. Even cabinet ministers go out and work on Sunday. In all Warsaw, there are not more than two or three concrete mixers and three or four electric hoists; in all Warsaw, not one bulldozer! A gang of men climb up a wall, fix an iron hook on the end of a rope to the topmost bricks, climb down and pull. Presto!—the wall crashes. Then some distorted bricks go into what is going up. The effect

is almost like that of double exposure in a film. No time for correct masonry!

So this catastrophically gutted city, probably the most savage ruin ever made by the hand of evil mankind anywhere, is being transformed into a new metropolis boiling and churning with vigour. Brick by brick, minute by minute, hand by hand. Warsaw is being made to live again through the fixed creative energy and imagination of immensely gifted and devoted people.

Quite different feelings were aroused in another visitor who observed the beginnings of German reconstruction on a journey through southern Germany. One will hardly be able to argue that Alfred Döblin's comments have lost any of their force in the course of the past decades.

A principal impression made by the country, and it provokes the greatest astonishment in someone arriving at the end of 1945, is that the people are running back and forward in the ruins like ants whose nest has been destroyed. Agitated and eager to work, their major grievance is that they cannot set to immediately, for the lack of materials, the lack of directions.

The destruction does not make them depressed, but acts as an intense stimulus to work. I am convinced that if they had the means that they lack, they would rejoice, only rejoice, that their old, out-of-date, badly planned towns have been destroyed, and that now they had been given the opportunity to put down something first class, altogether modern.

A populous town such as Stuttgart: crowds of people, their numbers further increased by an influx of refugees from other cities and regions, went about the streets among the dreadful ruins truly as if nothing had happened and as if the city had always looked as it does now. At any rate, the sight of the wrecked houses had no effect on them.

And if anyone believes, or once believed, that misfortune in one's own land and the sight of such devastation would cause people to think and have an educative effect on them—then he can see for himself that he was mistaken. People point out certain groups of houses, saying: 'Those were hit during this bomb-

> ing and the others were hit during that bombing,' and tell a few anecdotes. And that's all. No particular message follows, and there are certainly no further reflections. People go to their work, stand in queues here, as everywhere else, for food.
>
> Already there are theatres, concerts and cinemas here and there, and all apparently are well attended. The trams were running, horribly crowded as they are everywhere. People are practical and help one another. They are concerned with the immediate present in a way that is already troubling the thoughtful.
>
> Here lives, as before, an industrious, orderly people. They have always obeyed the government. They obeyed Hitler too, and by and large do not grasp why this time obedience is supposed to have been bad. It will be much easier to rebuild their cities than to get them to comprehend what it was they have experienced and to understand how it all happened.

It may appear unjust that the verdict on the reconstruction efforts of the people of Stuttgart turns out so ill-humoredly in comparison with the praise bestowed on those of Warsaw. But one cannot understand the puzzling energy of the Germans, if one resists the idea that they have turned their defects into virtues. Insensibility proved to be the condition of their future success. The tricky quality of this relationship emerges from the following report by Robert Thompson Pell, an American secret service officer, who, in the spring of 1945, was faced with the task of examining the activities during the Third Reich of the top managers of the I. G. Farben company.

> On the whole I gained the impression that the German leaders had gone over to accommodating themselves to necessity—but only to a limited extent. In the meanwhile, they are sounding out our weak points, putting us to the test at every opportunity, trying to find out if we really mean it when we thump the table, and offering as much resistance as they dare. They say almost openly that we will not be able to cope with the situation our-

selves and will have to turn to them again in the end. They are relying on us to make so many mistakes that it will be inevitable that they take charge again. Till then they will bide their time and look on, while we bungle everything. Apart from that, they play up the 'red peril' as much as they dare. As soon as one shows oneself to be even a little approachable—or if they believe they can see signs of it—they tell us again and again: 'We are so glad that you are here and not the Russians,' and in a few cases they've actually maintained that the German army withdrew so that we could save as much of West Germany from the Russians as could be saved.

The directors whom I fetched in my Jeep every day were itching to tell me that the German people had been the victim of a worldwide conspiracy that had intended to deliver up this lovely country to unknown forces; Germany had conducted a defensive war; the Allied 'terror raids' had united the German people, had no military value and had been a serious error; they were the true defenders of Western civilization against 'the Asiatic hordes'.

In short, the country was in chaos and the people were in a hysterical condition which quickly grew into an attitude of defiance and a feeling of being treated unjustly, and which was not clouded by the least trace of guilt. Most of these men of high, in some cases the highest, standing in society were ready to admit that Germany had lost the war, but were quick to add the reason was the superiority of the Allies in power and material; they then immediately added that in future they would try to make that good. The overall impression was, in short, disquieting. So far as I could ascertain, the attitude of the average manager was characterized by self-pity, fawning self-justification and an injured sense of innocence, which was accompanied by a yammering for pity and for aid in the reconstruction of his devastated country. Many of them, if not the majority, confidently expect that American capital will commit itself without delay to the work of reconstruction, and they declared themselves ready to place their labour power and their intellect at the service of these temporary masters; as a consequence they openly expect to

> rebuild a Germany more powerful and bigger than it was in the past.

Thanks to the irony of history or, rather, its mockery, these delusions of 1945 have, in a way, become reality. That those who were defeated then, the Germans and the Japanese, today feel like victors, is more than a moral scandal; it is a political provocation. Our leaders naturally never tire of protesting that in the meantime we have all become peaceable, democratic, and moderate—in a word, well-behaved. The most remarkable thing about this assertion is that it is true. This mutation has turned the Germans into what they once accused others of being: a nation of shopkeepers. In that, they are by no means alone. All the nations of Europe are, with varying success, trying to do the same. Since the end of the communist monopoly of power, the primacy of economics also appears to be establishing itself in the eastern part of the continent. Fifty years after World War II, this much is certain: not only did the German suicide attempt fail, but that of Europe as a whole. The more, however, our continent moves back into the center of world politics and of the world market, the more a new kind of Eurocentrism will gain ground. A slogan copyrighted by none other than Joseph Goebbels has reappeared in public debate: "Fortress Europe." It once had a military meaning; it returns as an economic and demographic concept. Under these circumstances a booming Europe will do well to remind itself of a Europe in ruins, from which it is separated by only a few decades.

1990

8) BRUSSELS OR EUROPE?

ON THE IDEOLOGICAL DRUG MARKET, a mixture by the name of "Europe" has been making the rounds, as if it were the amphetamine of the nineties. Business publications are particularly enthusiastic in their promotion; next to the dollar exchange rate and the stock-market index, they offer a little pink pill with the magical inscription "2001," the year in which the European Union is to be consummated, with the apparent intention of exciting euphoria in their readership.

But it seems that the desired effect has not transpired. Everyone complains about the public's lack of engagement. In Germany the project is perceived mostly as a lamentable but unavoidable side effect of the export business. The Germans are expecting a significant increase in taxes and—even more horrifying—the threat of an invasion of second-rate beer and meatless sausage. In Spain and Portugal, a vaguely hysterical enthusiasm seems to dominate, while the Swiss react with irritation and the Austrians with fear. In the Scandinavian countries, the question has been raised—in all seriousness—whether Norway, Sweden, Finland, and Iceland even belong in Europe, which proves that the so-called Idea of a United Europe has not inspired rapture in all corners of the continent.

This already somewhat dated notion was dragged onto

the political stage immediately after the Second World War, and is still trotted out happily on ceremonial occasions. It has a place in every political speech and can ornament any political platform. I still remember the role it played during the fifties for the West Germans, who (for obvious reasons) did not yet put any particular value on being German. The Idea of a United Europe offered Germans the prospect of a second, redemptive identity, promised a certain compensation for the fall of the Reich, and even held out for a greater, if somewhat vague, future.

Besides that, the Idea of a United Europe suggested something ideal or idealistic; it seemed to lend an air of divine consecration to the crude process of material reconstruction. Everyone believed it meant whatever seemed most useful for his own purposes, and the sincerity with which the Idea was mentioned made it clear to everyone (everyone who had not been dropped on his head as a child, that is) that this supposed Idea of a United Europe was not , in the end, meant to be taken so seriously, so no one had to be alarmed about the possible loss of personal privileges. It was, above all, the overblown nature of the idea that made it magic. It owed its success precisely to the fact that there was no such thing as a United Europe, and that there was no chance there would ever be one.

For in fact, there can be no one Idea of Europe, but there have been many Ideas, millions of them. The Europeans played a more than willing part in the dissemination of "Europe" throughout the globe, and so the Idea of Europe can no longer be considered in strict association with the European continent.

Forty years later, the propagandists of the European Union have wiped off all the make-up of Western pretension. No more Ideas. Interests have taken the place of the

Idea. Since we are now concerned with nothing more than an economic conglomerate, the once-so-sincerely-preached Idea has become dispensable. At least this renunciation has the advantage of clarity. The motivation behind the project is now clear.

As a consequence of the Second World War, the European market lost not only its old colonial territories, but its traditional spheres of influence as well. Politically, the two halves of the continent were absorbed by two empires, both of which, through quite disparate means, were intent upon incorporating their new protectorates into their own economic spheres. But the colonization of Europe soon hit a snag. Western European capitalism had remained intact, and despite its extreme dependence on the world market for import and export trade, it was capable of holding its own. But from 1945 on, it was forced to operate on a scale that could no longer be managed by the old nation-states. The European Union represents nothing more than the attempt to solve this economic problem through political means.

According to this logic, the future of our continent seems clear: in order for Europe to survive as an economic power, everything that distinguishes it from any other part of the world must be expunged as thoroughly and as rapidly as possible. A Europe capable of competition has to be faster, bigger, and more efficient, better organized and more homogenous. As a kind of synthetic super-power, it has to catch up with the pacesetters of the newest technology. If one believes the prophets of economics, the future of Europe lies in the American Sunbelt and in Japan.

And so, unity, finally, just fifty years after Yalta! But European unity only ratifies new divisions. The club is theoretically open to any applicant, but, in fact, it is exclusive; in the future, there will be two classes of nations on the continent: one of them will belong, and the other will be left in the cold. And even among the outsiders there are fine distinctions, reckoned according to the reasons for their exclusion. Some of them are simply too poor to be considered. Others remain outside because their citizens stubbornly refuse to surrender their neutrality. Why either of these facts should prevent a country's belonging to Europe has not been explained. The result is that we are dealing with a supposed European Union that has sixteen members, but excludes more than twenty other nations. That such a community should presume to speak for our continent is absurd.

Just as wrong-headed is the Europe rhetoric currently being spread throughout the media. It mixes two realities that ought to be kept distinct—indeed, they are utterly unreconciliable. On the one hand we have the Europe of day-to-day life, of which Riga, Cracow, and St. Petersburg are as much a part as Milan, Dublin, and Lisbon. On the other hand, we have the Europe of European institutions. This systematic confusion between a concrete world and a construct made up of treaties, regulations, and planned economy is intentional. Actual Europe has been overtaken by the "concept of Europe," and made over into a tool for propaganda by the institutions of Brussels, Strasbourg, and Luxembourg.

Only an expert in the field would be able to keep track of all of these institutions and their officials. We have a European Ministry, a European Commission with branches and subdivisions, an Institute for Coal, Steel, and Iron, a European High Court, a Parliament, and a European Council (which has nothing to do with the Union), and then we have a huge number of umbrella organizations and other bodies that no one can distinguish from one another except for the people who hold office in them.

The thing these institutions all have in common is their thorough lack of credibility, which stems from something that, strangely enough, is almost never mentioned. None of them possess either political competence or democratic legitimacy, and every survey on this issue has revealed that this is no secret to the European populace.

But it is the Brussels bureaucracy and its obscure decisions that attracts the greater part of peoples' dissatisfaction. Indeed, it is impossible to comprehend this morass of subventions, payments to equalize distribution, ordinances, guidelines, and regulations for exceptional cases. As understandable as the anger directed at this administrative labyrinth is, it falls short of the heart of the matter. It is a common error to believe that an industrial society like ours cannot get along without a bureaucracy of this type. The political problem of the Union has a deeper cause, and it is much graver. At the end of the twentieth century, Western Europe is threatening to revert to a pre-constitutional state. The European Union is governed by principles that date back before 1830, as if the constitutional struggles of the last century and a half had been in vain. These can be outlined as follows:

The constitution of the Union is negotiated by the participating nations through cabinet politics; there has been no assembly of a body assigned to write a constitution.

The government of the Union (the Council of Ministers) is not determined by the vote of the people or a parliament, but is named *in camera*. The Strasbourg parliament has no say in its composition, nor can it dissolve this government.

The Parliament is, in fact, elected by the people, but its function is purely symbolic and decorative. There is no normal legislative process. The oldest prerogative of every European parliament, namely, the right to determine taxation and the budget, has been abrogated in this case.

The only example of a similar body would have been the parliaments of the former East Bloc. There the functional counterpart of the Council of Ministers was called the Politburo, and the Strasbourg parliament had its opposite number in the People's Chamber or the Supreme Soviet.

So much for the political result of four decades of Western Europe integration. I imagine that the inhabitants of the sixteen member countries have yet to grasp fully the indignity being imposed upon them with this Union. Their lack of enthusiasm for the Strasbourg parliament does however indicate that they do suspect something—that they sense the political disenfranchisement that awaits them. In the long run, the Europeans will hardly want to accept a preconstitutional form of government. It is no coincidence that it is the oldest democracies of Europe that have offered the most decisive resistance to the Eurocratic project. It is in no small part for this reason that the Norwegians voted against joining, and in Denmark the feeling is still widespread that membership has limited the democratic rights of their country's citizens. The Swiss, too, seem to have little desire to sacrifice their rights on the altar of integration. And as unpleasant as it may be to agree with Mrs. Thatcher—when she refused to hand over the sovereignty of her nation to a body with no democratic legitimization, one cannot simply attribute her refusal to an insular mentality. Experts in the field of European law predict that seventy percent of all laws will be determined by Brussels. And so we will live under the rule of a legislature that operates largely beyond our control.

With all of this I do not mean to say that no useful work is done in Brussels. There is nothing to be said, in principle, against norms and agreements. But the negative effects of the mechanism in Brussels have become so evident, that not even its apologists have dared refute them. The debacle of the Union's agricultural policies has been lamented by all sides, and as far as the solution of ecological problems is concerned, the contribution from Brussels can best be typified as sabotage.

It would be naïve to characterize these catastrophic results as mistakes, typical of any new project. On the contrary, they arise naturally from the political logic of the entire enterprise. The systemic reasons for their occurrence can be described easily enough. In a democratic vacuum and in the absence of an effective parliamentary opposition, the decisions of the Union can take place in only one way: through negotiations between two groups of interested parties. These are, on the one side, professional politicians, and on the other, the lobbies of industry and the banks.

For these two groups of participants in the decision-making process, Brussels is a political paradise, because there they are entirely on their own. There they have finally succeeded in turning out the eternal static of the people's voice. What's good for Europe is good for the Politburo and for the management of businesses. That is the philosophy of the European institutions.

Still, I suspect that the Brussels colossus stands on feet of clay. The prematurely triumphant propaganda for the European currency cannot conceal the fact that the politicians have made their calculations without consulting their landlord. In the long run, the people of Europe will not put up with the rule of banking, armament, chemical, and agricultural lobbies. If they have more or less passively accepted the regulations of the Eurocrats up until now, it is only because they have not recognized their larger implications. Only after 2001 will the citizens get the picture, because at that point it will quickly become evident that these regulations are not of a purely technical nature—in fact, they have profound impact on the life of each individual. People will then begin to understand that the Brussels project, in which they have been denied a voice, threatens their social rights, their environment, and their culture. It is likely that the people's silent reservations will then turn to open resistance.

But the Japanization of Europe will not founder only because of the vehement opposition of the Europeans; the concept of the Union will be destroyed from within, by its own inner contradictions. Our continent, unlike a corporation, can never be ruled by a central government. Even the political leadership of the Soviet Union failed due to the fact that such a thorough centralization does not amalgamate power, but instead breaks it down. Besides, the idea that the European continent could be transformed into a homogenous super-power is utopian in the worst sense of that word. If this continent is to have a fighting chance in the coming century, it lies in the rich articulation of its various societies, in its complexity and wealth of traditions, attitudes, and abilities. Of this I am quite confident: the Eurocratic project is doomed to failure. Brussels or Europe—for Europeans faced with this alternative, the choice will not be difficult.

1989

9) BILLIONS OF ALL COUNTRIES, UNITE!

Notes on the World Bank and the International Monetary Fund

I

MURROW PARK, a few minutes from the White House in Washington, is not a park, but a traffic island around which the limousines roar, a tiny patch of burnt grass, where in the middle of the day black junkies and white winos sleep on torn cardboard boxes. Behind it rise two tall façades; nerve centers of world society, giant cubic brains that brood in the heat and year in, year out, reflect on an intangible substance—money.

Unlike vulgar mankind, their thoughts are not devoted to their own money; not those grubby notes which bear the likeness of a Washington, a Lenin, or a Fugger, but money as a value system, money pure and simple and as a whole—a subject, therefore, so general and esoteric that the most profound mind would become lost in thought over it.

But there are no scholastics meditating in these two concrete casings, nor any lamas, gurus or high priests, but almost eight thousand top-class bureaucrats, each one with a telephone and kept cool by the silent current of the air conditioning, without which not a single thought is possible in subtropical Washington.

The World Bank, more precisely, the International Bank for Reconstruction and Development (IBRD), has its home on the right-hand side of 19th Street. Opposite it, on the other side of the street, resides the International Monetary Fund (IMF). Insiders, who can allow themselves a certain familiarity, simply call the two institutions "the Fund" and "the Bank." From the outside they look more like two monsters. The IMF is considered the tough monster, the World Bank the soft monster.

II

Before we lose our way in the labyrinthine corridors of this brother and sister, it would perhaps be worth asking ourselves what a monster actually is. Where common sense only supposes a word of abuse, old lexicons and reliable dictionaries take us a little further; they inform us that we are dealing with a purely metaphysical phenomenon. "Something marvellous, extraordinary, that exceeds the bounds of nature," it says there; "actually in the language of religion a divine portent"; also admittedly "an unprecedented terrible event, a portent, an evil omen."

The word *monstrum* is presumably derived from *monere*, a Latin verb that means "to warn"; and only later did it come to mean "an imaginary being, half beast, half man, composed like a chimera, where in addition the idea of prodigious size and savagery is also present. Phrases like *a monster of perfection* indicate an unbelievable, unnatural, even repellent degree of perfection."

III

It's easier for the chance passer-by to gain entry to the White House, the Vatican, the Kremlin than to the headquarters of the International Monetary Fund. Only someone who has official business there—and what ordinary passer-by could claim that?—is admitted by the uniformed guards and the icily smiling ladies at reception. The visitor then discovers that half the volume of the building consists of air: because he steps into a luxurious vacuum, a thirteen-story-high atrium of shiny marble, decorated with flags and tropical plants.

He asks himself where he has ended up—a question that no one can answer in a single sentence. What is the whole thing for? What are the aims and duties of the Fund? Article I of the agreement setting up the Fund affords only meager information. According to it the Fund should:

> (a) *promote* (international co-operation, stability, maintenance of orderly arrangements, high levels of employment and real income);
> (b) *facilitate* (balanced growth);
> (c) *strengthen* (confidence of members);
> (d) *assist* (in the elimination of foreign exchange restrictions which hamper the growth of world trade);
> (e) *lessen* (the degree of disequilibrium in the international balances of payments of members); and finally,
> (f) *provide* (an international forum for the solution of problems).

Any Rotary Club could write the same pious wishes into its statutes. The padded prose in which they are expressed recurs in all the countless brochures, reports, and communiqués that the Fund publishes. The stylistic principle is the euphemism, the effect of kind of intellectual narcosis.

But anyone who would really like to know more is soon reeling from the jargon of international finance, a language that the internal dialect of the Fund constantly enriches with new inventions. Hard luck for anyone who is unable to tell the difference between an extended and a standby credit agreement, between a facility for compensatory financing and a supplementary finance facility, and shame on anyone who mixes up the Group of Five with the Group of Six, Seven, Ten, Twenty or even with the Club of Paris!

IV

So back to the beginning again, which is where a beginner should be. The small change in your pocket is one thing, but if you own a vegetable wholesale business then the figures in your books are already something quite different, that is, capital. Your money reaches the next stage of abstraction in the savings bank at the corner; it is transformed into credit. And so on in an ascending line via the municipal bank's clearing house and the provincial central bank up to the federal bank. At this stratospheric altitude, your solid pennies have changed into a medium and become cloaked in a secrecy that is hard to penetrate. No cucumbers are sold here; liquidity is "created," discount rates are fixed, minimum reserves laid down, money supply quantities proposed. The central bank simultaneously produces and controls our money.

V

In the middle of World War II, it occurred to some gentlemen, who were thinking about the international financial system, to crown this hierarchy of abstractions with one central overarching institution. The great crisis of 1929 had shown how unstable the condition of the world economy was. The famous "free play of forces" could lead to collapse overnight. The national control of the central banks had proved to be helpless in the face of the global integration of movements of capital. American and British experts, among them Harry Dexter White of the US Treasury Department and John Maynard Keynes from England, dreamt of a completely stable world currency system, in which a repetition of the catastrophe would be impossible.

They suggested setting up two institutions of a kind that had not been seen before: first a central bank of all nations, which would ensure stable rates of exchange, stable money values, free movement of capital, balanced international trading accounts, and sufficient liquidity; second, an international development bank, whose task it would be to lend a helping hand to the countries devastated and impoverished by the war, so that they could reach the economic level of the wealthy countries. Such institutions were only conceivable if the leading capitalist power took them under its wing. President Roosevelt was prepared to do so. In a message to Congress he said that the strongly developed American economy must be ready to stand by the rest of the world; such a posture would also bear a rich harvest for the United States.

The Fund and the Bank, the soft and the tough monster, are the result of these plans. They were founded in July 1944 in Bretton Woods, a small resort in New England, and set up business in 1946–47 in Washington. Almost every country on earth has joined them, with the exception of the Soviet Union and its vassals: the GDR, Czechoslovakia, Bulgaria, Mongolia. Also missing are: Albania, Angola, North Korea; Cuba left in 1960. An odd figure among these outsiders in Switzerland, which belongs to neither of the institutions, presumably because it is an international financial monster itself. However, relationships between the Swiss National Bank and the Fund can be described as altogether cordial.

VI

Every human institution has its own milieu, its physiognomy, its aroma. The atmosphere in a bakery is different from that in a police station. A quite distinct character is noticeable in "the Fund" and "the Bank"; yet the composite nature of the two monsters means that it is difficult to define.

The Fund, it could be said, is the bank of banks of banks. Indeed its halls are dominated by hints, an air of initiation, ambiguous smiles. A quite Victorian discretion is the rule here. If inquisitive questions are answered at all—and what question would not be delicate there?—then "off the record" or at least "not for attribution." Only the insignificant may be quoted. (Consequently, the information reproduced in this text must remain anonymous.) The businesslike, sophisticated, dynamic but always low-key tone is also reminiscent of the manners of international bankers. In the upper stories one meets almost exclusively men, encased in expensive and mercilessly impeccable suits. On the other hand, in contrast to the main halls of the Chase Manhattan or the Crédit Suisse, the customers are invisible.

Or are we in the headquarters of a multinational company? In favor of this second interpretation there is the strong sense of identity of the top managers and the concentrated expertise of specialists who are recruited from all over the world and know not only about money but also about oil and soya beans, road-building and fishing. Except that this business cannot display a single product and lacks the most important attributes of all: net profit. It is true that both the Fund and the Bank make balance sheet profits, yet yield is of no importance whatsoever; it is hardly mentioned, as if it were vulgar to make profits. In fact, the profits are not distributed to the member countries, but accumulated, that is, added to the reserves.

But, third, one might think of a government department. There is something bureaucratic in the air here. A breath of civil service tenure wafts down the corridors. Finally, the connoisseur will notice a certain extraterritorial halo, a trace of unreality, a strange bureaucratic rarefaction, which characterizes all supranational institutions, for example UNESCO or the Brussels Commission. In fact, in terms of international law, Bank and Fund are specialized agencies of the United Nations. However, anyone who studies the treaty that regulates this relationship more carefully will conclude that one thing, above all, is laid down in it: the fact that the United Nations has no say here.

In the World Bank and the Monetary Fund, unlike the glass box in New York, the noble principle of one member, one vote, does not hold. Here proceedings are conducted according to a rule that is as old as the world: Who pays the piper calls the tune. What gives the member states power and influence is the carefully balanced quota determined by capital invested and by the economic weight they can throw onto the scales. As a result, the United States enjoys a practically permanent veto right. Its quota amounts to just under 20 percent. A decision that went against its vote is inconceivable. It is no coincidence at all that the two monsters have set up their headquarters in the capital of the American empire.

Not all diplomats express themselves diplomatically. A German in the foreign service who knows his way around Washington doesn't mince words when he describes the World Bank and the Monetary Fund: "They're front organizations for the USA. Anyone who gets into a fight with the Americans only has himself to blame. After all, I don't start a fight either if I meet Mohammed Ali in a dark corner."

"Exaggerated," responds a highly paid insider. "Exaggerated out of all proportion! Your informant sees it all far too simply. In any case the power of our institutions is usually overestimated.

"Lord Keynes's pipe dreams have not come to fruition. Instead of becoming the fund of funds and the bank of banks, the IMF and the IBRD had to accustom themselves to a more modest role; as repair service and stopgap for a very unstable, susceptible system. There has been no reconstruction; instead we have to spend all our energies on patching up what already exists. The governments, who are all worried about their sovereignty, simply would not permit a fundamental change in the situation—quite apart from the fact that the politicians are far too ignorant to recognize in time the risks which the world economy faces.

"Consequently the functions of the Fund and of the Bank, like those of the fire brigade, can only be defined negatively. They are supposed to prevent the worst. Their big moments are the crises: currency instabilities, oil shocks, development catastrophes like the one in the Sahel zone, debt avalanches like the ones looming in the Third World, help the two sisters acquire new influence, new power. In such situations we are indispensable. We are there to get rid of crises, but without crises nobody would give a hoot about us. If it didn't sound too cynical, one could say that we need catastrophes just as the secret police needs terrorists. Nevertheless, I hardly think we need to worry ourselves about that. Anyone who has to deal with the negative things will never be out of a job."

VII

The two monsters have managed a positive achievement at least once in their history. In September 1967, at a joint session of the Monetary Fund and the World Bank, something completely new was created, a very special "facility": the so-called Special Drawing Right (SDR).

There is only one place in the world where it is possible to see this invention: the visitors' center of the IMF. Yes, the very same Fund that locks itself in like a Trappist monastery has also thought of the tourist, the taxpayer, the man in the street.

In front of the headquarters on 19th Street, a flight of steps leads down to a deep concrete vault, which is ready to welcome us. Admittedly, this space is hermetically sealed off from the padded corridors of headquarters. Mere laymen are left to themselves. The information that the visitors' center offers is correspondingly porous. No one reads the uplifting booklets displayed in the reading room, no one looks at the exhibition of Japanese calligraphy that decorates the walls. The executive board of the IMF can be looked at on a color photo, twenty-two men in giant office chairs. Gathered round an immense oval table, the gentlemen, somewhat distorted by the fish-eye lens of the camera, smile at the lonely guest.

The Special Drawing Right is displayed in a brightly lit glass case. The artist faced the difficult task of showing us an immaterial phenomenon. We gaze thoughtfully at a blue-white plastic chip, as large as a saucer, with the label 1 SDR. In front of it in a small bowl lie a few worn coins—pfennig, cent, penny, and yen pieces—which are supposed to make clear what one Special Drawing Right is worth. It has to be recalculated again every day according to the exchange rates of five leading currencies, which are weighted in a particular relationship to one another. The bowl with the coins is supposed to illustrate this "basket of currencies." But the plastic disc, which hovers in the glass case, betrays hardly anything of the boldness of the invention. For the Special Drawing Right is by no means hard cash.

Is it money at all? Its inventors, the gentlemen from the IMF, laugh evasively, if one asks them about it. No, one could not call the SDR a currency. It is not a legal means of payment; more a unit of account. But not just that! After all, liquidity is created through the SDR. It is a money surrogate, half book money, half credit limit. A hybrid. The question of its true nature must remain open. Whether credit or money, whether the zebra is black with white stripes or white with black stripes, is impossible to decide. It's best to stick to the official formulation, which, as always, remains obscure: it's described as an "international trustee reserve medium," which circulates according to certain highly complicated rules.

Of course, the SDR does not take the form of coins or notes. It only exists at all in the computers of the central banks. Beyond that, there are twenty-two other institutions of an arcane nature which use it, for instance the Bank for International Settlement (BIS) in Basel, a kind of discreet private clinic for central banks where, instead of rich heiresses, suffering currencies get face lifts or are operated on.

In a word, the Special Drawing Right is a "medium." The spiritualist connotation of the word is not altogether irrelevant. Around 21.4 billion SDRs were "created" in the course of the last twenty years, which corresponded at the time, depending on the exchange rate, to a sum roughly calculated of 50 billion dollars.

Created? Yes, it really is a case of something from nothing, of a miracle reminiscent of the miraculous increase of loaves. Where before there was an ebb, there is now a flood of credit. Billions are "authorized," "assigned," "drawn." Are the gentlemen in Washington alchemists who have discovered the philosopher's stone? That is an almost theological question, and like all theological questions defies a precise answer.

But, ultimately, is it not equivalent to what we carry in our wallets? The invention of the Special Drawing Right throws a surprising light on the nature of money as a whole. In Frankfurt am Main, too, there is a creating and a drawing with a vengeance! And it is far from clear what happens and how it all happens.

The German mark, too, is not just what the bank of issue has minted and printed. It exists beyond that in the invisible and phantomlike form of credits, bills of exchange, checks, claims. And so it is not surprising that the scholars distinguish up to twelve different money supply quantities: notes in circulation and central bank money, hard and soft money, M1, M2, M3, etc. Some statistical reports don't even flinch from the expression "quasi money."

The logical consequence is that no one, absolutely no one, no finance minister and no central bank director can possibly say how much money there is altogether. It's a question of faith. And until now, at any rate, not a single person has been found who doubts that the Special Drawing Right, this puzzling creation, is at least as good as the dollar, if not as good as gold.

VIII

Coded data, statistical curves, esoteric concepts; an almost otherworldly suspension far above the crude facts; the two monsters, so it seems, operate in the highest spheres of abstraction. And yet everything that is deliberated on, weighed up, voted on, decided here on 19th Street, in screened off rooms has tangible and very solid results.

In Xian (China) automatic signal boxes are introduced for the first time. In Zambia the price of maize flour, a staple food, rises by 120 percent because the state subsidies have been removed; fifteen people lose their lives in the disturbances this measure provokes. The completion of the Volta Dam in Ghana brought about changes in climate: since then, there has been drought in the north of the country. The city of Pusan (South Korea) is getting a new container harbor. More than two million inhabitants of the Narmada Valley (India) are to be made homeless. One single dam of this gigantic project will put 864,000 acres of forest under water. In Argentina, bus and rail fares are doubled. One hundred sixty thousand people in Burundi are at last supplied with tap water. In São Paulo, an angry crowd loots the supermarkets; the finance minister has to resign. The Ivory Coast follows the advice of the experts and stakes everything on one card, raising agricultural production for export. The world market price of cocoa, coffee, palm oil collapses; the government is bankrupt; thousands of government employees have to be dismissed. In the chemists' shops of Khartoum, there are no imported drugs any more. In Jordan, technical colleges are built, in Zaire roads. More than three million people are to be resettled in Indonesia; it is estimated that five million acres of rainforest will be destroyed as a result. Credits to the Bolivian government are traded at 11 percent of their nominal value. Governments fall, threshold countries penetrate the world market, whole nations declare themselves bankrupt, and all this would either not have happened, or would have happened differently, if the Fund and the Bank had not had a hand in events.

IX

No one turns to them of their own accord. If a country is having problems with its balance of payments, the Fund helps out in the short term with sums amounting to billions, at first only for a couple of months, at the very most for a couple of years. On the other hand, the World Bank, the largest development aid agency in the world, provides long-term credits for particular, precisely defined projects and for "structural adjustment measures" in virtually every developing country.

Neither the Fund nor the Bank has anything to give away. Their loans have to pay interest and be repaid when they fall due. For reasons that will be mentioned below, the payment morality of the debtors is beyond all criticism. (In 1986, the capital backflows at the IMF were a good two billion dollars higher than financial help provided.)

Yet the price that the two monsters demand for their aid cannot be expressed in figures. A commercial bank that lends money wants to see securities for it. However, states cannot be attached. Consequently, the two sisters make their readiness to step into the breach dependent on obligations and conditions that subsequently affect the political economy of the recipient countries. The technical term for it is "conditionality." In its purest form, this bitter medicine is prescribed by the Monetary Fund. As a rule, the patient doubts whether it's good for him. That's not surprising, because when one translates it from the secret language of the augurs into everyday terms, then the prescription amounts to a couple of truisms, which no one affected likes to hear: "No one can live permanently above their means! You must tighten your belts!"

Anyone who listens more carefully can hear in the background the voice of orthodoxy, of the true doctrine. It preaches against protectionism and for free competition, against excessive state expenditure and for the stability of currency values, against state intervention and for private initiative. In short, it advocates a pure capitalism, of a kind that is familiar only in rosy tracts from the nineteenth century, but not in reality.

Naturally, the practice of the Fund cannot conform to such postulates. In the first place, the IMF has to live with a number of members who shun its tenets as the devil shuns holy water: Vietnam and Romania, Poland and Ethiopia are hopeless cases from the ideological point of view. Second, there are countries in which the true doctrine must fail for lack of substance: Mauretania or Mozambique, for example, are simply too poor to be able to hold their own on the world market. Third, the Fund must pay attention to zones that are especially sensitive politically and strategically, where the full force of conditionality could smash too much crockery; for this reason Egypt, for example, can enjoy particularly lenient treatment.

But fourth—and this is the main point—economic orthodoxy founders on the wealthy, who would be very far from pleased if the Fund took it literally. This is true, above all, of the USA. The leading power of the West allows itself a considerable amount of protectionism, a chronically negative trade balance, an enormous foreign debt, and a huge budget deficit. According to the catechism of the IMF, these are all deadly economic sins that can only lead to a sad end. But, instead of placing the usual thumbscrews on the impenitent for his own good, the Fund in its annual report (the *World Economic Outlook*) contents itself with muttering a couple of timid subordinate clauses.

X

It is the composite nature of the beast which speaks through such contradictions. Its moral expression is hypocrisy. Yet this hypocrisy is no deviation from the rule, not an avoidable error but a systematic necessity; it deceives no one and conceals nothing. It expresses only the objective dilemma between pure principles and brute power relations.

The linguistic consequence is that everything has to be handled with kid gloves. When South Africa is mentioned in the IMF's printed material, one will look in vain for the word *apartheid.* Instead, the Fund speaks in sybilline fashion of "labor market rigidities, which are related to educational problems." And how are developments in Chile judged? "Very satisfactory. Of course no opinion on the political situation is associated with this assessment."

When hundreds of thousand of people in Latin America went onto the streets to demonstrate against the International Monetary Fund, the director at the time, Jacques de Larosière, had a brochure issued: "Does the IMF prescribe austerity?" He answered the question he himself had posed, with a resounding, "No." The measures that the Fund demanded certainly "involved social costs, but it is not the task of the Fund to decide how these costs are distributed among the population." Curious restraint! The IMF's conditions, which are laid down in contractlike letters of intent, are extremely detailed; they are concerned with prices, taxes, jobs. Economies of every kind are demanded. By contrast there is not a single known case, in which the Fund has called upon a Third World country to put a stop to its senseless arms purchases. In this respect, and in this respect alone, can any trust be placed in what de Larosière coyly declares: "An international institution like the Fund cannot presume to dictate social and political goals to sovereign governments."

"We don't have any machine guns," say the employees of the Fund to anyone who cares to listen. "We can only try to persuade, make recommendations, give technical advice." But what is a machine gun compared to the hand that turns the flow of money on and off? And where is the line between a recommendation and blackmail?

At any rate, the political neutrality that the Fund claims for itself is pure eyewash. The IMF requires, no more and no less, that the demands of foreign creditors should take precedence over the needs of the population. That is an eminently political demand.

The Fund's employees have to enforce them but are not allowed to call a spade a spade. They are left only with a flight into fiction. One could almost feel sorry for them. Really, they only want to do what's best. Really, they've only got one thing on their minds, that is "to pave the way for stronger and more sustained growth." But, instead of rewarding this good intention with tears of gratitude, "the Fund is allowed to come under fire" : that is M. de Larosière's troubled complaint. The injured undertone is unmistakable. It is the sad fate of a monster that no one takes it to his heart.

XI

Only, hypocrisy does not have a fixed address; it can't be pinned down, not to the pair of billion-dollar strongholds on 19th Street in Washington. It contaminates every continent, and nowhere does it express itself so callously and brutally as in the countries of the Third and Fourth World which, not without good historical reasons, portray themselves as victims of colonial domination. The word "elite" always has a fatal aftertaste, but in the poorest countries of Africa, Latin America, and Asia it sounds like utter contempt. Even if it is not good form in development politics to speak openly about it—these local elites consist almost entirely of criminals, who attempt to cover up their complete incompetence and their murderous greed with anti-imperialist phrases, a camouflage that grows more and more threadbare every year. These parasitic government apparatuses with their sinecures, their hot money, their endemic corruption are not only accomplices but protagonists of exploitation.

It would be naive to take the noisy argument between such "elites" and the International Monetary Fund at face value. A profound harmony is often concealed behind their ritual shadow boxing.

"It is our fate, that in the problem countries we usually have to play the role of villain. Basically it's part of the service which the Fund has to offer. If a government wants to do something sensible, but cannot push through its program politically, then we are, to a certain extent, prepared to take on the role of scapegoat. It's appropriate that we're in Washington. In many parts of the world this location has a negative symbolic value. Responsibility for unpopular measures is internationalized in this way. The politicians themselves don't need to be answerable for them. The Fund is to blame, an abbreviation, an anonymous power." The German Social Democrat Gustav Noske, who crushed the Spartakus revolt after World War I, expressed himself less circumspectly, but more clearly: "Someone has to be the bloodhound."

"Lately," it is said in Washington, "this game with divided roles has got out of control. It has lost its usefulness for both sides, because the politicians in the Third World have pushed it too far. That as a result the Fund has found itself in the firing line far too often, we could still perhaps put up with. But the spokesmen of the poor countries have become prisoners of their own demagogy. They have maneuvered themselves into a cul-de-sac. Anyone who turns the Fund into a bogeyman, responsible for all the ills of the world, can himself no longer come to terms with it, when he doesn't see any other way out. The best tactic can become counterproductive if one relies on it too much. Fortunately word is beginning to get around our members."

XII

The Fund finds comfort and compensation, for the unpleasantnesses to which it is exposed today, in the heroic moments of its forty-year history. The sixteenth of November, 1982 was one such legendary day. In August, the international financial world had been overtaken by a new nightmare—the debt crisis. What today is part of normal breakfast newspaper reading appeared that autumn as an unimaginable threat.

Mexico, one of the world's biggest debtors, was on the brink of bankruptcy. The country's liabilities amounted to 87 billion dollars. The demands of the foreign commercial banks alone had reached the dizzying height of 67.5 billion dollars; 28 billion of that was due within one year. There was the threat of a chain reaction if Mexico was forced to suspend payments. The biggest banks in the United States would have collapsed and pulled down the whole financial system with them. Neither the US Treasury Department nor the Federal Reserve Bank could cope with this situation. The creditor banks were not ready, or even seemed to be in a position, to throw new bridging credits after the money they had lost but not written off. A funding gap of more than

8 billion dollars had to be closed in order to avoid disaster. The American government and its allies wanted to commit 2 billion at most. The International Monetary Fund declared that it could make 1.3 billion available under the usual conditions. The Mexicans, in turn, had no other choice but to sign the required declaration of intent. They prepared themselves, even if with the greatest reluctance, to lower real wages, cut back subsidies, and to introduce higher taxes.

The director of the IMF scored his big coup on the afternoon of November sixteenth in the board room of the Federal Reserve Bank in New York. The representatives of the biggest creditor banks had been invited, among them the Citibank of New York, which alone had 3.3 billion dollars at risk; but there were also leading figures of English, French, Japanese, Swiss, and German banking capital. First to speak was the Mexican Finance Minister Jesús Silva Herzog, then it was Jacques de Larosière's turn. The governments were ready to help, the Fund too was going to step into the breach. "However," de Larosière continued, "5 billion dollars are still needed to clear up the situation. This money, gentlemen, can only come from you. I expect from you pledges corresponding to your share in the mass of debt, within four weeks, by 15 December to be precise. Should your pledges not have come in by this time, then the Fund will withdraw its Mexico program. I need not spell out the consequences to you. That is all. Good afternoon, gentlemen."

The assembled bankers are said to have been speechless. They were not used to such language. However, after they had recovered from the shock, it dawned on them that they had no choice. The pledges arrived punctually. The catastrophe had been averted for the time being. Today this form of crisis management has already become routine. The Fund has arranged similar rescheduling agreements with dozens of countries. One can say that it has become the biggest receiver in the world.

This new role also required new techniques. From now on, the Fund had not only to put the thumbscrews on the debtors but on the creditors as well. And those were the big banks who had become so thoughtlessly involved in the credit business with the Third World and accepted risks that no longer stood in any relationship to the performance of the debtors.

For years, the bankers had been stepping on one another's heels in São Paulo and Manila, Belgrade and Lagos, in order to force their credits on the administrators of distressed treasuries. They were inspired (if "inspired" is the right expression here) by only one wish: to invest the surplus petrodollars of the oil-producing countries as profitably as possible. In doing so, they fell victim to the illusion that a sovereign state cannot go bust. But the wealth of money that showered down upon the debtor countries brought another rule of the international credit business into the limelight. It is an open secret that a bank's loans are about twenty to twenty-five times greater than its assets. This is what is called *leverage*. This aspect of the miraculous multiplication of money makes the banks powerful but also extremely vulnerable. A large bank that, instead of spreading its risks, concentrates them—like the Bank of America, which had lent more than half of its corporate funds to Mexico—is finished if its principal creditor suspends payments.

It is one of the strengths of the International Monetary Fund that nothing similar can happen to it. It is obliged to operate only with its own resources, that is, with the quotas of the member countries and with special funds they agree to; it is therefore necessarily "more solid" than any bank. Its balance sheet total fluctuates around 140 billion dollars. The burden of debt of the so-called problem countries, on the other hand, is estimated at over 1.2 trillion dollars, an amount that is nine times greater than the Fund's resources. The Fund is rich, but far from rich enough to deal with global crises by itself. Its power does not derive from its own resources, but from its *de facto*, even if not *de jure*, control of access to the international capital markets. In its character as doorkeeper, it can impose conditions on both debtors and creditors. Anyone who falls out with the Fund is a financial pariah. To that extent, and only to that extent, the Fund really is what the international bankers' jargon calls *the lender of last resort*: the guarantor one clings to, when all the ropes break, the last hope, the lifeboat of the system.

XIII

In the Year of Our Lord 1462, in Perugia, a Franciscan monk called Barnaba founded a special kind of bank, the *Mons Pietatis* (in English, the Mount of Piety), in order to help the poor of the city. The initial capital was raised through charitable donations. Brother Barnaba's idea proved to be extremely successful. The Mount, originally only a small pile of coins, grew and grew, and the institution, half savings bank, half pawnbroker's shop, soon developed into an enterprise with a huge turnover. In the course of time, it found imitators in all the large cities of Italy, Spain, and Latin America. Its charitable aspect suffered, but its devout name was preserved, and so the *Montes de Piedad* flourish to the present day.

The soft monster of Washington, the World Bank, is distinguished by a similar consciousness. While the Fund attempts to cure "short-term imbalances" with technical and political interventions, the World Bank is concerned with long-term development aid. But it has as little to give away as its pious predecessor in Perugia. It offers credits earmarked for specific purposes. These have to be paid back, so that the capital circulates and doesn't dribble away. Apart from that, the banks takes completely normal rates of interest because it obtains the necessary money on the international financial markets, which are not known as philanthropic institutions. It issues loans with a yearly volume of approximately 12 billion dollars, and is considered by its investors, not without cause, as the very best address, for in contrast to the practice of other creditors, the borrowed funds it takes up are covered 100 percent by the member countries.

The World Bank's influence too, far exceeds its own financial possibilities. Just like the Fund, it occupies a key position, and does so through the virtuoso use of the method of co-funding. It draws into partnership in its projects and programs, development agencies and private banks from all over the world. In this way, aid cartels and consortia come into being under the World Bank's management and control, which at least triples its financial power and increases its political influence.

Financial operations are not enough, of course. One can even say that it is more difficult to dispense the funds than to raise them. A huge staff of experts investigates each project with respect to the technological, social, and recently also the ecological risks. Naturally, the Bank requires that each individual project must balance out. A long-term profitability of at least 10 percent is considered standard. But at the World Bank, in contrast to the Fund, it is not the bankers alone who make the decisions. Here agrarian experts, hydrologists, energy experts, geologists, engineers, educational planners, and doctors have a voice as well. And so in the

World Bank, which employs almost six thousand people and maintains forty-two outside offices from Rwanda to Bolivia, one meets a vast mixture of qualifications.

These people plough a difficult furrow. The aporias of development aid are well known. There is even disagreement over the question of who should define what is to be considered useful, the donor or the recipient. The list of objective difficulties is endless: it stretches from the fatal moods of the world market to overpopulation, from chronic shortage of capital to the constant political pressure that the export interests of the rich countries exercise, to say nothing of transcultural problems, educational deficiencies, military coups, the flight of capital, and corruption. And while no one knows the "right solution," the sources of error are countless.

In addition, there is the long-term nature of all development schemes. What may have seemed sensible on the adoption of a project, can turn out to be, when it is close to completion ten years later, pure madness—for example, the expansion of cattle raising in Botswana or the gigantic Polonoroeste Project in the rainforests of the Amazon.

The World Bank's dilemma is also expressed in the transformation of its ideology. It has always taken pride in having its own "philosophy." In the early years, this meant the classic doctrine of development as it had inspired the reconstruction of Europe. This teaching reflected the euphoria of the 1950s and 1960s, and the rise of the so-called threshold countries seemed for a while to confirm it. The problem of poverty would disappear of its own accord with solid growth rates, that is, through a social trickle-down effect. By the end of the 1960s, however, even the professors noticed that the reality of the Third World showed no sign of following this theory. The poor proved to be hard of hearing; they grew poorer each day.

When Robert McNamara took over the presidency of the World Bank in 1968 he wanted, like Brother Barnaba once upon a time in Perugia, to transform it into an instrument for fighting "absolute poverty." He advocated a new world economic order, fair *terms of trade*, the support of small peasants and craftsmen, and prioritizing self-sufficiency. This "intellectual breakthrough" was presumably honestly intended. McNamara is a man with a strong religious background. The fact that he wanted to manage his campaign against poverty in the same way as he had previously managed the Ford Motor Company and the Pentagon can only surprise a European. He paid particular attention to the International Development Association (IDA), a nominally independent body that is in fact an offshoot of the World Bank. The IDA is considered to be the last resort for hopelessly poor countries. It provides what neither the Fund nor the Bank are in a position to provide, that is, aid without guarantees, and distributes interest-free credits with a term of fifty years from a fund that is stocked by the wealthy member countries. Yet, measured by its tasks, the IDA is a midget, and what it provides is a drop of water on a hot stone.

After his resignation in 1981, McNamara had to admit that his "philosophy" had failed. Only his rhetoric has left a lasting mark: even today, there is still an oddly unctuous tone to the World Bank's publications, in contrast to those of the IMF.

And so the soft monster appears as a complete paradox. Where else does there exist an executive committee of world capital which presents itself as the friend and helper of the poor, a bank that raises the flag of philanthropy, a monster that subscribes to the principle of altruism?

Such an ambiguous enterprise is difficult to assess. The World Bank can point to a long list of successful projects. Its critics hold it responsible for an equally long list of development disasters. Whether the good outweighs the harm it causes is not only disputed, it can ultimately never be decided. That is due to the fundamentally contradictory nature of the institution.

This double nature also characterizes the people who work in the World Bank. Right next door to the tough manager who would indignantly reject the least suspicion that he allowed himself to be troubled by spasms of sentiment, one finds the committed supporter of development aid who problematizes his own role to the point of self torment. He identifies more or less secretly with his "target country," which he knows personally and with which he has many ties. Anyone who thinks and feels like that, is subjecting himself to an inner tension and becomes caught up in a hopeless struggle against the logic of the whole to which he has committed himself. His victories are minor and provisional, defeat normal, and there is no father confessor who could grant him absolution.

XIV

After his election victory in summer 1985, the new president of Peru, Alan García, kept the promise that had constituted the economic part of his program, without which he might perhaps never have come to power: he broke off relations with the International Monetary Fund and canceled all credit agreements his predecessor had made with the big international banks. Peru would undertake an "automatic debt conversion" according to its own criteria and in future unilaterally limit servicing of debt to 10 percent of its export earnings.

At this point the country's foreign debts amounted to 14.3 billion dollars (approximately 650 million dollars of that sum were IMF credits). Peruvian income per capita had sunk by one-third within three years. The interest and back-flow of capital threatened to bleed the economy completely dry.

The economic decline did not come out of the blue. It was the result of a long-term malformation whose roots stretch back into the nineteenth century, and even into the period of Spanish rule. The unfavorable starting position was exacerbated by numerous acute causes: collapse of raw material prices, decline of the fishing catch, natural disasters, high inflation, guerrilla warfare, the army's civil war–like strategies, incompetence, corruption, and extravagance of previous administrations, finally the route into the "debt trap" as a false solution to the problem. All in all, when Alan García came into office the country was in a typical spiral of impoverishment.

In the cool conference rooms of the International Monetary Fund, concern about the conflict with Peru remained within bounds.

"We have been working closely with the Peruvians for forty years and have experienced a number of ups and downs in that time. Our missions have negotiated regularly with the government in Lima. We even maintained permanent representation in the Peruvian capital. The co-operation was not always without friction, but on the whole we were satisfied. You know, the Peruvians suffer from a national over-sensitivity as far as external influences are concerned. That has occasionally led to implementation problems."

"You mean sabotage?"

"We prefer to talk about technical difficulties. But as far as the present problems are concerned, naturally we saw them coming. Really the end had already come by 1984. The commercial banks had recognized that the country was finished, and refused to finance the interest and repayments, which had become due, with new credits. At the same time the balance of payments rapidly worsened, inflation got out of control, one devaluation followed another, the standard of living sank dramatically, and who was the villain of the piece? We were. It became ever-more costly for the Peruvian politicians to work with us. This difficult situation offered an internal political opportunity, and Alan García seized it."

"How did the Fund respond?"

"In September 1985, Peru ceased its payments to the IMF. There's a carefully worked out procedure for such cases. It took almost a year until, following the prescribed warnings and reminders, and after the usual deadlines had expired, the right to draw on Fund credits was withdrawn from the Peruvians. The official statement sounds a bit clumsy, but the meaning is clear: The member in question will not get one more dollar from us and will in future have considerable difficulties on the international capital markets."

"What did the Peruvians think they were doing? Was it a rational decision?"

"Difficult to say. It is not always easy to distinguish between a nervous breakdown and a strategy. Alan García himself is a chrismatic politician. He believes he has been called upon to lead the Third World on to a new path. But around him there are also people who believed other debtor nations would follow the Peruvian example; then the problem would assume such large dimensions that the creditors would have to change the rules. But this gamble did not pay off. No one joined Peru, neither the Brazilians nor the Mexicans, and the Peruvian debts are simply not large enough to send anyone into a panic."

"Perhaps the till was empty, and the García government had no other choice?"

"It would be wrong to say that. On the contrary, the Peruvians had made careful preparations for their action. They had accumulated considerable currency reserves beforehand."

"And what did they do next?"

"What one always does in such situations. Currency controls, price fixing, freezing foreign currency accounts, import restrictions, split exchange rates. They deployed all the instruments of state economic management and in the short term certainly achieved success. Real growth in 1986 was 8.5 percent, a fantastic rate, and the income of the masses rose correspondingly. Wonderful! But the internal boom was stoked up at the expense of the level of savings, there are hardly any new investments and the flow of foreign capital has practically dried up. The Peruvians are living on their reserves."

"And how long can that go on?"

"We are not prophets, but the country's currency reserves are declining month by month. Take a look: at the end of 1985, 1,830 million dollars; mid 1986, 1,620; by the end of 1986, 1,430. If things go on at this rate, then I see the crunch coming by the end of the eighties."

"So you only need to sit and wait. Bankruptcy or capitulation."

"Well, we're always available to our members, and we

won't leave Peru in the lurch either if the government should turn to us."

XV

On the opposite side of the street, developments in Peru are not regarded so calmly. The soft monster has more problems with sanctions. Even someone who has fallen out with the Monetary Fund can continue to enjoy the help of the World Bank. It is used to being flexible—with the inevitable terms and conditions—in order not to put its long-term projects at risk. Nevertheless here too the rule is: Only those who pay on time can count on further remittances. But even after the announcement of the moratorium by the García government, interest and redemptions continued to arrive punctually at the World Bank, further monies flowed, as agreed, to Peru, the game was not yet up.

Until, in spring 1987, even this last thread threatened to break. Since the beginning of March the regular payments from Lima had no longer come in. No explanation was given. Preliminary requests for further information remained unanswered. No mention of the problem was made in the corridors of the World Bank. There was a slightly irritated silence. Perhaps only the very old hands concluded from the anxious expression of this or that official that there was something in the air. To the outside world the catchword was "Let's not break any china!" At most, a handful of insiders in Lima and Washington could say how such a crisis unfolds; but they are not only party to the knowledge but also actors, and they have good reason to remain silent.

On the other hand, one doesn't need the talents of a clairvoyant to reconstruct the course of events. It is damp and pretty hot in Lima at this time of year, and the air conditioning in the Finance Minister is unreliable. The state secretary is at his wits' end. He is just phoning the president's personal assistance. The mood in the palace is hectic. According to the constitution, Alan García cannot be reelected. The candidates for the succession are preparing their first battles of position. The lights in the capital go out every night. The guerillas of the Shining Path have already established themselves in the more affluent residential areas. The president of the National Bank does not know how he is supposed to finance the most essential imports. Yet again the military are threatening to stage a coup. Alan García cannot be reached, and his assistant tries to get rid of the tiresome caller. But the latter insists on explaining that at present more than twenty programs under World Bank management are currently in progress in Peru; total volume more than 1.9 billion dollars. What kind of projects? Well, for example, Bajo Piura, irrigation of 86,000 acres, cost 180 million, or the airport at Pucallpa, 47 million. Also 360 miles of road, the eighth section of the plan. . . . Where? In the highlands, Cerro de Pasco, La Merced and so on. . . . Never heard of them. . . . Then go and ask the Transport Ministry what that means! You must make clear to the president what is at stake. . . . Didn't you hear his speech last Sunday? We are not putting up with any more outside interference. We're not paying any more, not even to the World Bank!

The nervous official in Washington has not failed to notice García's speech either. His contact in Lima assures him, it's a mistake, the president was speaking spontaneously, it mustn't be taken too seriously. . . . A few days later the Peruvian minister of finance visits Washington, but he doesn't put in an appearance at the World Bank. Dinner with the gentlemen of the Treasury Department, negotiations in New York, all very unofficial. Privately, he promises Peru will pay, the difficulties are merely temporary . . . meanwhile, the official has informed the management of the Bank, that cannot be avoided. The decision is to say nothing for the time being. . . . But already the first Hong Kong investors are getting in touch with the Finance Section. The Far Eastern investors are sensitive, as sensitive as mimosas. . . . No, there is no question at all of a rupture between the Peruvians and the World Bank, there are technical reasons for the delay in payment, no cause for concern.

The official, however, is already considering what may happen if the worst comes to the worst. He thinks of the agrarian experts, who will soon perhaps have to pack their bags, of the doctors who will leave their station in the jungle if their salaries don't arrive, and of the twenty thousand families in the Ceja de Selva, among them two thousand Indians. More than half live in extreme poverty. He can imagine it all very clearly, after all he's been there. The project in this jungle area, it's called Satipo-Chanchamayo, has been going on for three years, a satellite photo of the district hangs on the wall somewhere, feeder roads, fruit and coffee growing, afforestation, cheap loans, land for the small peasants. It all looked very promising, but now. . . . Meanwhile the date of payment is long past, and it's only a matter of days before the telex has to be sent to Lima. The last warning, the ultimatum. . . . Someone or other high up in the hierarchy will perhaps still try to reach the responsible minister by phone, but then Lima doesn't call back, because the air force is causing trouble again or because it just happens to be a holiday in Peru. . . .

Finally, our official learns by chance that a Peruvian delegation has arrived in Canada, senior people, who are supposed to give lectures in Montreal and Toronto on the "Peruvian Model." Half officially, half on his own initiative he takes the next flight, and in Ottawa he arranges to meet one of these gentlemen, whom he has known for years, in some bar. The delegate has good connections, a direct line to the president. . . . Our man from the World Bank explains the whole thing to him from the very beginning again: Don't you understand that there are people in Washington who are only waiting for the opportunity to make an example of you? That's crazy! After 180 days we have to stop payments, and then a tiny footnote, which only the experts can understand, appears in our annual report, but the consequences for Peru will be disastrous. So you must try to get something done in Lima today, immediately. It's the last chance. I need your consent by morning!

The man with the direct line will see what can be done, but before that he still has to put in an appearance at a reception at the embassy. Of course he'll call back! He's managed harder things before now!

The man from the World Bank, in fact quite unimportant, because other people make the final decision, returns to his hotel room; he's hardly shut his eyes during the last few nights; while he waits for the redeeming phone call, he asks himself where he really belongs. At last, at about two o'clock, the phone rings, but it's only his wife in Washington, who's been worrying about him for some time.

Probably it was more or less like that.

XVI

He has already been "with the firm" for more than ten years, a hardheaded currency expert who knows both the Fund and the Bank inside out. He's opening up a bit—not because of his little weakness—he likes to drink vintage champagne now and again, but due to the fact that his days in Washington are numbered. He has a lucrative offer from London, from the City, in his pocket.

"Most of the problems we have to deal with," he says, "are quite simply insoluble. Our reports exist mainly to chloroform the public. In reality everything looks much worse. We are objectively overstretched. Take the debt crisis. Servicing the debts of the developing countries costs more than 150 billion dollars a year; if one believes the official figures, that amounts to more than 21 percent of their export earnings; with the so-called problem countries it averages 36 percent. In reality the proportion is even higher than that. As it is no one is thinking about repayment any more, but even the interest alone and the interest on the interest grows like a snowball with each rescheduling. We're simply happy if we manage to stop things falling apart from case to case and from quarter to quarter.

"But on top of these objective difficulties there are also our own internal failings. They are hardly visible from the outside, and naturally in general we take care not to mention them. For example no one would dream of admitting that we are simply too big. A large proportion of what is invested in the Fund and in the Bank gets lost through autodigestion, as it does in all organizations that are too large, especially if they have a monopoly position. I estimate our efficiency to be 40 percent, or at most 50 percent.

"A management discussion has been going on in the World Bank as to whether the whole thing should be organized centrally or decentrally, by regions or by sectors. More and more new cost analyses, disputes over competence, motivation studies, restructuring plans. In 1973 McNamara set up a staff department with the sole purpose of getting a grip on this bureaucratic muddle, in fact in the first place to find out what was going on in his own house—a kind of commercial espionage on his own account. But that only increased the confusion. Now it's a new president's turn. So new consultancy companies will be engaged, old employees fired, new brooms tried out, but it would be naive to believe that one can deal with a forty-year-old rut in that way.

"Take our concrete experts, people who decades ago fell in love with the idea that dams are the most beautiful thing in the world. That is their purpose in life. They want to continue building their monuments without any regard for the losses, and you cannot believe how difficult it is to stop them.

"Forty years is a long time for an institution which neither has to prove itself on the market, nor is subject to any kind of effective external control. It can pursue its principal purpose, of perpetuating itself, to the point of arteriosclerosis. It's sensitive and defensive in the face of criticism from the outside, on the inside Parkinson's disease runs wild.

"You should take a look at our *manuals* some time. These are enormous folio volumes in which every single activity in the innards of the institution is standardized right down to the smallest detail. Taxes, salary, bonuses, holidays, travel regulations, who can fly when to where and at what rate, or everything that has to be observed when someone picks up the telephone. The endless cost analyses, savings recommendations and checks and controls on this one subject have probably cost us more than our telephone bills. Do you know, by the way, that the relationship between bank and Fund is nowhere formally laid down? Officially the cooperation is praised in lofty language, but in fact the Bank cannot stand the Fund and vice versa. The frictions and complaints are never ending. The rivalry is expressed in the most petty details. The Fund is said to be arrogant and snobbish, because there even the secretaries fly first class, and until 1980 the poor relations from the World Bank were not even allowed to use the IMF's country club in Maryland.

"Yet the two institutions have a great deal in common. It's not only that there are outstanding people and a lot of expert knowledge in both, they both have to grapple with the same contradictions. The Fund, just like the Bank, set out to export the priorities of the market economy all over the world, following the motto that what's good for us must be good for everyone else too. But the World Bank and the Fund are themselves para-state institutions, which are by no means run according to the principles of free-business enterprise, quite the reverse. Hence their bureaucratic habits, their formalism, their deeply rooted planning ideology. It's no wonder that their preferred interlocuters, especially in the most problematic countries of the Third World, are the local planning bureaucracies, and where these are missing, they simply have to be invented. The World Bank has drawn up what are effectively five-year plans for all kinds of states, especially in Africa. They train the required administrators in their own training programs. Yes, it even happens that whole ministerial bureaucracies, right up to the level of state secretary, are exported in a kind of leasing procedure. The World Bank dispatches these bureaucratic pyramids ready for immediate use, as it were, to Tanzania or Jamaica, and the Fund establishes central banks in exotic dwarf states, a luxury which was quite unknown there, and which until then no one had missed.

"Besides, one must grant the World Bank one thing: it proceeds much more flexibly than the Monetary Fund, which can't escape its internal orthodoxy and is always worried about covering itself. But here, just as over there, one is busy day in, day out, collecting an impressive amount of information—to the extent that both houses can be seen as news agencies. Everyone pretends they believe the figures which their computers print out, although we all know that statistics are pure magic, especially in the countries of the Third World. In this way a second reality comes into existence, which consists of abstract magnitudes, of indicators, indices and projections. Our missions are constantly en route across all continents, but wherever they happen to arrive, they sit in their hotels, as if in a terrarium, completely isolated from the facts of the society they are supposed to pass judgment on. We have replaced reality with data. It's a good thing that I'm not a philosopher, but only a currency dealer. I know what's on my screen."

XVII

It is not the purpose in life of the two monsters to be popular. The question is: Whom does their existence benefit and whom does it harm? The Left critique has always made things easy for itself. An organization that is dominated by the rich can only benefit the rich; it exists to exploit the poor; that is all. This argument has at least one advantage: it is persuasive and brief.

Strange then that the Right, especially the American Right, sees things quite differently. The extreme wing of the Republican Party hates all international organizations, from the United Nations to the World Bank. A considerable proportion of the American population shares this aversion. Every form of regulation that subjects private initiative to rules of some kind or another, is suspect to them, and if on top of that foreigners have got some say, then it borders on socialism. According to this point of view, the opaque machinations of international institutions serve only one purpose: to stuff the taxpayers' money into the mouths of some faraway parasites, the *gooks* or the *dagos*.

A deep mistrust is also not alien to American liberals when it comes to international finance. Here, admittedly, it's not a case of anticommunist paranoia that scents a capitulation in every agreement with a foreign state, but of a populist conspiracy theory, according to which the bankers alone are to blame for the sufferings of the little man. For someone who believes that, even the name, the World Bank, is a provocation.

These hostile views are amplified by established special interests in the American Congress. The farming and copper lobbies conduct a constant guerilla war against the World Bank's projects, and every quota increase meets bitter resistance from the representatives of the people.

In addition to all of that, there is the boundless ignorance of American politicians when it comes to the world economy. The international currency system is of no interest to them, and they simply have no idea about the vulnerability of the financial network. Years ago, when the Italians got into balance of payments difficulties, the unforgettable Richard Nixon said, "I shit on the lira." "Enlightened capital" is often in a difficult position when faced by the stupidity and ignorance of the professional politicians.

Admittedly, the attacks from the Right are acknowledged with a satisfied smile in the Monetary Fund. Although the constant tug-of-war with Congress can assume very wearisome forms, the symmetry of right-wing and left-wing criticism serves the gentlemen as proof that they are walking on the path of virtue.

Yet the truth by no means lies in the middle but, rather, in the logic of capitalism, which as we all know has quite simply been victorious throughout the world. Today there is no longer any life outside what was once, in 1968, called "the system" and today goes by the more modest name of "the world market." Every attempt to definitively exclude oneself is doomed to failure in the long run. The last country to test a total disconnection was Cambodia. The consequences of the experiment were deadly. The reasons that have persuaded almost every country on earth to join the Fund and the Bank are therefore quite elementary ones. The only important exception is the Soviet Union. But the Moscow leadership too, long ago confidentially let it be known that it is interested in joining soon; the question is only whether the Americans will give their consent.

Anyone who has accepted these premises should be careful about casting accusations of guilt, in case the moral protest that is raised rebounds on the accuser. The double standard of morality that confronts one in the glossy brochures from Washington is one thing, the demagogy of corrupt ruling elites in the Third World is another. But there is also a hypocrisy of the third kind, which likes to express itself on recycled paper, which wants to give itself a clear conscience by making others responsible for the miserable state of world society.

Only someone who seriously hopes for the collapse of the global economy, with all the consequences that entails, and who is capable of thinking another option through to its conclusion, can expect something good from the abolition of the two monsters. Anyone who is not prepared and capable of going so far, is himself sitting in a glass house. He can criticize the gentlemen in the two big glass houses on 19th Street in Washington as much as he likes, but he would do well to remember that they are his delegates.

XVIII

Everyone who enters the atrium of the International Monetary Fund has to pass a large wooden sculpture standing by the entrance. The statue's face is painted copper. It has a savage expression.

It is a present from the National Bank of Indonesia, and was delivered one day without prior warning, in an enormous box. "Just between the two of us, it was not a very welcome gift. But what could we do? It would have been discourteous to send it back. We have got used to the thing, we don't even see it any more."

The statue represents Garuda, a mythological figure in the Hindu tradition. The Garuda is a winged monster that carries the sun god Vishnu on his journey around the world. "The Garuda," say the Indonesians, "is always victorious. He looks evil, but he stands for all the good things in the world."

Its head, its claws and its wings are those of an eagle, its body and its limbs those of a human being. The warlike monster eats a snake daily. Its face is white, its wings are red, its body is golden. The staring apparition at the gate will continue to guard the sacred relics of our economy for a long time to come, and no one will be able to avoid him.

1988

10) HITLER WALKS AGAIN

When Adolf Hitler came to his end, in the bunker on 30 April 1945, most of those who survived him believed in his singularity; he was a figure who seemed to allow for no comparison with other violent criminals of history. This conviction, in which horror was coupled with hope, has proven to be an illusion. Hitler was not unique. As long as millions of people passionately await his return, it is only a matter of time before their wish is fulfilled.

With good reason, the postwar period has insisted on the unique nature of Germany's crimes and has made taboo any comparison with other examples of state terror. All too often, such parallels are drawn only to absolve some perpetrator. For that reason, the censorship of comparisons has seemed reasonable, even though in the end it can be justified only on moral and not on intellectual grounds, for, of course, any attempt to understand historical events rests on experience—that is, comparison. In cases where there are substantial similarities, comparison is not just permissible, it is required. Calling Saddam Hussein a successor to Hitler is no journalistic metaphor, no propagandistic bombast, but instead goes to the heart of the matter.

It would be unfair to the leader of Iraq, and an underestimation of the danger he poses, to consider him simply a traditional despot or a modern dictator. Unlike figures such as Franco, Batista, Marcos, Pinochet, and fifty others who hold power today throughout the world, Saddam Hussein does not merely intend to oppress a people, to dominate and exploit them, and to wring out the last possible drop of pleasure he can derive from all that. Autocrats of that ilk are part of history's standard repertoire. Indeed, one is tempted to say they belong to the normal world of nation-states as we know it. These monsters pose no riddles. They simply allow themselves to be guided by their instinct for self-preservation. For that reason, they act according to a calculation of their self-interest, and that makes them calculable, too.

Hitler knew that he was free from such considerations. And it is in this respect that Saddam Hussein is Hitler's genuine successor. He is not battling any particular domestic or foreign opponent, his enemy is the world. The determination to attack is his primary drive; objects, motivations, and reasons are picked up as he finds them. The next group to have its turn at destruction, whether it is Iranians or Kurds, Saudis or Palestinians, Kuwaitis or Israelis, depends only on opportunity. Even his own people do not occupy a privileged position in his plans; their destruction will be the closing act of the mission to which Saddam feels he has been called. His motive is his death wish, his method of governing is destruction. All of his actions are geared toward this aim. The rest is planning and organization. He himself only wants the privilege of dying last.

The parallel to Hitler is obvious. The German leader, too, was not interested in defeating any particular internal or external opponent. He was not only the mortal enemy of the Jews, the Czechs, the Poles, the English, the French, the Dutch, Belgians, Scandinavians, Balkan peoples, Russians, and Americans but also, in the end, the Germans. Let us call him them, not intending to demonize but only to describe, an enemy of humanity. The obscene images depicting Saddam as he dandles the children he has captured are identical down to the last detail of body language with the ones taken in the Bavarian Alps fifty years before.

Taken on his own, as an isolated subject, the enemy of humanity is a banal—one is tempted to say, unremarkable—creature. We will never now how many people of his kind live among us, as failed artists or crazed gunmen run amok, a block away or in the deepest jungle village. A Hitler, a Saddam, can emerge in history only when entire peoples desire their advent. Their power comes not down the barrel of a gun but from the boundless love of their followers, their devotees' lust for self-sacrifice.

Thus, any comparison between Hitler and Saddam necessarily leads to a second comparison between the masses who offered themselves up to each man as his murderers or victims. *The Nazis were the Iraqis of 1938–1945.* That this conclusion has not been drawn by any of the German tabloids is all too understandable, though it not only has logic on its side; it could also illuminate the Gulf War like a flash of lightening. Nothing could be further from the mind of today's German than to recognize himself in those Arab masses. An insight like that would pull the rug out from under any racist interpretation of the conflict. Besides, it would bring hidden continuities to light, remnants of fascism that nobody wants to be reminded about.

(German industrialists never regretted the dedicated service they provided for Adolf Hitler; that they hurry to aid his successor with the same zeal is therefore only logical. And when a significant portion of Germany's youth identifies with the Palestinians rather than the Israelis, when they would rather protest against George Bush than against Saddam Hussein, one can hardly dismiss it as simple ignorance.)

On the basis of their own experience, the German people are better qualified than any other to understand what is happening in the Arab world today. Every second interview conducted from Rabat to Baghdad must sound like an echo of their own voices: "We will go on marching until everything lies in ruins." The devastation of cities, the fanatic hate, the "greatest battle of all time"; the talk of a "fight to the finish" or a "final victory": who can forget the frenetic cheers that greeted these slogans, the thousands of cheers that answered the famous question "Do you want total war?"

The thing that excited the Germans was not just the license to kill but, even more, the prospect of being killed. Just as passionately, millions of Arabs today express the wish to die for Saddam. "We long," said Assad el-Tamini, a Muslim priest in Jordan, "to smell Saddam Hussein's gas." The leader will do everything in his power to grant his followers' final wish. "The German people do not deserve to survive," said Hitler at the end of his career. This is precisely what Saddam thinks of his people.

It was not the fault of the German people that Hitler could not successfully complete his program. The energy of the leader and his followers was sufficient to bring about unimaginable crimes and to transform Europe into a field of rubble. But despite the German determination to send even the very last Hitler youth into the fire, not only the victorious Allies but the Germans, too, survived.

Posterity was occupied for decades with an explanation for the behavior of the Germans. An entire generation of scholars sought to blame Hitler and the consequences of his rule on a singular moment in history, a peculiar character, a supposedly alien culture. One is reminded of the hapless attempts of historians to create a concrete explanation for the inexplicable in the deeds of kings or chancellors, or in the thought of Nietzsche, Wagner, or Luther.

Today, Mideast experts and Orientalists come out with the same arguments. We are simply dealing with a completely different culture in the Middle East, an incomparable culture, a mentality that has to be decoded, with religious conditions of which the ignorant outside world can have no conception.

These are comforting hypotheses, because they give the impression that the problem can be dismissed as local. If the blood lust of Hitler and his followers had been reducible simply to some peculiarity of the German character, it would have been sufficient to put the territory under quarantine and subject it to perpetual supervision. Then the rest of the world would have been able to live unmolested until the end of time. If the determination to commit genocide were a cultural or religious peculiarity of the Iraqis, that is exactly how we would have to treat Saddam and his followers.

It is time for us to part with such illusions once and for all. The new enemy of humanity does not behave any differently from his predecessors. Despite differing conditions, the impulses of his devotees are identical to those of our fathers and grandfathers, and they pursue the same goal. This continuity proves that we are dealing with neither a German nor an Arab phenomenon, but an anthropological one.

That is not to say that an enemy of humanity could appear suddenly out of the darkness, under arbitrary circumstances, without certain preexistent conditions. To find followers who long for destruction, the sense of long-standing, collective insult is required, an insult that undermines the basic feeling of self-worth in millions of people. On this point, too, the Germans would be able to recognize themselves in the Arabs, if they had a better memory.

In *The Germans*, Norbert Elias describes why it is that the German people perceive themselves as eternal losers, at least since the Thirty Years' War. Their sense of humiliation, he shows, grew virulent after the Treaty of Versailles, and became an overwhelming obsession during the world economic crisis of 1929. The parallel to the peoples of the Near East is obvious. When a group sees no further chance to compensate on its own for (both real *and* imaginary) degradation, it devotes all of its psychic energy to laying up immeasurable stores of hate and envy, resentment and vengefulness. It sees itself as the pawn and victim of circumstances and denies any personal responsibility for the situation in which it finds itself. The search for the guilty parties can now commence.

Then the hour of the leader has arrived. The enemy of humanity can arm himself with the accumulated death wish of the masses. And he will bring a talent to this role that borders on genius: an unerring sense for the unconscious impulses of his followers. For that reason he uses not logical arguments, but emotions that defy all logic.

That is why all attempts to interpret or even refute him ideologically are doomed to fail. His project is driven not by ideas but by obsessions. The closer the ideas he exploits border on insanity, the more powerful they are. The paranoia that is not able to see real events as anything other than conspiracy or betrayal is not the leader's individual disease but the necessary prerequisite for his actions and for the echo he hears from his followers. The hatred of the Jews was an ideal vehicle for this, an emotion that consumed Hitler and his followers as it does their successors.

Moreover, the enemy of humanity must keep his followers far from anything resembling a thought. He produces an intellectual vacuum that can be filled with meaningless and arbitrary fragments of tradition. Thus, Hitler exploited German nationalistic and anticapitalistic sentiments, swaggering around with his *Vaterland* and *Blut und Boden* (Blood and Soil), while Saddam prefers anticolonial, pan-Arabic, and Muslim motifs. These ideological dummies can be switched at will. Content is unimportant to the leader, which allows him to change enemies at will. Hitler could first declare Bolshevism a deadly enemy, then an ally, and finally a deadly enemy again, without harming himself in the eyes of his followers. For Saddam, the eight-year-long war of aggression against Iran, which probably cost a million people their lives, was an inconsequential bagatelle; nothing would suit him better than a brotherly alliance with Teheran.

It is a fatal mistake to ascribe convictions to Hitler or Saddam. Tradition is nothing more than an explosives depot for them. The runic magic of the one and the prayer rug of the other have tricked many contemporaries into seeing something atavistic in their behavior, a "relapse" to a supposed Middle Ages or the barbarism of some prehistory. That is dangerous miscalculation. The modern enemy of humanity is a twentieth-century phenomenon, and the gasses and the missiles he uses in order to achieve his goals are just as modern as the newest forms of media.

The pacifists are right when they say that diplomacy has failed with Saddam Hussein. It was no different in Hitler's case. For a long time the world, then as now, did not want to grasp what confronted it. In foreign offices, Hitler was regarded as a statesman who represented "justifiable national concerns," to whom concessions had to be made, and with whom one must negotiate. To the victors of World War II, he was welcome as a business partner, as a balance to the Soviet threat, as someone who bought "order." In other words, they approached him through normal political means and trusted that this was a matter of a conflict of interest, a conflict that had to be solved.

But such actions tacitly assume that all participating parties are interested in their own survival. With this assumption, the world thoroughly misjudged Hitler. Only he knew what he wanted: total destruction through terror. What seemed like a misperception of reality to the rest of the world was only his determination to pursue that goal by every available means. For that reason, Hitler could only understand a willingness to negotiate as a sign of weakness. The idea of mutual exchange was incomprehensible to him, compromise filled him with revulsion, contractual solutions aroused his contempt; and he reacted with rage to any concession that hindered the pursuit of his final aim.

There is no conceivable political approach, no matter how wise or circumspect, that could initiate relations with such an enemy. In the end, he will always get what he wants: war. His success in taking the entire world hostage, including his followers, is his triumph. Even in dying, he has the pleasure of knowing that he managed to make millions die before him.

The elimination of Hitler cost the lives of innumerable people. The price for removing Saddam Hussein from the face of the earth will be astronomical, even if his desire to set loose an atomic war perhaps remains unfulfilled.

His successors will scarcely suffer the same limitation. It is foreseeable in the future that other nations will cheer for executioners, their own and ours. Eternal losers can be found in every corner of the earth. Their feelings of degradation and collective suicidal urges increase with every year. A nuclear arsenal stands ready on the Indian subcontinent and in the former Soviet Union. Where Hitler and Saddam failed, in their lack of final victory, that is, their final solution—their next incarnations could succeed.

Postscript. After the publication of my essay, the report of an eyewitness reached me. I reproduce it here with his permission. Georg Kahn-Ackermann is the retired General Secretary of the European Council:

> Because of my excellent contacts, in 1967 I was sent to Baghdad by the foreign office on a secret mission to reinstate relations, which were broken off at that time, between the Federal Republic of Germany and Iraq. At one of my preliminary discussions in the office of the Ministry of the President, I met a young officer of the Baath party named Saddam Hussein, who was standing in one of the anterooms. He asked me, among other things, whether I had read Hitler's *Mein Kampf.* I explained to him that this book was usually a wedding present from the justice of the peace to young married couples, and it remained, as a rule, unread. I myself had only glanced at it a few times as a boy. Saddam Hussein: "Very unfortunate! That is the most important book to have been written in our century." He claimed to know large passages of it by heart. Adolf Hitler, he said, was his model. It was a great mistake that the Germans had not completely exterminated the Jews. The Jews ought to have been torn out, root and branch.
>
> In those remarks, by the way, Saddam reflected the view of nearly all of the Iraqi government officials with whom I spoke at the time. The exception was the President, who shortly thereafter was deposed by his bodyguards, with the aid of Saddam.

1991

11) PITY THE POLITICIANS

A Conciliatory Gesture

PERHAPS IT IS TIME for us to stop abusing politicians. The heckling has long since moved beyond its origins in the political arena and turned into a pastime for the grumbling masses. Since that metamorphosis, it appears in all the media as a kind of amusing diversion. And as always, when everything has already been revealed, revelation becomes nothing more than a boring industry. It turns a profit when the ratings need a lift. But after a while, even this marginal kind of usefulness expires, the tasty morsel becomes a binge, outrage burns itself out, and in a consensus of contempt, we turn away with a shrug of the shoulders.

The field research of industrious sociologists, the investigations of state attorneys, and the reports of hard-charging journalists leave no doubt that the accusations are true: the group we call, in a phrase more puzzling than accurate, the "political class," is not a pretty sight. Not only in Germany but all over the world it is reproached—to varying degrees but with depressing unanimity—for its rule of mediocrity, breakdown in good judgment, shortsighted thinking, conceptual ignorance, lust for power, greed, addiction to big government, corruption, and arrogance.

Hardly anyone, from the meticulous political scientist to the blubbering bar-stool moralist, would contest the accuracy of this diagnosis. Regardless, the pettiness with which the press exposes the average officeholder's little extravagances is disturbing. The shabbiness of the sums in question, at least in Germany, speaks for itself. Our own West German politicians' homes bear an alarming similarity to the middle-class pretense of Wandlitz, that hellish neighborhood of East Berlin where the top politicos of the GDR fulfilled their petit-bourgeois dreams. Besides, expense-account padding and tax evasion are considered amusing national sports in every Western society, and if we want to discuss the incomes of politicians we also ought to take a look at the take-home pay of tabloid editors, who consider the pharisees a legitimate source of income.

No, accusations borrowed from gangster jargon—skimming off, cashing in, and gambling away—probably say more about the accusers than the guilty. They betray a secret envy of our sponging soldiers of fortune and an impaired sense of economic reality. Because as long as our discussion revolves around fudged fuel bills and pleasure jaunts on account, we are really only debating style, and in that arena it is difficult to decide between mud-slinging rivals.

Chancellor Helmut Kohl is not the notorious Mobutu, and Baden-Württemberg still has a long way to go before it reaches the scale of Italian corruption. As long as there are only dribs and drabs seeping from the public domain into politicians' pockets, the subject does not offer much to investigation, especially compared to the usual potlatch of organized waste that goes on for the benefit of political lobbies and parties. The capital that is squandered on campaigns, party donations, special funds, and legislative guarantees beats any of the perks politicians can award themselves by a factor of ten thousand.

The real problems are obscured rather than illuminated by the degree of national outrage in Germany. For example, it does not make sense that politicians should be slower on the uptake than other people. But it has been shown time and again that even unambiguous signals and major defeats at the polls do not suffice to teach anything to officeholders. After the debacle of the Danish "no" to the European Union, the unanimous reflex of all the politicians was: "OK, that does it! Damn the torpedoes, full speed ahead!" After police riots at the so-called economic summit in Munich, hooliganism was proclaimed a state virtue. Examples can be added ad infinitum and are not limited to Germany. The American government has proved to be just as hard-of-hearing concerning the uprisings in Los Angeles, ditto the single-party Japanese state in the face of corruption that borders on highway robbery; ditto the capitulation of the Italian state and its Roman multiparty circus in the face of deficit, the mafia, and government criminality.

Now, on the basis of statistics alone, it is improbable that a given population, in this case the political class, would be afflicted with defects from which the remaining population remains free. Genetic characteristics follow the Gaussian law of probability distribution. That explains why giants and lilliputians are less common than people of normal size. It is similar in the case of intelligence.

Sociological explanations are more promising. How and to what end does a person become a politician? A look at the development of politicians in Bonn, Paris, and Madrid shows that professional politicians are, as a rule, people without a profession. Already as adolescents, they spend their days in high school or college organizations. Only a person who neglects his studies, and thus learns as little as possible, makes it as a spokesperson, a delegate, a chair. It is a hard school in which the primary concern is to develop a killer instinct. As soon as the backwoods tour of duty through the community association, district committee, and municipal council has been completed, and the leap into the regional government has been successful, the search for gainful employment becomes superfluous.

One can describe such careers from two sides. Seen from the outside, we are looking at a full-time job that requires eternal vigilance; the constant struggle to maintain an image and the dogged, mortal campaign fights leave no breathing space. On the other hand, a political career is nothing more than a special form of unemployment. The organization of voting blocs, debates on the rules of procedure, and backroom intrigues create a peculiar emptiness where experience should be. Anyone who finally succeeds in wrangling a spot on the ballot or ascends to the chair representing this or that troop, will, as a rule, have reconciled himself to a reality deficit that must then be defended against all comers.

This political mechanism for recruitment can be seen not only in the biographies of politicians, but also through comparison with other career patterns. If one looks at the leadership in banking and industry, where a considerable shift has occurred in the past ten years, one will find people who lack neither ambition nor a sense of power. However, it is impossible to maintain such positions without knowledge of both a field and the world, without perceptive power and the ability to make decisions, without thought for the long-term. From what one hears, even moral criteria play a role now and then.

One imagines these people, when they speak among themselves, expressing barely concealed disdain for the political class, not only because they consider professional politicians fools, but also because the idle nature of the political enterprise strikes them as unbearable. The average businessman would never be content with the limited playing field and time frame prescribed by parties. The construction of an assembly line, the development of a new airplane, even the redevelopment of a middle-sized shipping firm involve lead times of which a politician, who hardly dares look beyond the next election, can only dream.

And so even if recruitment and professional development might make certain deviations from the statistical norm comprehensible, these selection mechanisms do not explain everything. In the end, every profession involves certain professional quirks, though in the case of locksmiths, undertakers, and veterinarians the consequences are not so disturbing. For that reason it is time to speak of the misery of politicians instead of abusing them. This misery is of an existential nature. To express it with a certain amount of pathos: The entry into politics is the departure from life, the kiss of death.

The first striking thing about the daily existence of these marked individuals is the unheard-of boredom to which they are subjected. Politics as profession is the Kingdom of Sameness, of merciless repetition. Anyone who has had the misfortune to take part in a political meeting knows the paralysis that seizes even the best-intentioned person when he is forced to listen to the circumspect, utterly banal series of remarks, admissions, discussion, and consideration produced on such occasions. Now, it is undoubtedly the case that the primary concern of a politician is to sit in meetings. Everybody sits. Bodies of experts sit, factions sit, committees, subcommittees, advisory committees, boards of trustees, presiding committees, boards of directors, city, county, state, and economic commissions, unions, chambers, discussion groups, supergroups. A professional politician spends years, possibly even decades of his life in such meetings. The consequences are unavoidable.

Second, a quick look into the office or even just the in-box of a representative reveals how the majority of his non-meeting time is spent with the reading of an interminable flood of documents—files, circulars, bills, motions, opinions, written statements, parliamentary questions, decisions, guidelines, bulletins, dossiers, resolutions, protocols, poll results, budgets, platforms, research reports, drafts of bills, position papers. . . . only those familiar with the horrific prose of such writing can fully appreciate what this means. The sheer volume excludes any other reading—except for tabloids, which are favored because of their small amount of text. Reasonably enough, the politician *has someone else* read the newspapers and magazines so that he at least knows what is being printed about himself. For that purpose he hires a personal assistant; in a pinch his secretary, his press secretary, or a clipping service can help him out.

Yet the indirect form of his reading only aggravates the problem instead of solving it. The boss only discovers what the filter, who is supposed to protect him, allows to pass. The higher he rises, surrounding himself with ever-more-reliable staff, the more reliably he will be shielded from unpleasant information. It is only too natural for him to punish the messenger who brings bad news; it is only too natural for the messenger to spare him from what he does not like to hear.

Third, it is not only true that much escapes the politician, but he also must not allow much to escape from him. At best he is allowed to share what he thinks, if he thinks, with his most inner circle. On the other hand, he is also not allowed to remain silent. In fact, it is demanded of him that he speak continuously. The emptiness of these speeches is, under such circumstances, not a flaw but an advantage. Even the most practiced person cannot produce this stream of words on his own power. Specialists are there to see that he never runs dry. It is the speaker's job to look over the manuscript carefully and to delete anything that could be interpreted as an independent thought. If he happens to overlook a turn of phrase that could awaken such a suspicion, punishment will be swift. The howl of public opinion will rob him of his rest, and his own comrades-in-arms will shun him.

The discipline necessary to avoid this risk would be better devoted to something else. It comes as no surprise that under such stress, the long-term public speaker is eventually robbed of his ability to express himself normally. Loss of language is one of the many casualties of the political profession.

Fourth, continual self-promotion is perhaps the most painful embarrassment to which a person can be subjected. It is, alas, one of the professional duties of politicians to deck themselves out with everything from little Alpine hats to Indian headdress, to kiss infants and elephants, to tap beer kegs, to participate in the dreariest carnivals and the most repellant talk shows. No cleaning lady, no mechanic would contemplate such degradation. Yet stoic self-denial, pasted-on smiles, and shameless boot-licking are the natural duties of a candidate running for office.

And it is not just outsiders but even his own kind who subject the professional politician to constant and boundless humiliation. One has to ask oneself what makes a person able to withstand the rituals of the political pecking order, what inures him to the penetrating stench of the manure shoveled at political meetings, what makes him put on the straitjacket of the party line?

Fifth, a further penance placed on the professional politician is the complete loss of control over his own time. The only thing he is allowed to observe during his waking hours is his appointment schedule. His calender is filled down to the minute for months, if not years, in advance. There are no empty pages. Even his vacation is a fiction: it is fully taken up with interviews, meetings, appearances. Bosses, great and small, all live under the compulsion to be continuously on the move, like a gyroscope, literally spinning until they fall over. There is no labor union that would not respond to this type of demand with a general strike. In comparison, any hobo enjoys an unimaginable freedom.

It would be possible to continue an enumeration of the adversities suffered by politicians, but only with diminishing returns. And it would not be possible in this way to grasp the decisive point, the thing that makes up the most profound reason for their misery, namely, their complete social isolation. This condition is paradoxical, because it applies in this case to people who are not allowed to be alone. Just the denial of this elementary right must, taken on its own, lead to serious psychic damage. But if one forces a person to spend all of his time in a mob and *at the same time* closes him out of all normal communication, he falls into a hopeless dilemma.

There is a scientific form of torture called sensory deprivation, in which the subject, perhaps in a water tank, is removed from all sensory stimulation. The chamber in which he is enclosed is soundproof, odorless; the sense of touch is neutralized by the liquid in which he floats. The social analogy to this experiment would be the peculiar encapsulation to which the professional politician is subjected. The higher he ascends, the more radically his social contacts are restricted. What goes on "out there in the country" remains as good as completely hidden from him. He has no idea what a pound of sugar or a pint of beer costs, nor how one goes about extending a passport or getting a train ticket.

A state visit exemplifies the compulsory deprivation of experience. After a long journey in his private plane, accompanied always by the same cohort of advisers, the chief hurries through empty streets in a city in which he gets to see nothing more than his police motorcade to the presidential palace, which looks exactly like every other presidential palace. From that moment on he must listen to speeches, speak, eat, speak, listen to speeches, eat, listen to speeches, speak. This is all. The next day he is brought to the airport without having gotten the slightest impression of the place he has visited.

This relatively harmless example only gives a small idea of the isolation of a politician. It is this solitude that deprives him of any sense of reality; that explains why he, regardless of his intellectual capacity, is usually the last one to understand what is happening in society.

Even his privileges, for which people never tire of condemning him, are nothing more than salt in his wounds. A characteristic example is the ominous status symbol of the bodyguard. It is easy to see that this figure not only protects the politician from the world but protects the world from the politician, preventing him from breaking through the membrane that separates him from his surroundings. The security agent is at once bodyguard and prison guard.

This kind of situation is, of course, not unique. Some analogies present themselves for comparison. In some respects, the life of a politician resembles that of the terrorist, his most dangerous enemy. Terrorists, too, are excluded from social life as a result of the demands of conspiracy; they, too, must make use of an extremely deformed language. (The loss of language and the loss of reality are but two sides of the same coin.)

However, a more productive comparison presents itself from a less exotic milieu, the "total-care institution": nursing homes, hospices, hospitals, prisons, psychiatric clinics, and the like. Many of the motifs that make up the existence of the professional politician can be found in such institutions: the inmates cannot dispose of time as they wish; appointments and routines are prescribed, there is no such thing as a private sphere; those who are locked up are always isolated but never alone; ritual humiliations are part of the order of the day; the loss of a sense of reality increases with the length of the stay.

After years of captivity, damages appear that may be collectively described as "institutional psychosis." Lack of sociability, apathy, disturbances in thought, language, and potency, weepiness, restlessness, and aggressiveness are among the most common symptoms. Occasionally it can go as far as delusions and hallucinations. The patients almost always suffer from anxiety, though their anxiety usually has quite real causes, as well.

Just like the inmate of an asylum, the politician is constantly watched. In his case the peephole or panopticon of the classical penitentiary becomes the eye of the camera, and in place of a guard, journalists and state attorneys appear. And since even the politician with personal integrity is forced to move in the gray areas of party finance, in the jungle of vested interests and weapon exports and in the morass of intelligence agencies, anxiety is his constant companion.

However, the most important system of institutional psychosis is depression. For the most part it appears in a disguised form, because the professional politician is not allowed to show it. Only mania, the reverse of depression, can be acted out. The drive for validation displayed in diplomatic events that are apparently called "summits" because of their flatness, the politician's infantile dreams of glory, his naive vanity, his extravagance—it is a mistake to believe that this has anything to do with pleasure, or even happiness. Such a suspicion would be misleading. The crude traveling circus staged by politicians only serves as compensation. In clinical literature, the transition from the depressive to the manic phase is described as follows:

> The diseased frame of mind colors all of the experience and the behavior of the patients so much that they believe that they are in their best mental condition. The lack of insight and an exaggerated capacity for activity lead to an explosive situation. In this state, the patient is impatient, obtrusive and annoying and reacts to resistance with aggressive irritability. Thoughts and actions are compounded and can advance to a clear case of megalomania. For example, patients can be convinced of their personal power and genius, or they can temporarily take on an ostentatious identity. Manic persons perform a variety of actions inexhaustibly, impulsively, and excessively without recognizing the social dangers associated with such behavior. In extreme cases their activity is so hectic, that any comprehensible connection between mood and behavior is lost.

A patient who attempts in this way to cope with a hopeless emotional state—how is he supposed to understand why people then blame him for his desperate actions?

Anyone who decides—even just as an experiment—to take the side of a professional politician, must be prepared for two objections that are so obvious that it is advisable to respond to them immediately.

The first objection is that it is the enjoyment of power that compensates the professional politician for all of the adversities he suffers. For some people, power is supposed to be an irresistible aphrodisiac. This observation might be correct historically. Time after time, absolute monarchs and despots approached the fulfillment of that infantile dream that the world no longer offers any resistance to their individual will.

But it is hard to understand how someone sitting in the government offices of Washington, Bonn, or Tokyo could succumb to such an ecstasy of power. For each of these leaders resembles Gulliver, tied down by a thousand threads. In the web of interests formed by parties, lobbies, unions, bureaucracies, he can only move an inch this way, then an inch the other way. A person bearing the proud title of commander-in-chief has to expect that the dispatch of even an unarmed airplane will get him a complaint of unconstitutionality. And questions such as whether a patient on government assistance should have to pay a few pennies extra for a prescription, or whether the taxation on widows' pensions can be modified—these provoke month-long titanic struggles within the political apparatus. The deletion of a tax loophole can succeed only with the help of diabolical tricks carried out behind the backs of those affected.

Any truly power-hungry person would flee in the face of such impediments. He would probably have more to say as the representative of a wholesale steel firm. In this way, reality takes its revenge on the politicians who abandoned it.

The other argument for the prosecution is the objection that the politicians are at fault for their own situation. In the end, they chose their profession of their own free will, the profession that is at the same time a nonprofession. And that is doubtless true.

But wouldn't it be malicious to insist upon that? For this spiteful judgment fails to take into consideration that the political career is like a lobster pot. It is easy to enter, but the chances are much smaller of getting out alive. A person trapped within it must imagine that there is only one way out: up. And if he succeeds, using all of his power, to rise, one day he will realize that he has been the victim of an illusion, for his ascendance did not free him from the situation, intensified it. But that will become clear only when it is too late.

Perhaps an even more desolate fate awaits the rare party politician released from his harness. In the best case, he ends as a well-paid unemployed person on the eleventh floor of a high-rise in Brussels, or he is assigned to be overseer of the city works, though he has not the least interest in burst pipes or public toilets. After all, who would, of his own free will, hire people who know nothing about anything in particular? So the prospect of a respectable pension is the only comfort for many of those who fell during the storming of the command post of society. They are still living in the heart of the country.

Certainly, most of us believe that it would be an extravagance to waste our sympathy on people who, without blushing, allow themselves to be identified as top politicians. But like all marginal groups—like alcoholics, gamblers, and skinheads—they too deserve pity and the consideration it takes to understand their misery.

1992

12) THE HERO AS DEMOLITION MAN

AT THE SPOT in every European capital where symbolism is densest—that is, in the center of the city—one always finds peculiar, obese centaurs cast in metal. They are Roman emperors, great princes, eternally victorious leaders on pedestals, and under their hooves, officials scurry to their ministries, spectators to their operas, believers to their houses of worship. The chimera mounted high on its steed represents the European hero, an imaginary figure without whom it is impossible to imagine the history of this continent. The invention of the automobile threw this *Weltgeist* on horseback from its saddle—Lenin and Mussolini, Franco and Stalin had to get along without a whinnying foundation—but our modern heroes made up for it in the number and size of their monuments. Our stone heroes now populate Caribbean islands and Siberian factories, and their shoe size often exceeds the scale of a single-family dwelling. The very bloat of their monuments announced the approaching demise of those heroes who had never been concerned with anything other than conquest, triumph, and megalomania.

Writers anticipated this change. More than a century ago, literature abandoned the larger-than-life figures it had helped to create. Panegyrics and heroic sagas now belong to literature's ancient history, and writers have long since turned away from Augustus and Alexander to embrace

Bouvard and Pécuchet, Vladimir and Estragon. Today, Napoleon and Friedrich of Prussia have been buried in literature's basement, to say nothing of those Hitler-hymns and Stalin-odes that were destined for the garbage heap from the very beginning.

So-called power politics has clung tenaciously and helplessly to the classical heroic model until today. As of old, we gild the victors and dream of unachievable triumphs. But the hero's loss of symbolic force heralds the traditional model's imminent collapse, and there is a pragmatic sign of the hero's decline as well, in the modest scope of the contemporary leader's power. Democracy's proclivity toward the banal somewhat restricts arrogance and the thirst for glory, no doubt to the frustration of our political leaders. They realize that not a world empire but, at best, a constituency is theirs for the taking, and the military genius finds himself limited to islands such as Grenada or the Falklands, which can hardly be located on the globe without a magnifying glass. Anyone who doubts the phenomenon of the incredible shrinking hero need only compare Churchill to Thatcher, de Gaulle to Mitterand, Adenauer to Kohl. A whiff of drama has always surrounded the hero in his or her role as representative of the state; the current power elite in Western Europe has dropped its ferocity and become a laughable imitation. The cast of this unintentional comedy, constantly imagining itself on some "summit," is but a caricature of the classical heroes of history.

In their place other and, to my mind, more important protagonists have entered the scene in recent decades—a new breed of hero, a hero of retreat who represents not victory, conquest, or triumph, but resignation, withdrawal, and devolution. We must all pay close attention to these demolition experts, because Europe depends upon them if it is to survive at all.

The great classical strategist Clausewitz showed that retreat is the most difficult of all maneuvers in war. It is the same in politics. The ultimate act in the art of the possible is being able to surrender an untenable position. If the greatness of a hero is measured by the difficulty of the task he faces, we must not only revise our notion of heroism, but reverse it. Any cretin can throw a bomb. It is a thousand times more difficult to disarm one.

In any case, military prowess and competence alone no longer make a hero. It is the moral dimension of his actions that makes a protagonist worthy of notice. But it is precisely in this regard that the heroes of retreat encounter a massive and stubborn resistance. Popular opinion, especially in Germany, champions the old heroic model. The people, as always, insist upon the importance of an infallible character, and they want a political morality that places tenacity and resolve above all things—even if their hero has to walk over a few dead bodies to achieve his goals. It is precisely this singularity of purpose that the hero of retreat is under no circumstances able to provide. Anyone who abandons his own position gives up not only territory but also a piece of himself. An action of this kind cannot succeed unless the person separates himself from the role he plays. The ethos of this hero lies in his ambivalence. The demolition expert shows his moral courage in assuming this ambiguity as part of his persona.

The antiheroic paradigm I describe here has come to light historically in the aftermath of the totalitarian dictatorships of the twentieth century. The pioneers of retreat allow us to understand their role only obscurely and indistinctly. One can claim of Nikita Khrushchev that he did not know what he was doing, that he was unclear as to the implications of his acts; after all, he did speak of perfecting communism rather than doing away with it. But all the same, with his famous speech before the Twentieth Party Congress, he planted the seed of his own downfall. His intellectual horizons were limited, his strategy clumsy, his style self-aggrandizing, but his civil courage exceeded that of any other politician of his generation. It was precisely that peculiar instability in his character that qualified him for his task. Today, the subversive logic of his heroic career has been brought to light; it was with him that the dismantling of the Soviet Empire began.

The divided nature of the demolition expert comes out even more clearly in the figure of Hungary's János Kádár. This man, who was buried without ceremony in Budapest in 1989, came to terms with the Soviet occupational forces after the failed uprising in 1956. Eight hundred death sentences can be placed on his account. But hardly were the victims of repression buried, when Kádár began the life's work that would occupy him for nearly thirty years. This consisted of the patient and stubborn undermining of the Communist Party's control of his country. The remarkable thing is how this process unfolded without significant turbulence, setbacks and self-delusions accompanied it, tactical maneuvers and compromises fueled it. Without the precedent of Hungary, the dissolution of the East Bloc would hardly have had a chance to get started, and that Kádár was a trailblazer in this regard cannot be contested. But it is just as obvious that he was not able to deal with the forces he set free. The work of the demolition expert always undermines his own position. The process he sets into motion typically casts him aside, and he is defeated by his own success.

Adolfo Suáez, General Secretary of the Spanish Falange, became prime minister after Franco's death. In a carefully orchestrated coup, he dragged the dictatorial regime down with him, gutted his own party, and got a democratic constitution passed—an operation as difficult as it was dangerous, which Suárez led with personal courage and political brilliance. Unlike Khrushchev, his was not a dull understanding of history and a vague premonition of the things to come, but an utter awareness of the state of things. It was not only necessary for him to outmaneuver the political apparatus, but to keep the army at bay: a military putsch would have led to bloody repression and perhaps even another civil war.

This case, too, cannot be understood with a simplistic black-and-white moral view. Suárez was a participant in and beneficiary of Franco's regime; had he not been part of the inner circle of power, he would not have been in the position to do away with the dictatorship. At the same time, has past ensured that any democrat would regard him with unshakable mistrust. Indeed, Spain has not yet forgiven him. In the eyes of his former comrades, he was a traitor; in the eyes of those for whom he made way, he was an opportunist. Ever since he stepped down, a typical "transitional figure," he has never been able to regain support. The role he played in the party system of the republic remains obscure. There is only one thing of which the hero of retreat can be sure: the ingratitude of his fatherland.

In the case of Wojciech Jaruzelski of Poland, this moral aporia takes on nearly tragic features. He was the one who saved Poland from an imminent Soviet invasion in 1981. The price for this was the declaration of martial law and the internment of the opposition group that would later rule the land under his presidency. His striking political success did not save him from the fact that a significant portion of Polish society holds him in quiet contempt. No one cheers for him; he will never escape the shadow of his actions. His moral strength lies in the fact he had reckoned with his fate from the beginning. No one has ever seen him smile. With his gestures stiffened to the point of lifelessness and his eyes hidden behind dark glasses, he represents the patriot as martyr. This Saint Sebastian of politics is a figure of Shakespearean proportions.

One cannot say the same of his successors. Egon Krenz of East Germany and Ladislav Adamec of Czechoslovakia will probably take up no more than a footnote in history: one of them as a clown, the other as the comfortable bourgeois version of the hero of retreat. But neither the antics of the German nor the fatherly countenance of the Czech can conceal that they are indispensable. The inconstancy for which they are scorned is their only value. In the oppressive silence of the pregnant moment, in which each person waits for the other to do something and thus nothing happens, somebody has to be the first to clear his throat, to produce that first, tiny, half-choked sound that sets off the avalanche. "Someone," a German Social Democrat once said, "someone has to be the bloodhound." Seventy years later someone had to fall into the clutches of the bloodhounds, even if it was a communist Pulcinell who broke the deadly silence. No one will think of him with mercy. And that is precisely what makes him worthy of consideration.

The heroes of retreat are outcasts. They act under a pressure that comes both from below and outside. But the true hero of retreat is himself the driving force. Mikhail Gorbachev set a process into motion with which others tried, more or less voluntarily, to keep pace. He is, to be sure, not a saint. But the sheer dimensions of the task he had set himself were nearly inconceivable: he dismantled the next-to-last monolithic empire of the twentieth century without violence, without panic, without war. No one had thought it possible. It took a very long time for the world to even begin to comprehend his project. The superior intelligence, the moral daring, the far-reaching perspective of this man—all of this lay so far beyond the ken of politicians in the East as in the West that there was no government that dared to take him at his word.

Nor could Gorbachev have any illusions about his popularity in his own country. This greatest of all renunciatory politicians found himself confronted at every step with the question of the positive, as if his task were a matter of proclaiming yet another brilliant future to his people, a future that would offer soap, missiles, and brotherhood to each according to his need—as if there were any other form of progress other than retreat, as if any future chance did not depend on the disarmament of the Leviathan and the return from nightmare into reality. It can be taken for granted that every step along this road presented a mortal danger. To the right as well as to the left, Gorbachev was surrounded by old and new, loud and mute enemies. He is a rather solitary man, as becomes a hero.

By all of this I do not mean to argue that we ought to pay homage to the great and small heroes of retreat, an honor they do not expect. New monuments are superfluous. But on the other hand, it is time to take this new breed of protagonist seriously and to recognize what unites them, and what distinguishes them one from the other. A political morality that sees only black or white hats cannot be the judge of this.

A German philosopher once said that by the end of this

century we will want not to have improved the world but to have saved it. This applies not only to those dictatorships that have been scrapped, peacefully or not, before our eyes, but also to those Western democracies that face an impending and unprecedented disarmament. Military disengagement is only one of the forms of retreat to consider. Other untenable positions have to be abandoned in our economic war against the Third World, and the most difficult of all our retreats will take place in the war we have been waging against our own biosphere since the Industrial Revolution.

For that reason, it is time for our tiny men of state to take on the task of demolition. The work that stands before us demands abilities that can best be studied in the examples I have given. Only through a strategic retreat can an energy and transportation policy be introduced worthy of the name. Such a policy will demand the closure of key industries, which in the long run are no less threatening than a central party, and the civil courage necessary for this will hardly be any less than that summoned up by the communist functionary when placed in the position of gutting his party's power.

Instead, however, our politicians prefer foolish victory poses and self-satisfied lies. They triumph by walling themselves off from the world, and they believe that they can become the masters of the future by waiting it out. They sense nothing of the moral imperative of renunciation. The art of retreat is foreign to them. They still have a lot to learn.

1989

Part Three

13) THE INDUSTRIALIZATION OF THE MIND

ALL OF US, no matter how irresolute we are, like to think that we reign supreme in our own consciousness, that we are masters of what our minds accept or reject. Since the Soul is not much mentioned any more, except by priests, poets, and pop musicians, the last refuge a man can take from the catastrophic world at large seems to be his own mind. Where else can he expect to withstand the daily siege, if not within himself? Even under the conditions of totalitarian rule, where no one can fancy any more that his home is his castle, the mind of the individual is considered a kind of last citadel and hotly defended, though this imaginary fortress may have been long since taken over by an ingenious enemy.

No illusion is more stubbornly upheld than the sovereignty of the mind. It is a good example of the impact of philosophy on people who ignore it; for the idea that men can "make up their minds" individually and by themselves is essentially derived from the tenets of bourgeois philosophy: secondhand Descartes, run-down Husserl, armchair idealism; and all it amounts to is a sort of metaphysical do-it-yourself.

We might do worse, I think, than dust off the admirably laconic statement one of our classics made more than a century ago: "What is going on in our minds has always been, and will always be, a product of society." This is a comparatively recent insight. Though it is valid for all human history ever since the division of labor came into being, it could not be formulated before the time of Karl Marx. In a society where communication was largely oral, the dependence of the pupil on the teacher, the disciple on the master, the flock on the priest was taken for granted. That the few thought and judged and decided for the many was a matter of course and not a matter for investigation. Medieval man was probably other-directed to an extent that our sociology would be at a loss to fathom. His mind was, to an enormous degree, fashioned and processed from "without." But the business of teaching and of indoctrination was perfectly straightforward and transparent—so transparent indeed that it became invisible as a problem. Only when the processes that shape our minds became opaque, enigmatic, inscrutable for the common man, only with the advent of industrialization, did the question of how our minds are shaped arise in earnest.

The mind-making industry is really a product of the last hundred years. It has developed at such a pace, and assumed such varied forms, that it has outgrown our understanding and our control. Our current discussion of the "media" seems to suffer from severe theoretical limitations. Newsprint, films, television, public relations tend to be evaluated separately, in terms of their specific technologies, conditions, and possibilities. Every new branch of the industry starts off a new crop of theories. Hardly anyone seems to be aware of the phenomenon as a whole: the industrialization of the human mind. This is a process that cannot be understood by a mere examination of its machinery.

Equally inadequate is the term "cultural industry,"

which has become common usage in Europe after World War II. It reflects, more than the scope of the phenomenon itself, the social status of those who have tried to analyze it: university professors and academic writers, people whom the power elite has relegated to the reservations of what passes as "cultural life" and who consequently have resigned themselves to bear the unfortunate name of cultural critics. In other words, they are certified as harmless; they are supposed to think in terms of *Kultur* and not in terms of power.

Yet the vague and insufficient name "cultural industry" serves to remind us of a paradox inherent in all media work. Consciousness, however false, can be induced and reproduced by industrial means, but it cannot be industrially produced. It is a "social product" made up by people: its origin is the dialogue. No industrial process can replace the persons who generate it. And it is precisely this truism of which the archaic term "culture" tries, however vainly, to remind us. The mind industry is monstrous and difficult to understand because it does not, strictly speaking, produce anything. It is an intermediary, engaged only in production's secondary and tertiary derivatives, in transmission and infiltration, in the fungible aspect of what it multiplies and delivers to the customer.

The mind industry can take on anything, digest it, reproduce it, and pour it out. Whatever our minds can conceive of is grist to its mill; nothing will leave it unadulterated—it is capable of turning any idea into a slogan and any work of the imagination into a hit. This is its overwhelming power, yet it is also its most vulnerable spot: it thrives on a stuff it cannot manufacture by itself. It depends on the very substance it must fear most, and must suppress what it feeds on: the creative productivity of people. Hence the ambiguity of the term "cultural industry," which takes at face value the claims of culture, in the ancient sense of the word, and the claims of an industrial process that has all but eaten it up. To insist on these claims would be naive; to criticize the industry from the vantage point of a "liberal education" and to raise comfortable outcries against its vulgarity will neither change it nor revive the dead souls of culture: it will merely help to fortify the ghettos of educational programs and to fill the backward, highbrow section of the Sunday papers. At the same time, the indictment of the mind industry on purely aesthetic grounds will tend to obscure its larger social and political meaning.

On the other extreme we find the ideological critics of the mind industry. Their attention is usually limited to its role as an instrument of straightforward or hidden political propaganda, and from the messages reproduced by it they try to distill the political content. More often than not, the underlying understanding of politics is extremely narrow, as if it were just a matter of taking sides in everyday contests of power. Just as in the case of the "cultural critic," this attitude cannot hope to catch up with the far-reaching effects of the industrialization of the mind, since it is a process that will abolish the distinction between private and public consciousness.

Thus, while radio, cinema, television, recording, advertising, and public relations, new techniques of manipulation and propaganda, are being keenly discussed, each on its own terms, the mind industry, taken as a whole, is disregarded. Newsprint and publishing, its oldest and in many respects still its most interesting branch, hardly comes up for serious comment any longer, presumably because it lacks the appeal of technological novelty. Yet much of the analysis provided in Balzac's *Lost Illusions* is as pertinent today as it was a hundred years ago, as any copywriter from Hollywood who happens to know the book will testify. Other, more recent branches of the industry still remain largely unexplored: fashion and industrial design, the propagation of established religions and esoteric cults, opinion polls, simulation and, last but not least, tourism, which can be considered as a mass medium in its own right.

Above all, though, we are not sufficiently aware of the fact that the full deployment of the mind industry still lies ahead. Up to now it has not managed to seize control of its most essential sphere, which is education. The industrialization of instruction, on all levels, has barely begun. While we still indulge in controversies over curricula, school systems, college and university reforms, and shortages in the teaching professions, technological systems are being perfected that will make nonsense of all the adjustments we are now considering. The language laboratory and the closed-circuit TV are only the forerunners of a fully industrialized educational system that will make use of increasingly centralized programming and of recent advances in the study of learning In that process, education will become a mass media, the most powerful of all, and a billion-dollar business.

Whether we realize it or not, the mind industry is growing faster than any other, not excluding armament. It has become the key industry of the twentieth century. Those who are concerned in the power game of today, political leaders, intelligence men, and revolutionaries, have very well grasped this crucial fact. Whenever an industrially developed country is occupied or liberated today, whenever there is a coup d'état, a revolution, or a counterrevolution, the crack police units, the paratroopers, the guerilla fighters do not any longer descend on the main squares of the city or seize the centers of heavy industry, as in the nineteenth century, or symbolic sites like the royal palace; the new regime will instead take over, first of all, the radio and television stations, the telephone and telex exchanges, and the printing presses. And after having entrenched itself, it will, by and large, leave alone those who manage the public services and the manufacturing industries, at least in the beginning, while all the functionaries who run the mind industry will be immediately replaced. In such extreme situation the industry's key position becomes quite clear.

There are four conditions that are necessary to its existence; briefly, they are as follows:

1. Enlightenment, in the broadcast sense, is the philosophical prerequisite of the industrialization of the mind. It cannot get under way until the rule of theocracy, and with it people's faith in revelation and inspiration, in the Holy Book or the Holy Ghost as taught by the priesthood, is broken. The mind industry presupposes independent minds, even when it is out to deprive them of their independence; this is another of its paradoxes. The last theocracy to vanish has been Tibet; ever since, the philosophical condition is met with throughout the world.

2. Politically, the industrialization of the mind presupposes the proclamation of human rights, of equality and liberty in particular. In Europe, this threshold has been passed by the French Revolution; in the communist world, by the October Revolution; and in America, Asia, and Africa, by the wars of liberation from colonial rule. Obviously, the industry does not depend on the realization of these rights; for most people, they have never been more than a pretense or, at best, a distant promise. On the contrary, it is just the margin between fiction and reality which provides the mind industry with its theater of operations. Consciousness, both individual and social, has become a political issue only from

the moment when the conviction arose in people's minds that everyone should have a say in his own destiny as well as in that of society at large. From the same moment any authority had to justify itself in the eyes of those it would govern; coercion alone would no longer do the trick; he who ruled must persuade, lay claim to people's minds and change them, in an industrial age, by every industrial means at hand.

3. Economically, the mind industry cannot come of age unless a measure of primary accumulation has been achieved. A society that cannot provide the necessary surplus capital neither needs it nor can afford it. During the first half of the nineteenth century in Western Europe, and under similar conditions in other parts of the world, which prevails until fairly recently, peasants and workers lived at a level of bare subsistence. During this stage of economic development the fiction that the working class is able to determine the conditions of its own existence is meaningless; the proletariat is subjected by physical constraint and undisguised force. Archaic methods of manipulation, as used by the school and by the church, the law and the army, together with old customs and conventions, are quite sufficient for the ruling minority to maintain its position during the earlier stages of industrial development. As soon as the basic industries have been firmly established and the mass production of consumer goods is beginning to reach out to the majority of the population, the ruling classes will face a dilemma. More sophisticated methods of production demand a constantly rising standard of education, not only for the privileged but also for the masses. The immediate compulsion that kept the working class "in their place" will slowly decrease. Working hours are reduced, and the standard of living rises. inevitably, people will become aware of their

own situation; they can now afford the luxury of having a mind of their own. For the first time, they become conscious of themselves in more than the most primitive and hazy sense of the word. In this process, enormous human energies are released, energies that inevitably threaten the established political and economic order. Today, this revolutionary process can be seen at work in a great number of emergent nations, where it has long been artificially retarded by imperialist powers; in these countries the political if not the economic conditions for the development of mind industries can be realized overnight.

4. Given a certain level of economic development, industrialization brings with it the last condition for the rise of a mind industry: the technology on which it depends. The first industrial uses of electricity were concerned with power and not with communications: the dynamo and the electrical motor proceeded the amplifying valve and the film camera. There are economic reasons for this time lag: the foundations of radio, film, recording, television, and computing techniques could not be laid before the advent of the mass production of commodities and the general availability of electrical power.

In our time, the technological conditions for the industrialization of the mind exist anywhere on the planet. The same cannot be said for the political and economic prerequisites; however, it is only a matter of time until they will be met. The process is irreversible. Therefore, all criticism of the mind industry which is abolitionist in its essence is inept and beside the point, since the idea of arresting and liquidating industrialization itself (which such criticism implies) is suicidal. There is a macabre irony to any such proposal, for it is indeed no longer a technical problem for our civilization to abolish itself. However, this is hardly what conservative critics have in mind when they complain about the loss of "values," the depravity of mass civilization, and the degeneration of traditional culture by the media. The idea is, rather, to do away with all these nasty things, and to survive, as an elite of happy pundits, in the nicer comforts offered by a country house.

Nonetheless, the workings of the mind industry have been analyzed, in part, over and over again, sometimes with great ingenuity and insight. So far as the capitalist countries are concerned, the critics have leveled their attacks mainly against the newer media and commercial advertising. Conservatives and Marxists alike have been all too ready to deplore their venal side. It is an objection that hardly touches the heart of the matter. Apart from the fact that it is perhaps no more immoral to profit from the mass production of news or symphonies than from the mass production of soap and tires, objections of this kind overlook the very characteristics of the mind industry. Its more advanced sectors have long since ceased to sell any goods at all. With increasing technological maturity, the material substrata, paper or plastic or celluloid, tend to vanish. Only in the more old-fashioned offshoots of the business, as for example in the book trade, does the commodity aspect of the product play an important economic role. In this respect, a radio station has nothing in common with a match factory. With the disappearance of the material substratum the product becomes more and more abstract, and the industry depends less and less on selling it to its customers. If you buy a book, you pay for it in terms of its real cost of production; if you pick up a magazine, you pay only a fraction thereof; if you tune in on a radio or television program, you get it virtually free; direct advertising and political propaganda is something nobody buys—on the contrary, it is crammed down our throats. The products of the mind industry can no longer be understood in terms of a sellers' and buyers' market, or in terms of production costs: they are, as it were, priceless. The capitalist exploitation of the media is accidental and not intrinsic; to concentrate on their commercialization is to miss the point and to overlook the specific service the mind industry performs for modern societies. This service is essentially the same all over the world, no matter how the industry is operated: under state, public, or private management, within a capitalist or a socialist economy, on a profit or nonprofit basis. The mind industry's main business and concern is not to sell its product: it is to "sell" the existing order, to perpetuate the prevailing pattern of man's domination by man, no matter who runs the society, and by what means. Its main task is to expand and train our consciousness—in order to exploit it.

Since "immaterial exploitation" is not a familiar concept, it might be well to explain its meaning. Classical Marxism has defined very clearly the material exploitation to which the working classes have been subjected ever since the industrial revolution. In its crudest form, it is a characteristic of the period of the primary accumulation of capital. This holds true even for Socialist countries, as is evident from the example of Stalinist Russia and the early stages of the development of Red China. As soon as the bases of industrialization are laid, however, it becomes clear that material exploitation alone is insufficient to guarantee the continuity of the system. When the production of goods expands beyond the most immediate needs, the old proclamations of human rights, however watered down by the rhetoric of the establishment and however eclipsed by decades of hardship, famine, crises, forced labor, and political terror, will now unfold their potential strength. It is in their very nature that, once proclaimed, they cannot be revoked. Again and again, people will try to take them at their face value and, eventually, to fight for their realization. Thus, ever since the great declarations of the eighteenth century, every rule of the few over the many, however organized, has faced the threat of revolution. Real democracy, as opposed to the formal façades of parliamentary democracy, does not exist anywhere in the world, but its ghost haunts every existing regime. Consequently, all the existing power structures must seek to obtain the consent, however passive, of their subjects. Even regimes that depend on the force of arms for their survival feel the need to justify themselves in the eyes of the world. Control of capital, of the means of production, and of the armed forces is therefore no longer enough. The self-appointed elites who run modern societies must try to control people's minds. What each of us accepts or rejects, what we think and decide is now, here as well as in Vietnam, a matter of prime political concern: it would be too dangerous to leave these matters to ourselves. Material exploitation must camouflage itself in order to survive; immaterial exploitation has become its necessary corollary. The few cannot go on accumulating wealth unless they accumulate the power to manipulate the minds of the many. To expropriate manpower they have to expropriate the brain. What is being abolished in today's affluent societies, from Moscow to Los Angeles, is not exploitation, but our awareness of it.

It takes quite a lot of effort to maintain this state of affairs. There are alternatives to it. But since all of them would inevitably overthrow the prevailing powers, an entire industry is engaged in doing away with them, eliminating possible futures and reinforcing the present pattern of domination. There are several ways to achieve this end: on the one hand, we find downright censorship, bans, and a state monopoly on all the means of production of the mind industry; on the other hand, economic pressures, systematic distribution of "punishment and reward," and human engineering can do the job just as well and much more smoothly. The material pauperization of the last century is followed and replaced by the immaterial pauperization of today. Its most obvious manifestation is the decline in political options available to the citizen of the most advanced nations: a mass of political nobodies, over whose heads even collective suicide can be decreed, is opposed by an ever-decreasing number of political moguls. That this state of affairs is readily accepted and voluntarily endured by the majority is the greatest achievement of the mind industry.

To describe its effects on present-day society is not, however, to describe its essence. The emergence of the textile industry has ruined the craftsman of India and caused widespread child labor in England, but these consequences do not necessarily follow from the existence of the mechanical loom. There is no more reason to suppose that the industrialization of the human mind must produce immaterial exploitation. It would even be fair to say that it will eventually, by its own logic, do away with the very results it has today. For this is the most fundamental of all its contradictions: in order to obtain consent, you have to grant a choice, no matter how marginal and deceptive; in order to harness the faculties of the human mind, you have to develop them, no matter how narrowly and how deformed. It may be a measure of the overwhelming power of the mind industry that none of us can escape its influence. Whether we like it or not, it enlists our participation in the system as a whole. But this participation may very well veer, one day, from the passive to the active, and turn out to threaten the very order it was supposed to uphold. The mind industry has a dynamic of its own which it cannot arrest, and it is not by chance but by necessity that in this movement there are currents that run contrary to its present mission of stabilizing the status quo. A corollary of its dialectical progress is that the mind industry, however closely supervised in its individual operations, is never completely controllable as a whole. There are always leaks in it, cracks in the armor; no administration will ever trust it all the way.

In order to exploit people's intellectual, moral, and political faculties, you have got to develop them first. This is, as we have seen, the basic dilemma faced by today's media. When we turn our attention from the industry's consumers to its producers, the intellectuals, we find this dilemma aggravated and intensified. In terms of power, of course, there can be no question as to who runs the business. Certainly it is not the intellectuals who control the industrial establishment but the establishment that controls them. There is precious little chance for the people who are productive to take over their means of production; this is just what the present structure is designed to prevent. However, even under present circumstances, the relationship is not without a certain ambiguity, since there is no way of running the mind industry without enlisting the services of at least a minority of men who can create something. To exclude them would be self-defeating. Of course, it is perfectly possible to use the whole stock of accumulated original work and have it adapted, diluted, and processed for media use, and it may be well to remember that much of what purports to be new is in fact derivative. If we examine the harmonic and melodic structure of any popular song hit, it will most likely turn out to employ inventions of serious composers centuries ago. The same is true of the dramaturgical clichés of mediocre screenplays: watered down beyond recognition, they repeat traditional patterns taken from the drama and the novel of the past. In the long run, however, the parasitic use of inherited work is not sufficient to nourish the industry. However large a stock, you cannot sell out forever without replenishment; hence the need "to make it new," the media's dependence on men capable of innovation, in other words, on potential troublemakers. It is inherent in the process of creation that there is not way to predict its results. Consequently, intellectuals are, from the viewpoint of any power structure bent on its own perpetuation, a security risk. It takes consummate skill to "handle" them and neutralize their subversive influence. All sorts of techniques, from the crudest to the most sophisticated, have been developed to this end: physical threat, blacklisting, moral and economic pressure, on the one hand, overexposure, star-cult, co-optation into the power elite on the other, are the extremes of a whole gamut of manipulation. It would be worthwhile to write a manual analyzing these techniques. They have one thing in common, and that is that they offer short-term tactical answers to a problem that in principle, cannot be resolved. This is an industry that has to rely, as its primary source, on the very minorities with whose elimination it is entrusted: those whose aim it is to invent and produce *alternatives.* Unless it succeeds in exploiting and manipulating its producers, the mind industry cannot hope to exploit and manipulate its consumers. On the level of production, even more than on the level of consumption, it has to deal with partners who are potential enemies. Engaged in the proliferation of human consciousness, the media proliferate their own contradictions.

Criticism of the mind industry which fails to recognize its central ambiguities is either idle or dangerous. It is a measure of their limitations that many media critics never seem to reflect on their own position, just as if their work were not itself a part of what it criticizes. The truth is that no one can nowadays express any opinion at all without making use of the industry, or rather, without being used by it.

Anyone incapable of dialectical thinking is doomed as soon as he starts grappling with this subject. He will be trapped to a point where even retreat is no longer possible. There are many who feel revolted at the thought of entering a studio or negotiating with the slick executives who run the networks. They detest, or profess to detest, the very machinery of the industry, and would like to withdraw into some abode of refinement. Of course, no such refuge really exists. The seemingly exclusive is just another, slightly more expensive line of styling within the same giant industrial combine.

Let us, rather, try to draw the line between intellectual integrity and defeatism. To opt out of the mind industry, to refuse any dealings with it, may well turn out to be a reactionary course. There is no hermitage left for those whose job is to speak out and to seek innovation. Retreat from the media will not even save the intellectual's precious soul from corruption. It might be a better idea to enter the dangerous game, to take and calculate our risks. Instead of innocence, we need determination. We must know very precisely the monster we are dealing with, and we must be continually on our guard to resist the overt or subtle pressures that are brought to bear on us.

The rapid development of the mind industry, its rise to a key position in modern society, has profoundly changed the role of the intellectual. He finds himself confronted with new threats and new opportunities. Whether he knows it or not, whether he likes it or not, he has become the accomplice of a huge industrial complex that depends for its survival on him, as he depends on it for his own. He must try, at any cost, to use it for his own purposes, which are incompatible with the purposes of the mind machine. What it upholds he must subvert. He may play it crooked or straight, he may win or lose the game; but he would do well to remember that there is more at stake than his own future.

1962

14) THE APORIAS OF THE AVANT-GARDE

TO COUNT ONESELF A MEMBER of the avant-garde has for several lifetimes now been the privilege of everyone who covers empty surfaces with paint or sets down letters or notes on paper. Not everyone has availed himself of this opportunity. Whoever undauntedly sticks the label *avant-gardist* on an author like Franz Kafka is already seduced into negligence by that mouthful of a word; it would have stuck in Kafka's craw. Neither Marcel Proust nor William Faulkner, neither Bertolt Brecht nor Samuel Beckett—none of them, as far as we know, has invoked that vocable, which nowadays, to be sure, every laundry list lays claim to, but on whose meaning, as if it were settled once and for all, hardly anyone of the crowd who mouth it stops to reflect.

This is true of the partisans of the avant-garde no less than of its enemies. They differ in their judgment but not in their premises. Both sides help themselves uncritically to a critical concept that struck it rich in Paris over a hundred years ago, and has since passed for a touchstone of which it has not been expected or demanded that it undergo a test itself. The minds that it separates from one another have a way of lapsing into a permanent debate whose beginnings are lost in a mist and whose end can be held off ad libitum. Names and catch phrases change; the schema remains the same. Since Swift's *Full and True Account of the Battle Be-*

tween the Ancient and the Modern Books (1710), this controversy has lost some of its originality and brilliance; what remains is that modest abstraction for which, all along, it was willing to settle. The cast-iron stances of the contenders, no matter on which side, are of a depressing innocuousness; they remind one of the figures of middle-class family drama to whose antiquated conflict between father and son they would reduce the march of history. Commonplace like the ones about the impetuous youngster whose ears will yet be pinned back, about the excesses of youth and the wisdom of maturity, and about the enlightened traditionalism of age that looks back with a wink on its own rebellious past are characteristic of the entire sphere of such discussion, with their lack of a sense of history. Unhistoric, not merely hackneyed, is the blind trust they are happy to put in the threadbare concept of generations, quite as if it were the life of the arts, rather than that of trichinae, that is subject to the biological law of the life cycle; or as if the content of a hymn by Hölderlin or a play by Brecht could be read off the author's "vintage." Whoever distinguishes between old and new, or old and young, in such comfortable fashion, agrees by his very choice of criteria with the philistines. To him, the simplest dialectical propositions must remain inaccessible. That the durability of works is always determined only by their immanence in today's creation, which simultaneously and rejuvenates them, remains unfathomed, indeed unfathomable, even though this insight could be gleaned at the starting point of all European thought: "The old, veering round, becomes the new, and the latter, veering back, the former." The statement is to be found in Heraclitus.

The argument between the partisans of the old and those of the new is unendurable, not so much because it drags on endlessly, unresolved and irresoluble, but because its schema itself is worthless. The choice that it invites is not only banal, it is a priori factitious. The semblance of a timeless symmetry with which it surrounds itself is invalidated by history, which has so far overtaken every unhistoric position and given it the lie. For no sooner do the arts enter the gravitational field of totalitarianism than the harmless tug of war about the avant-garde, or rather what passes for it, assumes murderous traits. The symmetry of the old and the new, that timeless mirror image, is brutally broken in two, and its real substratum becomes manifest. No avant-garde has thus far called for the police to rid it of its opponents. The "healthy forces of preservation" are the ones that have persistently sanctioned censorship, book burning, bans on publishing, indeed murder, as the extension of their criticism to other means; they purport to be liberal only until the political conditions permit or, rather, command them to talk of a breach.

Only when it has come to that (but it has always come to that on the other side of the fence) do the categories of "progressive" and "reactionary" in the arts come into their own. To be sure, they are scarcely less questionable and shabby than those of the Old and the New; moreover, so many cardsharps have been operating with them that there are indelible black marks against them on the books. Nevertheless, they can lay claim to their historicity; they are suited to the analysis not of biological but of historic processes. So long as somewhere in the world aesthetic questions are settled by force—so long, indeed, as such a procedure can be reckoned with as a real possibility—they are indispensable; in other words, everywhere and for an unforeseeable length of time. They require no metaphysical foundation. Their usefulness is simply and solely heuristic. They require, therefore, constant reappraisal; like every indispensable device, they imperil the user as soon as he relies on them blindly. What most profoundly distinguishes the progressive attitude from every reactionary one is precisely its relation to doubt. The readiness to revise all solidified theses, to examine endlessly its own premises, is the essence of all progressive criticism. Reactionary criticism, on the contrary, considers itself, so to speak, naturally and everlastingly in the right. It is exempt from reflecting on its presuppositions. As complaisantly as it adapts its judgment, from case to case, to the nature of the powers that be, as unshakably has it established what is to be considered beautiful, sane, and constructive.

Only after coming into power does it reveal its brutal countenance. Until then it operates in the underbrush of conventicles, on the unserveyable terrain of textbooks and "education in the arts"; it observes certain precautions. Under democratic conditions, reactionary criticism sees itself constrained to deny its own existence. It even admits tacitly to its canon of imperishables what it previously denigrated: the moment a modern work is no longer new, no longer risky, it is claimed as a "contemporary classic" by that very criticism which for decades tried in vain to strike it dead with its "rigid yardstick." Once annexed to the heritage that must be preserved, it is truly deprived of its life, that is, removed from criticism and exhibited as an embalmed holy relic. Whatever he cannot lick, the reactionary critic will join, and even thinks thereby to demonstrate his magnanimity. As long as he cannot enforce his doctrine with police assistance, he finds himself willing even to sign a truce and passes himself off as a mediator and man of common sense who stands "above the press of things." Social pluralism becomes, for the time being, an aesthetic pillow; in the dark of freedom, all cats are gray. Every work has its justification along with every other one, trash "complements" the masterpiece, and with the obligingness of all judgments the critical faculty itself is made to vanish by sleight of hand.

Neutrality of this ilk, which likes to answer to the name of "openmindedness," condemns itself. At the first sign that aesthetic questions are about to be adjudicated by the power of the state, it flaps over into what it has secretly been all along. In the face of a rule of terror, whether exercised by a Goebbels or a Zhdanov, there can be no tolerance; which, for reactionary criticism, means that tolerance for the victims of that terror can be dispensed with. Such criticism rests untroubled on its certitudes as long as it sees to it that the yardsticks of its Beckmesserdom are always calibrated according to regulation.

The prescriptions are always the same: "The emphasis must be placed on questions pertaining to a world view." The work of art is nothing in itself; it functions merely as the "representative" of the currently demanded "Weltanschauung," which it must "adequately reproduce." "What matters is not the specific, artistically formal manner of writing, but this stand in terms of an ultimate worldview." Opportunism that makes common cause with the stronger battalions is candidly appealed to: "Affiliation with the determinant tendencies of the times, which, sooner or later, will be the ruling ones," is what the writer must seek, placing himself "on the ground" designated to him by reactionary criticism. He is thus given the "concrete plumb line" by which he can hang himself, and "the justified, world historic optimism, so extraordinarily fruitful for art" will then come about on its own. The arts are there to supply "lifelike realism" and "all-embracing positivism" and "to fashion man's future from within." "The will and aptitude for the creation of such a positive, new reality" facilitate "the choice between social health and sickness." "From that there follows"—verbatim!—"such a heightening of the watchtower" that it can no longer be doubted what sort of straitjacket the watchman intends for the arts; the avant-garde, whatever that term means to him, is "decadent," "perverse," "cynical," "nihilistic," and "sickly." This vocabulary will be well remembered from the *Völkische Beobachter*, and that the state of mind it expresses has not died out in our land is demonstrated by every second glance into the newspapers that appear between Bonn and Passau. The quoted phrases did not, however, sprout from façist dung; they were not culled from the *Neues Deutschland*, either. The man who wrote them passes for the most intelligent, distinguished, and courageous literary critic whom communism can point to anywhere; they appear in Georg Lukács's book, *Against Misunderstood Realism*, which could not be published on the other side of the Elbe, for to the cultural police that have the final word there is seemed still not reactionary enough. To be sure, Lukács objects—in a language that, probably unjustly, claims to derive from Schiller and Goethe—to the "ever more pronounced stepping-into-the-foreground of the pathological in literature," but he does not opt for the therapy that customarily follows on such pronouncements and consists of liquidating the patient. Lukács does not by any means reach for his gun when he hears the "culture." He has kept within him a remnant of that bad conscience that the most intelligent "representatives" of reactionary criticism bring to it as a dowry. It stirs in vain.

The "artistic striving" of such criticism does not manifest itself only in that its language, under whatever party insignia, gets tattered and rotten. This criticism can dispense even with the knowledge of what it defames. The goat turned gardener need not concern itself with botany. It separates herbs from weeds with its horns. What passes for healthy is most likely to be the mediocre: Theodore Dreiser, Sinclair Lewis, Norman Mailer, Romain Rolland, and Roger Martin du Gard are for Lukács the quintessence of modern literature. To what unhappy misconception Thomas and Heinrich Mann may owe their appearance on this roster of those given a clean bill of health remains inscrutable. Sickly and decadent, however, in contradistinction to the apple-cheeked author of *The Black Swan*, are Dos Passos and Beckett, Motherlant and Kafka, Proust and Jens Rehn, Koeppen and Jünger, Gide and Faulkner—about as nonsensical a collocation of names as could possibly be conceived. Tonsure is administered with the self-same unclean comb to heads that, for content and quality, for style and provenance, simply cannot be compared. Lukács calls this pocket comb "avant-gardism"—naturally without taking the trouble to analyze the term. Nor have Hanns Johst and Will Vesper made the art of discrimination any harder for themselves.

Neither Western nor Eastern exponents of such criticism, on whatever bastions they may ply their trade, are competent to criticize the avant-garde. Their verdict about what is healthy or sick—about the meritorious or the degenerate—must be implemented by the police, or it remains without significance. With every one of their anathemas, they attest to their lack of authority.

In the face of their censure, whose aim is nothing other than censorship, solidarity goes without saying. Every work deserves to be defended against its suppressors: this tenet precedes all aesthetic probing, and event he most superfluous, "experiment" may have recourse to it. A criticism that considers itself progressive must weigh all the more carefully its rights and duties precisely as regards the most advanced production. If it is content with turning the verdicts of the culture wardens upside down, it thereby makes them seem only most justified. Whoever denies the bailiffs of unjust power their competence cannot simultaneously vindicate himself by reference to their pronouncements. Solidarity can be valid in the arts only so long as it is not used as a carte blanche. What proclaims itself the avant-garde is by no means immune to criticism. There is much evidence for this term's having become nowadays a talisman, which is to make its wearers proof against all objections and to intimidate perplexed reviewers. What is most revealing is that the term, to this day, has not been analyzed. Those who would be happiest to eradicate it have never specially concerned themselves with what the avant-garde actually is. That is understandable. What is queerer is that its followers have hardly contributed more to the definition of that which they admire than have its foes. The concept "avant-garde" is in need of elucidation.

Under that catchword, there appears in all [German] dictionaries, in token of its military derivation, a pair of crossed daggers. Older works of reference do not even recognize the figurative meaning:

> *Avant-garde, advance guard, vanguard,* that segment of a marching troop which the letter (the main body) sends more distance forward. . . . An a. subdivides itself frontward into ever smaller divisions, down to the spearhead marching at the very forefront. Each of these subdivisions serves the purpose of gaining for the larger one following it more security and time. . . . The flung-out smaller divisions must govern themselves as to their movement according to the larger ones that follow them.

The transfer of this strategic concept to the arts was first effected in the fifties of the past century in France. The metaphor has since dislodged and obscured the original sense of the term: it must, however, accept the fact of being taken at its word. The objection that it wasn't meant that way comes ready to hand but does not matter. The figure of speech preserves what its users have forgotten; analysis merely brings to light what presuppositions it drags along. The concept of the avant-garde is, like the word itself, a composite.

Its first component poses no conundrum. The field in which the avant-garde moves is history. The preposition *avant*, conceived spatially in the technical military sense, returns in the metaphor to its original temporal significance. The arts are regarded not as historically unvarying activities of mankind or as an arsenal of timelessly extant "cultural goods" but as a continually advancing process, as a work in progress, in which every single production participates.

Now, this process has a single direction. Only this makes it possible to differentiate advance guard, main body, and rear guard. Not all works are equally far "forward," and it is by no means a matter of indifference which position they occupy. The pathos of the concept feeds on the notion that the place at the spearhead of the process distinguishes a work, endows it with a rating denied other works. What is being compared is not really present performance with the past. To be sure, the avant-garde metaphor does not exclude the dull and inferior view that whatever came earlier can, for that very reason, be thrown on the junkheap. But it cannot be reduced to vulgar worship of the latest thing. Included in the concept is the nonsimultaneity of the simultaneous: precursors and stragglers are, at every moment of the process, simultaneously present. External and internal contemporaneity fall apart. The *en avant* of the avant-garde would, as it were, realize the future in the present, anticipate the course of history.

This conception has its justification in the fact that art

without a moment of anticipation cannot even be thought of. It is contained in the very process of creation: the work is preceded by the design. The design, the project, does not disappear in its realization. Every work of art, and the masterwork in particular, has in it something unfinished; indeed, this necessary residue makes up its durability: only when it fades does the work fade with it. An inkling of it is the prerequisite of all productivity. The idea of fame has its roots here. It has always been the notion of posthumous fame, not to be compared with mere celebrity during one's lifetime. Only subsequent generations can fulfill the work of art that juts, uncompleted, into the future; only they can, so to speak, redeem anticipation through fame. The works of antiquity were created in this confidence. It is stated explicitly in a widespread literary topos: the poet's apostrophe to posterity.

With the development of historical consciousness, this faith in posterity begins to decline. No doubt, there opens before any work, even the least significant, a prospect of a new immorality: everything can, indeed must, be preserved in mankind's memory—but as a "memorial," as a relic. That brings up the question of surpassability. Eternal survival in the museum is being bought with the prospect that henceforth the march of history can stride across everything without extinguishing it. Everyone becomes aware of the process of steady advance, and this awareness, in turn, becomes the motor that accelerates the process. The arts no longer find protection in their future: it confronts them as a threat and makes them dependent on itself. Faster and faster, history devours the works it brings to fruition.

From now on, the arts are cognizant of their own historicity as a stimulant and a threat, but this change of consciousness is not all there is to it. The triumph of capitalism turns it into a hard economic fact: it brings the work of art into the marketplace. It thus enters into a state of competition not only with other merchandise but also with every other work of art. The historic contest for future recognition becomes a competition for present purchase. The mechanics of the market imitates the devouring course of history on a smaller scale: it is geared to a rapid turnover in accord with the scant breath and crude eye of planned economy. The anticipatory moment of art is cut down to a mere speculation; its future is charted like that of stocks and shares. Historic movement is observed, comprehended, and discounted—a market trend upon whose correct prediction economic success depends. In the long run, though, the consciousness industry does not content itself with merely letting its augurs survey the marketplace of the arts. It attempts to insure itself against changes in the weather by creating it. If it does not exactly invent tomorrow's trend, it certainly proclaims and promotes it. The future of the work of art is sold before it has even occurred. What is steadily being offered for sale is, as in other industries, next year's model. But this future has not only always begun; it is also, when tossed out into the market, always already past. Tomorrow's aesthetic product offered for sale today proves, the day after tomorrow, a white elephant and, no longer sellable, wanders into the archives in the hope of the possibility that, ten years later, it might still be palmed off as the object of a sentimental revival. Thus, the work of art too is subject to the industrial procedure of built-in obsolescence; its afterlife is immediately cashed in on and cashiered; indeed, it is transmogrified, by way of publicity, into a forelife, which the work inherits before it even appears on the scene. Its afterlife is factory-made. The proposition concerning the nonsimultaneity of the simultaneous is realized by training the clientele to become a vanguard that insists on being served the newest thing and demands the future, so to speak, as consumer goods.

As suppliers of this industry, writers, painters, composers assume, economically speaking, the traits of employees. They must "keep in step with the times" and always nose out the competitors. To keep in the forefront, they must not "fail to connect." This explains why fifty-year-olds let themselves be described as young authors. Such an economic disposition obviously invites contemptible maneuvering. It gives rise to an avant-garde as bluff, as escape forward, with which the main body, for fear of being left behind, falls in. The type of the fellow traveler who would like to pass for a forerunner becomes prominent; in the rush for the future, every ram fancies himself the bellwether. The man on the treadmill remains unremittingly the object of a process that he thinks he is, as subject, in control of.

These economic consequences, however, merely reveal an aporia that is posited with the very concept of an avant-garde in the arts. What is questionable is not just its commercial exploitation but also the very *en avant* wit which the avant-garde presents itself. For just who, other than the avant-garde itself, is to determine what at any given time is "to the fore" remains an open question. "The flung-out smaller divisions must govern themselves as to their movement," if we may trust the Brockhaus, "according to the larger ones that follow them": but that means, as soon as a spatial movement is translated into a temporal one, governing themselves according to an unknown body.

Of course, it is possible to verify without much trouble that there exists at all times a rear guard. It coincides without fail with what reactionary criticism recommends as healthy. Its physiognomy can be described down to its minutest traits, for in them it is only the all-too-familiar that epigonously recurs. An extreme, very well explored example is the popular novel, which always reiterates older, exhausted patterns in distorted fashion. This does not actually devaluate what previous epochs have produced; devaluated, rather, are the suppliers of this rear guard, which likes to justify itself—but always unjustly—with reference to tradition. its unassuming, petit-bourgeois wing is shielded from every objection by its stupidity; in communist countries, it enjoys state protection; in neocapitalist society, it supplies, hardly observed by the public eye, the proletariat, which, by universal demand, has been rechristened "lower-middle class." How this majority of the population is being provided for, without dissension, with fifth-hand aesthetics, can be studied in the catalogs of the large department stores and mail-order houses. At the forefront of this inarticulate rear guard is to be placed that "elevated" group, which consists of "culture bearers." Its speciality is the aristocratic gesture with which it purports to "attend to spiritual interests" and defend "values"; its shadowboxing with modernity, of many decades' standing, needs to elucidation, and its points of view have become known ad nauseam.

On the other hand, it is not possible to discern a vantage point form which one could determine what is avant-garde and what isn't. All the efforts of the consciousness industry to detect a trend in the historic movement of the arts and elevate its prognostications to the level of a dictate misfire as speculation; at best, it is by chance that it scores any bull's-eyes. The actual process puts to shame not only the impotent attempts of the communists to plan it but also the cleverer endeavors of capitalist economy, which would steer it by means of advertising and market manipulations. All that can be affirmed is what *was* "out front," not what *is* there.

The work of Kleist or Kafka remained invisible to their contemporaries not because they refused to "go with the times" but because they went with the times. This does not mean that, in the arts, what contains futurity must go unrecognized. The notion of the unrecognized has, in any case, taken on an old-fashioned coloring, ever since the capacity of the reproducing apparatus has become greater than existing production, and since, consequently, anything at all that anyone writes or paints is indiscriminately and suspiciously publicized. That in this way every work—let alone one that anticipates the future—is done justice to cannot for a moment be entertained; there is no authority before which such justice can be pleaded or, like a tariff regulation, implemented. Where the word "avant-garde" is being construed in the present tense, a doctrinaire formulation results. Whoever becomes rigid about objective necessity, the demands of the medium, and compulsory evolution is already in the wrong. Every such doctrine relies on the method of extrapolation: it projects lines into the unknown. Such a procedure, however, will not get even at a political or economic process, because it is applicable only to linear, not to dialectical operations, to say nothing of an aesthetic process, which can be apprehended through no prognosis, not even a statistical one, because its characteristics are determined by leaps. Their spontaneous appearance defies any theory of futurity

The model according to which the concept of the avant-garde orients itself is invalid. The forward march of the arts through history is conceived of as a linear, perspicuous, and surveyable movement in which everyone can himself determine his place, at the forefront or with the hangers-on. What is overlooked is that this movement leads from the known into the unknown; that, therefore, only the stragglers can indicate where they are. Nobody knows what is up front, least of all he who has reached unknown territory. Against this uncertainty there is no instance. Only someone willing to suffer the consequences of error can get involved with the future. The *avant* of the avant-garde contains its own contradiction: it can be marked out only a posteriori.

The metaphor of the avant-garde, however, contains not only temporal but also sociological determinants. These are expressed in the second component of the compound term.

> *Guards* is the name given, other than to the bodyguards of princes, in many armies, to elite troops distinguished by excellent supplies and especially brilliant uniforms (cf. *Elite*); they are usually garrisoned in capitals and royal residential towns. Guard means originally an enclosure. . . . Napoleon I must be considered the actual creator of the g. Tradition puts into the mouth of its commander, General Gambronne (to be sure, without foundation), the saying, "The guard dies, but does not surrender."

Every guard is a collective; that is the first thing that can be deduced from this word. First the group, and only then the individual, whose decisions are of no consequence in the undertaking of the guard, unless he be its leader. For every guard is most rigorously divided into the one who issues the commands and pass them on, and obey them. What all who belong to it have in common is discipline. Without dictates and regulations, it cannot manage. To abide by them is not always easy, but it does relieve the member of the guard of many worries. Along with his freedom, he delegates to the collective body doubt, fear, and insecurity; he feels surer about his cause, which is no longer his concern but that of the whole. The protection that the guard vouchsafes is enjoyed, in the first place, by the guard itself. The guardsman has not only duties but also rights—to be exact, perogatives. To belong to the guard is a distinction. It is an exclusive league of men; the enclosure keeps others out. Every guard, and so too the avant-garde, considers itself an elite. It is proud not only of being ahead of and further on than the others but also of belonging to a distinguished minority.

The guard's vocation is combat. In it, and only in it, does the guard prove its worth. Not productivity but contest is its raison d'être: it is always militant. Here the transfer of the concept to the arts leads into some difficulties. What adversary does the vanguard expect to encounter on the terrain of history if it alone, and nobody else, operates in, or into, the future? What enemy army could it meet there? Enemies should not be lacking to anyone who forsakes the safe, allegedly so "healthy" grounds of mediocrity; but these adversaries seem to be located in back of him, and aside from the fact he will not exactly see his purpose in life as fighting the likes of them, it just will not jibe with the idea of a guard that its only foe should be the tail of that very column it has the privilege of leading.

The concept of the avant-garde was applied not only to the arts but also, over half a century later, more felicitously and sensibly to politics. In 1919, Lenin defined the Communist Party as the avant-garde of the proletariat. This formula became part of the international communist vocabulary. It pinpoints what the avant-garde metaphor sociologically comprehends, or rather, uncomprehendingly drags along. The role played by Sorel's concept of an elite in the development of Lenin's theories is well known. Very much in Sorel's sense, the party is to Lenin a strictly organized, elite combat unit, where absolute discipline is a matter of course; no less obviously, it is entitled to a privileged position vis-à-vis the outsiders, the mass of nonparty members. Here the avant-garde metaphor is thought out with sharp consistency down to its last detail. At one point only does the figurative meaning diverge from the literal one. The communist avant-garde need not "govern itself as to its movement" according to the main body, but conversely, it is at the same time the general staff according to whose plans the entire operation must proceed: it enforces the dictatorship not only *of* but also *over* the proletariat. Understandably, if the revolution is to be "carried out" in the name of the majority but against its will, what is required is not so much muses as a bodyguard. In all other particulars, however, the communist concept of an avant-garde is strictly relevant. What is "forward" is determined once and for all by an infallible doctrine, and the adversary at whom the vanguard action is directed is established and really there.

Beside Lenin's well-defined application of it to politics, the concept of the avant-garde in the arts appears to be somewhat confused. Least convincing is its collective trait. Clearly, a historic process has many collaborators, so many that it would be ridiculous to speculate about just how many individuals at a given period "constitute" a literature. But as much as every literature is a collective effort, as little is it to be visualized as a troop organized along disciplinary lines and sworn to a doctrine. Whoever participates in it enters forthwith into a direct relationship with the process as a whole; he can consign his freedom and risks to no group outside of himself.

The avant-garde metaphor does not contain the slightest reference to a revolutionary or even rebellious intent. Nothing is more glaring than this lack. Yet so far every group that made use of the concept, in the arts as in politics, viewed itself as a *Fronte* and proclaimed the overthrow of existing conditions. No avant-garde program fails to protest the inertia of the merely extant, and all of them promise to burst aesthetic and political bonds, throw off established rule, liberate suppressed energies. Freedom, gained through revolution, is heralded by all avant-garde movements. It is to this claim, which it does not even express, rather than to its future-orientedness, rather than to its promise to form an elite, that the concept of the avant-garde owes its emotional appeal. This aspect too was thought out more acutely and thoroughly by Lenin than by all the writers and painters. From what the communist avant-garde would free its partisans and everybody else is made clear beyond any doubt; its revolutionary character will not be denied by its worst enemy. By contrast, it remains vague and blurry just what freedom the mainifestos of the artistic avant-garde have in mind and what the word "revolution," frequently though it may appear in them, is supposed to mean there. All too often these manifestos sound both grandiloquent and innocuous, as if they had no other concern than to scare off bourgeois conventions, which, in any case, are nothing more than ghosts. The cry for absolute freedom rings peculiar when the question involved is whether or not fish may be eaten with a knife. The propensity of revolutionary rhetoric may reveal the surface nakedness of the avant-garde; it does, however, cover up its central aporias. Only where it ruthlessly formulates its aims and methods, as with Lenin, do these aporias become apparent.

In much the same way as communism in society, the avant-garde in the arts would enforce freedom in doctrinaire fashion. Just like the Party, it believes itself to have taken, as a revolutionary elite, which is to say as a collective, a lease on the future. It disposes with the indefinable in the most definite manner. It arbitrarily dictates what will be valid tomorrow and, simultaneously, submits, disciplined and will-less, to the commands of a future of its very own contriving. It proclaims as its goal total freedom, and surrenders, unresisting, to the historic process, which is to relieve it of that self-same freedom.

These aporias lie in the concept "avant-garde" itself. They can be verified empirically in all groups that have had recourse to it, but they have never become more flagrantly apparent than in that which today exhibits itself as the avant-garde: in tachism, in *art informel*, and in monochrome painting; in serial and electronic music; in the so-called concrete poetry; and in the literature of the beat generation. These movements have in common the more or less obstreperously announced conviction of being "out front," their doctrinaire bias, and their collective state. That their names have become, in the course of a few years, catchwords, indeed trademarks, stems not merely from their accord with the consciousness industry; these terms were launched with premeditation as handy slogans. Avant-gardism, nowadays, is brought into currency overnight as coin of the realm. All the more reason for examining the coinage a little more closely.

It is to Jack Kerouac, the supreme commander of the Beatnik sect, canonized by his partisans as Holy Jack, that we owe the following maxim, which he posited in his "Credo" together with a "List of Indispensable Remedies" for the writer: "Be always idiotically absentminded!" The sentence can serve as motto for the current mass productions of tachism, *art informel*, action painting, concrete poetry in toto, as well as for a large part of the latest music. Kerouac goes on: "My style is based on spontaneous get-with-it, unrepressed wordslinging. . . . Push aside literary, grammatical and syntactic obstacles! Strike as deep as you can strike! Visionary spasms shoot through the breast. You are at all times a genius." To be sure, the avant-garde bares its breast with so much naiveté (even if false) only between New York and San Francisco. The harmless simplicity with which it proclaims barbarism has a downright endearing effect in contrast to its European counterpart. Here indeterminacy expresses itself in a petrified academic jargon that dishes out delirium like a seminar report: the proffered texts form "a system of words, letters or signs, which obtain their meaning only through the personal contribution of the reader. . . . They are arbitrarily disposed in the sixteen directions of the quadratic square and aligned in a chance sequence . . . they possess stringency only: through the swirls of motion and the assent they evoke in the reader . . . when carried through with rigorous consistency, they debouch into the black stone, the last standstill, as the no-further-enhanceable complex motion. Are, thereby, concrete form, uninterruptedly centered point, objective duration in nature (as material-1 sine qua non) guess whyyyy."

That reads like a translation of Kerouac's catechism into occidental culture-gibberish. The translator keeps strictly to the prescription of the original, which, to be sure, is garnished with eruditional flotsam, but to whose intellectual exiguity he remains absolutely faithful. Mobility raised to an end in itself reappears as "swirls of the no-further-enhanceable complex motion," and the "visionary spasms" turn into "the black stone guess whyyyy." In both cases, mystification demands "carrying through with rigorous consistency," and the precept "Be always idiotically absent-minded" lays claim to stringency. An idea of the possibilities this avant-garde opens up may be gleaned from the following "text":

ra ra ra ra ra ar ra ra ra ra ar ar er ir
ra ra ra ra ar ar ar ka ra ra ar ar ar er
ra ra ra ar ar ar ak af ka ra ar ar ar ra
ra ra ar ar ar ak af ab af ka ar ar ra ra

ra ar ar ar ak af ab af ab af ak ra ra ra

This result does not stand in isolation. Works of the same stamp are available in such quantities that it would be unjust to name the begetter of the specimen, even though he has already made a bit of a name for himself with his output. Since, however, it is hardly distinguishable from the outpourings of his companions, rather, what should be considered the author, insofar as this word still applies, is the collective: in such texts the guard brings itself into being. It can be seen at a glance (and this in itself justifies the reproduction of a specimen) that the sociological aporias of the avant-garde are repeated in these texts quite accurately on the formal level; indeed, they perfectly consume themselves in their reproduction. Indeterminacy appears as doctrine, retrogression as progress. The milkman's bill masquerades as inspirited madness, quietism as action, chance as prescription.

That these characteristics apply not only to "concrete poetry" and the literature of the beat generation but also to the self-declared avant-garde in all the arts is demonstrated by an international album in which it draws its self-portrait and which purports to be "at once account, documentation, analysis and program." it contains a list of basic concepts and categories, which are supposed to be equally valid for literature and painting, music and sculpture, film and architecture (insofar as such distinctions are still permissible). The following should be noted: improvisation, chance, moment of imprecision, interchangeability, indefiniteness, emptiness; reduction to pure motion, pure action, absolute motion, motoricity, *mouvement pur*. Arbitrary, blind movement is the guiding principle of the entire album, as emerges already from its title. That title applies insofar as the avant-garde was all along bent on movement, as conceived not only by the philosophy of history but also by sociology. Each one of its groups not only believed itself to be anticipating a phase of the historic process but also saw itself always as movement, motion. This movement, in both senses of the word, now proclaims itself an end in itself. The kinship with totalitarian movements lies close to hand, their center being precisely, as Hannah Arendt has shown, empty kinetic activity, which spews forth thoroughly arbitrary, indeed manifestly absurd, ideological demands and proceeds to implement them. Kerouac's appeal, "Strike as deep as you can strike!" is so utterly innocuous only because it is directed at literature, and because literature, like all arts, cannot be terrorized by the likes of him. Transposed onto the plane of politics, it could serve as a device for any fascist organization. The impotent avant-garde must content itself with obliterating its own products. Quite consistently, the Japanese painter Murakami contrives a large painted paper screen destined for his work, which is "the piercing of several holes in one instant"; "the work of Murakami made a mighty noise as it was being pierced. Six holes were torn into the strong eightfold paper screen. This was done with such speed, in a single moment, that the cameraman [!] missed the exact instant. When the six holes were there, he had an attack of bloodlessness of the brain. 'I've been a new man ever since,' he later murmured."

All avant-garde groups incline toward the adoption of obscure doctrines of salvation. They are, characteristically, defenseless against Zen Buddhism, which, within a few years, spread rapidly among writers, painters, and musicians of this cast. In its imported form, Zen Buddhism serves to confer upon blind action an occult, quasi-religious consecration. Its teachings are transmitted in exempla, the so-called *mondo*. The punch line of the best-known exemplum consists in the master's answering the metaphysical questions of a disciple with a stick or a slap in the face. Murakami's "action" too may be considered a Zen precept. It points to the latent acts of violence in avant-garde "movements," which, to be sure, are directed first against the "materials" with which they are dealing: they blindly toss about paints, tones, or word fragments rather than hurling hand grenades or Molotov cocktails.

The reverse side of this susceptibility to extremely irrational, supposedly mystical teachings is the no less extreme faith in science that the avant-garde proudly sports. The indeterminacy of its "actions" always pretends to be exact. It tries to convey this impression by means of a terminology for which the most diverse disciplines have been ransacked: along with *vacuum* and *absolute motion*, there are catchwords like *constellation*, *material structure*, *correlogram*, *coordination*, *rotomodulation*, *microarticulation*, *phase-shift*, *autodetermination*, *transformation*, and so on and so forth. A laboratory smock enfolds the breast shot through with visionary spasms: and what the avant-garde produces, whether it be poems, novels, pictures, movies, constructions, or pieces of music, is and remains "experimental."

Experiment as an aesthetic concept has long since become part of the vocabulary of the consciousness industry. Put in circulation by the avant-garde, used as an adjuration, worn threadbare and unelucidated, it haunts artistic conferences and cultural panels and reproduces itself through reviews and essays. The obligatory modifier is "bold," but the choice of the ennobling epithet "courageous" is also permitted. The most modest reflection reveals that it is a case of plain bluff.

Experimentum means "that which has been experienced." In modern language, the Latin word designates a scientific procedure for the verification of theories or hypotheses through methodical observation of natural phenomena. The process to be explained must be isolable. An experiment is meaningful only when the variables that appear are known and can be controlled. There is the additional requisite that every experiment must be susceptible for rechecking and must at every repetition yield the same unequivocal result. That is to say, an experiment can succeed or miscarry only with regard to a previously exactly defined goal. It presupposes reflection and contains an experience. It can in no way be an end in itself: its intrinsic worth equals zero. Let us also set down that a genuine experiment has nothing to do with boldness. It is a very simple and indispensable procedure for the investigation of laws. It requires, above all, patience, acuteness, circumspection, and diligence.

Pictures, poems, performances do not satisfy these requirements. The experiment is a procedure for bringing about scientific insights, not for bringing about art. (Of course, every publication can be considered an economic or sociological experiment. Under this heading, success and failure can be established quite accurately, and most publishers, art dealers, and theatrical managers do not hesitate to derive from that the theory and practice of their enterprises. To be sure, viewed from this angle, Karl May, the German author of popular cowboy-and-Indian novels, is every bit as experimental as Jack Kerouac. The difference between the two experiments lies in the result, that is, in the number of copies sold. That such experiments possess aesthetic relevance may be doubted.) Experiment as bluff does, indeed, flirt with the scientific method and its demands, but has not the least intention of getting seriously involved with it. It is unconditional "pure action"; intentions of any kind are not to be attributed to it. Method, possibility of proof, stringency have no share in it. The farther removed from any sort of experience they are, the more the experiments of the avant-garde are "experimental."

That proves that this concept is nonsensical and unusable. What has yet to be explained is what makes it so popular. That is not hard to say. A biologist who undertakes an experiment on a guinea pig cannot be held accountable for its behavior. He is answerable only for the irreproachable observance of the conditions of the experiment. The result is out of his hands: the experimenter is literally obligated to interfere as little as possible in the process he is observing. The moral immunity he enjoys is precisely what appeals to the avant-garde. Though it is by no means ready to adhere to the methodical demands to which the scientist submits, it does wish to avoid all responsibility, both for its activities and their results. It hopes to achieve this by referring to the "experimental" character of its work. The borrowings from science serve as an excuse. With the designation "experiment," the avant-garde excuses its results, takes back, as it were, its "actions," and unloads all responsibility on the receiver. Every boldness suits the avant-garde perfectly so long as it itself remains safe. The concept of the experiment is to insure it against the risk of all aesthetic production. It serves both as trademark and as camouflage.

What is under investigation here is the aporias of the avant-garde, its concept, its assumptions, and its postures. Such an analysis reveals the claims made in behalf of concrete poetry, the beat generation, tachism, and other present-day avant-garde groupings to be untenable, each and all. On the other hand, it can by no means serve the purpose of condemning the productions of such groups as a whole. It does not unmask doctrinaire fraud only to fall prey to it itself. Not a single work can be dismissed by pointing to the fact that its creator has joined up with such-and-such a guard, and even the silliest aesthetic program does not ipso facto vitiate the potency of those who subscribe to it. The person who demolishes the terminological tricks and doctrinal screens with which today's avant-garde tries to shield itself does not thereby save himself the trouble of critically examining its products; he merely makes such a critical examination possible in the first place. Such examination must be insisted upon all the more determinedly the more advanced a work claims to be; and the more assiduously it appeals to a collective, the more it must affirm its individuality. Every popular movie deserves more leniency than an avant-garde that would simultaneously overpower critical judgment and timorously rid itself of the responsibility for its own works.

The aporias that have rent it and delivered it into the hands of charlatans have always been contained in the concept of the avant-garde. They were not first dragged in by hangers-on and stragglers. Already the first futurist manifesto of 1909, one of the earliest documents of an organized "movement," makes "*dynamisme perpétuel*" into an end in itself: "We live," Marinetti writes, "already in the absolute: we have created permanent and omnipresent speed. . . . We extol aggressive motion, feverish sleeplessness, marching on the double, the slap of the palm and the blow of the fist above all things. . . . There is no beauty but that of battle. . . . Only in war can the world recover its health." (The last sentence in the original: "*La guerre seule hygiène du monde.*")

In futurism, the avant-garde organized itself for the first time as a doctrinaire clan, and already then it lauded blind action and open violence. That in 1924 the nucleus of the movement collectively rushed into the fascist camp is no accident. In formal matters, the futurists, exactly as did their descendants, advocated the removal of all "literary, grammatical and syntactic barriers." Even the disconnected slapping together of pseudo-mathematics and questionable mysticism can already be found among them. The painters of the movement declared in 1912 that they wished to "reinforce the emotions of the viewer according to a law of inner mathematics"; there is talk also of visions and ecstasies. In the futurist texts, mathematical formulas crop up alongside occult incantations and chaotic verbal debris. The catechism of the avant-garde of 1961 contains hardly a sentence that was not formulated fifty years earlier by Marinetti and his circle. Be it mentioned in passing that the few significant authors of the movement left it shortly after the publication of the first manifestos, and that the manifestos are the only texts futurism has left us.

An extensive survey of the countless avant-garde collectives of the first half of the twentieth century is neither possible nor called for here. The role of most of them is overestimated. Literary and art historians, who, as is known, enumerate "currents" and "-isms" with passionate fondness because that relieves them of concern with details, have accepted too many such group appellations as gospel truth instead of sticking to the particulars of the given works; indeed, they even, as it were, invented such movements a posteriori. Thus, German expressionism became hypostatized into a collective manifestation that in reality, never existed: many expressionists did not even live to hear the word "expressionism," introduced into German literature in 1914 by Hermann Bahr. Heym and Trakl died before it came up; as late as 1955, Gottfried Benn declared that he did not know what it was supposed to mean; Brecht and Kafka, Döblin and Jahn never "joined a movement" that went by that name. Every historian can claim for himself the right to tie together manifestations and lump the manifold under one heading, but only on the condition of not confusing his auxiliary constructs with reality, whose representation they are meant to subserve.

In contrast to expressionism, surrealism was, from the outset, a collective enterprise that had at its disposal a well-developed doctrine. All previous and subsequent groupings seem, compared to it, impoverished, dilettantish, and inarticulate. Surrealism is the paradigm, the perfect model of all avant-gardist movements: once and for all it thought through to the end all their possibilities and limitations and unfurled all the aporias inherent in such movements.

"Only the word freedom can still fill me with enthusiasm. I consider it suited to keep the old human fanaticism upright for an indefinite length of time yet to come." With these words, André Breton, in the year 1924, opens the first surrealist manifesto. The new doctrine crystallizes, as always, around its yearning for absolute freedom. The word "fanaticism" is already an indication that this freedom can be acquired only at the price of absolute discipline: within a few years, the surrealist guard spins itself into a cocoon of regulations. The tighter the bond to the collective, the blinder the "pure action": "The simplest surrealist deed consists," we read in Breton, "in walking out into the street with guns in the hand and shooting as long as possible blindly into the crowd." A few years were yet to pass before this maxim was realized in Germany. In any case, even before World War II broke out, Salvador Dali reached the conclusion that "Hitler is the greatest surrealist."

Long before the coming to power of this surrealist, inner

aporias had split open the movement. Its sociology would deserve more detailed consideration. At the end of the 1920s, the intrigues, declarations of apostasy, bickerings, and "purges" within the group reached their high point. Its development into a narrow-minded sect strikes one as both ridiculous and tragic; yet it cannot be stemmed by the energy and self-sacrifice of the members because it follows of necessity from the presuppositions of the movement. Its commander-in-chief assumes more and more the features of a revolutionary pope; he sees himself compelled solemnly to excommunicate his companions-in-arms one after another. Occasionally this turns into show trials that, in retrospect, seem like bloodless parodies of the later Stalinist purges. At the outbreak of World War II, the surrealist movement lost all its best brains without exception: Artaud, Desnos, Soupault, Duchamp, Aragon, Éluard, Char, Queneau, Leiris, and many others turned their backs on it. Since then, the group ekes out a shadowy existence.

The party-line surrealist literature is faded and forgotten; the above-named authors have, with the exception of Breton, produced nothing worth mentioning while submitting to the group's discipline. Surrealism was destined to have an enormous effect, but it became productive only in those who freed themselves from its doctrine.

We see no reason for gloating over its foundering. Every backward glance at an avant-garde whose future is known has an easy time of it. Everyone today participates in the historical experiences of surrealism. No one has the right to encounter it with condescension or to take pleasure in its plight; it is, however, our duty to draw conclusions from its downfall. The law of increasing reflection is inexorable. Whoever tries to dodge it ends up offered for sale at a discount by the consciousness industry. Every avant-garde of today spells repetition, deception, or self-deception. The movement as a doctrinairely conceived collective, as invented fifty or thirty years ago for the purpose of shattering the resistance of a compact society, did not survive the historic conditions that elicited it. Conspiring in the name of the arts is only possible where they are being suppressed. An avant-garde that suffers itself to be furthered by the state has forfeited its rights.

The historic avant-garde perished by its aporias. It was questionable, but it was not craven. Never did it try to play it safe with the excuse that what it was doing was nothing more than an "experiment"; it never cloaked itself in science in order to be absolved of its results. That distinguishes it from the company of limited responsibility that is its successor; therein lies its greatness. In 1942, when, except for him, nobody believed in surrealism any more, Breton raised his voice against "all those who do not know that there is no great departure in art that does not take place in mortal peril, that the road to be taken quite obviously is not protected by a breastwork, and that every artist must set out all alone on the quest for the Golden Fleece."

This is no plea for a "middle way" and no cure for an about-face. The path of the modern arts is not reversible. Let others harbor hopes for the end of modernity, for conversions, and "re-integrations." What is to be chalked up against today's avant-garde is not that it has gone too far but that it keeps the back doors open for itself, that it seeks support in doctrines and collectives, and that it does not become aware of its own aporias, long since disposed of by history. It deals in a future that does not belong to it. Its movement is regression. The avant-garde has become its opposite: anachronism. That inconspicuous, limitless risk, by which the artists' future lives—it cannot sustain it.

1962

15) LITERATURE AS INSTITUTION

or, The Aspirin Effect

A WRITER WHO OFFERS his own theory of literature seldom cuts a happy figure. Hardly has he begun to erect the house of cards of his poetics than he's already blushing, feeling clumsy, beginning to stammer. But he has already gone too far; logic requires that he goes on talking, and so he becomes ever louder and more categorical. The audience nods, but he himself no longer believes what he's saying. Why doesn't he leave this thankless task to the specialists who are only waiting to storm the hall with their little instrument cases full of drills and forceps? Ah, when they take the floor, then his heart really sinks.

From that I conclude that it's better not to lay down any definitions, proclaim any laws, formulate any principles. A couple of suggestions, that's all; a couple of hints. I make do with sowing a doubt here and there, with presenting some product or other of the writing brain, in order to satisfy your curiosity.

If you examine the literature about literature, you will discover that it usually divides its object into three parts. It deals first of all with a series of works, second with a series of authors and thirdly with a series of readers, who for some time now have also gone by the name of recipients. That sounds reasonable, because this trinity is what we see. What I'm holding up in front of you is a book; what I see in front of me is the public, and what you have in front of you looks like a writer. Except that none of these three elements, taken by itself, constitutes a whole; because each one presupposes the existence of both the others. It will therefore be necessary to put the cart before the horse, if things are to get moving. The resulting arrangement looks rather like a carousel. I ask you to consider whether such a system is not best called an institution.

One could easily start worrying about what an institution actually is. As far as I know, there's no agreement. I only vaguely remember the relevant theories, but I believe they can be divided into two principal kinds. There are those which maintain that the human being is a much too dangerous, simple, and weak beast to be left to his own devices. Institutions exist to control his wicked instincts, to simplify an all-too-complex world sufficiently for him to find his way around it, despite his limited power of comprehension, and to take the burden of freedom from his shoulders: these are the doctrines of Thomas Hobbes, certain systems theorists and of the cleverest of all German fascists, Professor Arnold Gehlen. On the other side there are people who, like the venerable Dr. Marx, regard them more as tools of oppression. Both views have also, from time to time, been asserted of the institution with which we are dealing here, so that the augurs were assured of a good supply of material to disagree about.

What actually has to be present before one can talk of an institution? I think that everything we need is at hand. First, a definable group of people who practice a particular profession, and a corresponding group of clients, both, in an active or a passive sense, more or less closely involved with the same practice. Second, a stock of established rules or rituals.

And third, a particular competence, and that means not only a craft or a technique but a social purpose, which is reserved to this specific institution by law or by a tacit agreement. But here, with this last condition, I'm afraid is the rub.

Because it was never so very simple to say what constitutes the competence of literature. It's easy to fall flat on one's face trying. We would do well to remember that in the course of history institutions lead a life of their own. So that there were times when the Catholic Church principally concerned itself with religious matters, schools served to pass on knowledge, and parliaments were sovereign in the exercise of their power. These examples show that institutions are quite able to go on existing, even long after they have lost sight of their original purpose. Therefore, I would like to take the precaution of limiting my object. The carousel that I'm talking about is literature as we know it, a practice that emerged with bourgeois society, among whose inventions, as I continue to believe, it was one of the happiest.

Why did the bourgeoisie bring forth literature? What was it good for? What was its competence? The traditional Marxist answer amounts to this, that literature was to serve a new ruling class as an ideological instrument to secure its hegemony. At the same time, these very same Marxists have made every effort to search out among the products of the nineteenth century authors and texts they held to be politically progressive. In this way they separated the white sheep from the black within the fold of the literary institution, and the modest portion of criticism which has survived to the present day has never quite freed itself from this distinction. Such a reading has its merits, yet I fear that ultimately it has been led astray by a misunderstanding, because it misses what constitutes the actual competence of literature.

When it comes to class conflict it is especially weak as an institution. Quite other means were needed to defeat the aristocracy or hold down the working class: older institutions like the university and the army, justice and the schools were remodeled for these purposes, and new ones created, like the political parties, the mass-circulation press and the employers' associations. It is true that again and again there were people who wanted to spread an ideology with the help of literature, but this enterprise is like trying to move a brick with a feather. The achievements of literature are less conspicuous but also more subtle and enduring. Its work was to invent and manufacture historically new feelings and perceptions. In making this statement, I do not wish to sing a song in praise of irrationalism in literature, and still less do I want to reduce it to a medium of psychology. When I say new feelings and perceptions, I mean altogether intelligible, even if nondiscursive learning processes.

Viewed from this standpoint, states that we call "love," "mourning," "happiness," and so on—and I'm deliberately sticking to the most simple and banal examples—are extremely odd and unnatural social innovations; and I'll risk putting forward the thesis that a distinct, highly specialized institution was required in order to produce, shape, disseminate and regulate them.

Literature has taken over, to quote a classic bourgeois writer, the *éducation sentimentale et sensible* of our civilization. Its results go far beyond the modest proofs I have mentioned. The largest part of this effort has cultivated forms of sensibility and capacities of perception so complex that they can be expressed neither in everyday vocabulary nor in traditional concepts. Consequently, anyone who mentions them usually resorts to allusion or to quotation: "But that's pure Kafka!" or "This bicycle bell is my madeleine." Yet even such innocent associations are still too crude to allow the reach of literature to be estimated. Because the process by which "life" imitates "art"—and here that means imitates literature—is usually a hidden, yes, even unconscious one.

It could be objected against such a line of reasoning that literature is by no means the only agency or institution dedicated to the task I have indicated. Indeed, there were times in which, for example, the Church did its utmost to teach the people what they should feel; it can just as little be denied that the schools continue to trouble themselves about our perceptive faculties up to the present day. However, these establishments proceed in a somewhat dilettante manner, and so the effects are rather superficial. Literature in its heyday went a lot deeper. Its power was so great because participation in its game was voluntary; from that there developed an odd complicity, which would have been inconceivable with a compulsory arrangement. Also, reading was a private, not to say, a secret relationship, a circumstance that greatly encourages the corresponding learning process. This intimacy allowed the reader to forget that he was involved in a social practice, and gave him the illusion of a completely individual, direct, personal discovery, a deception that no other institution could hope to achieve. Now, of course other arts too can claim a similar competence, but none has exercised such a highly *articulated* influence. The effect of music is buffered by numerous mediations, and that weakens the consequences it has for a person's life, when he exposes himself to it as participant or listener.

I do not know if you can make anything of the notes that I'm sketching here. I have only scribbled a few characters or signs to serve as a drop scene for the second part of my talk.

It is dedicated to the notorious "crisis of literature," a theme that pops up and disappears again and again, something like the Loch Ness monster. The first noticeable thing about the often-proclaimed death of literature is the extraordinary duration of this agony. In this respect, it strongly resembles the collapse of capitalism, which as we know, has been on the agenda for a good hundred years, and which certainly looks as if it will keep us waiting for a while yet. It would presumably be asking too much of an institution to think of dying out or disappearing of its own accord. On the contrary, it will do everything it can in order to exist for ever. Even the demonstration of its own superfluousness cannot force it to throw in the towel; it will, rather, transform itself beyond recognition; it will spare no effort or trick to keep going, and it will stand on its head if it has to, only it will not disappear.

If this is the way things are, then it's tempting simply to let the subject drop. The crisis of literature is not new. It has been talked to death. It bores us. And yet it remains true that something has happened to our institution, and we would look ridiculous if we did not admit that. It has lost weight. It is conceding ever more territory. Its importance is not what it was. The subinstitutions that are dependent on it are feeling the pinch too. The literary critics feel their power crumbling, the bishops and popes of the trade have abdicated, and the professors are plagued by all kinds of frustrations and doubts about the meaning of their activity. Their academic fortresses are like outposts to which no one is laying siege any more, and which are encircled only by a dull tolerance.

How is this decline to be explained? Various explanations are offered. Someone who wants to make things easy for himself, simply asserts that no good books are being written any more. This proposition is easy to refute, and even if it could be proved, it would not provide an explanation. Rather, what it proposes would itself require explanation. The same is true of two further conjectures: that the best minds are turning to other goals, and that the public is running away from literature. The loss of meaning that concerns us is not a statistical phenomenon; and it's not the future of the publishing industry and of the book trade we are racking our brains about here. Apart from that, it's well known that the trade isn't doing so badly.

Perhaps an answer that is more to the point will occur to us if we remind ourselves that we are dealing with an institution. What is the worst thing that can happen to an institution? The invasion of its traditional areas of competence by another institution. On the day on which the establishment of a new Ministry of Education is decided, panic breaks out in the Ministry of Culture. A mood of catastrophe from the boss's anteroom to the most junior official! Not only are their jobs at risk, the whole gang's territory is threatened, their legitimacy, their responsibility, their authority. The institution is being disemboweled alive. Something very similar has happened to literature.

I have a preference for examples that are close at hand. Allow me, therefore, to tell you about my grandparents' love life. When I was a child I once came across their letters. I found them, carefully tied up, in the attic of their house. These love letters were pure literature. My grandparents expressed their most intimate concerns in sentences that a writer had made available to them. Their tone, their metaphors, their sensibility were the property of some forgotten second-rate poet of the 1890s. My grandparents had appropriated his output. They had drawn from this repertoire whatever seemed useful to them in their particular situation and reassembled it for their own purposes.

In the case of my daughter, a radically different picture presents itself. It's not only that she isn't used to communicating by letter. Her dialogue on the telephone makes use of codes in which literary signs as good as never appear. An undercover agent who was condemned to record her conversations and listen to them, would be confronted by an enormous quantity of elements that derive from quite different sources: by forms of perception, of feeling and of expression invented and propagated not by writers but by TV stars, rock musicians, feminists, journalists, and by the countless constantly changing spokespersons of one scene or another. She would be more likely to quote a TV advertisement than a poem, *Der Spiegel* than Samuel Beckett, and Woody Allen than Adorno. Now, don't imagine that my daughter is illiterate; she is very well aware of what's in the books. Only, for the greatest part they have lost the power over her life.

The conclusion is obvious. You see this glass of water; now look at this crumbly white aspirin pill and watch closely what happens. The institution dissolves, yet it does not disappear. It still exists, but it's no longer conspicuous. Finely distributed, it continues to exist as solution and as dispersion. The concentration has decreased, but instead it is now omnipresent. Note another detail that could prove to be significant, although we cannot be sure. I mean the sediment. If you look carefully you will notice a whitish deposit at the bottom of the glass, the persistent residue of the original concentrate. This remainder has evidently resisted dissolution. You can ignore it, this mere remnant, which seems to be insignificant compared with the great aspirin mainstream. But who knows. . . .

* * *

In other words, in the words of Dr. Marx: What we have before us is a socialization process. This operation has nothing to do with the state or with a party taking over production. It does not assume any kind of transition to socialism. In the course of the last two hundred years, capitalist society has taken it to an ever-higher level. The interdependence of our labor and the labor of other people, our mutual dependency, has increased throughout history.

In Dr. Marx's view, it was inevitable that this process would continue ever further until it met the limits of our contemporary social constitution: a critical point would then have been reached—the old structures would no longer be able to cope with it, and new ones would have to take their place, within whose framework the socialization of labor would increase until all activities would be interchangeable. At this point of development, it would be open to everyone to do what he felt like doing; engineers could, if they enjoyed it, write poems, and if the mood took them, the poets could drive tractors or bake rolls. A pleasant vision, which some of us still mourn today.

In any case, as far as the socialization of labor is concerned, this is a process whose end is not in sight. Dr. Marx has proved right. The literary institution is only one of the more modest victims it has claimed. Its former privileged position, its special competence, has dissolved like an aspirin. Poetry is spreading everywhere, in the headlines, in pop music, in the advertisement; that its quality leaves something to be desired is beside the point. Unfamiliar feelings, new forms of perception, are invented in the cinema, in fashion, in music, in political action, in sects and subcultures, in the crazy spectacle that the streets of our metropolises offer. In this sense, literature has fallen victim to socialization. It is not finished; it is everywhere. The socialization of literature has brought with it the literarization of society. But that's another subject, which is perhaps too important to be left to the writers. What is left to them, and what no one can deny them, is the sediment in the glass.

1972

16) IN PRAISE OF THE ILLITERATE

LADIES AND GENTLEMEN, I should like to link the thanks that I owe you with a question that is prompted by the occasion. The question is whether you, the taxpayers and elected representatives of the City of Cologne, have given this honor to a threatened species, whether you have honored an anachronism. From the morning papers of recent months, I gather that what is called "reading culture" or "written culture" is threatened with extinction everywhere on the planet. As someone who lives from writing, and therefore from reading, this frightening news cannot leave me indifferent. But you too, as citizens of a city which is not only the home of Heinrich Böll but also of the WDR, the largest media establishment on the European mainland, will perhaps be concerned about such a prediction. If I am not mistaken, then a personal interest coincides here with a public one, a local with a universal interest.

Are written words superfluous? That is the question. Anyone who raises it must talk about illiteracy. Only there's a small catch. The illiterate is never on the spot when discussion turns to him. He simply does not turn up, he takes no notice of our arguments, he remains silent. For that reason, I should like to undertake his defense, even if he has by no means entrusted me with it.

Every third inhabitant of our planet gets by without the arts of reading and writing. Approximately one billion people find themselves in this position, and their numbers will almost certainly increase. That is a very impressive figure, but a misleading one. For the human race includes not only the living and the unborn but also the dead. Anyone who does not forget them must come to the conclusion that illiteracy is not the exception but the rule.

It could only occur to us—that is, a tiny minority of people who read and write—to consider people who are not in the habit of doing so to be a tiny minority. This belief displays an ignorance that I do not find acceptable.

On the contrary, when I think about it, the illiterate now appears to me to be an admirable figure. I envy him for his memory, his ability to concentrate, his cunning, his inventiveness, his tenacity, and his acute sense of hearing. Please do not accuse me of dreaming about the noble savage. I am not talking about a romantic phantom but about people I have met. I have no intention of idealizing them. I can also see the narrowness of their horizons, their illusions, their stubbornness, their crankiness.

You will perhaps wonder why a writer, of all people, is taking up the cause of those who cannot read. . . . But the answer is quite obvious: It was the illiterate who invented literature. Its elementary forms, from the myth to the nursery rhyme, from the fairy tale to the song, from the prayer to the riddle, are all older than writing. Without oral transmission there would be no poetry, and without the illiterate no books.

But the Enlightenment, you will object. . . . Agreed! . . . The oppressiveness of a tradition that excluded the poor from all progress! You don't need to tell me that social misfortune is based not only on the material but also on the immaterial privileges of the rulers. It was the great intellectuals of the eighteenth century who uncovered this state of affairs. They believed that the immaturity of the people was due not only to its political suppression and economic exploitation but also to ignorance. Later generations have drawn the conclusion from these premises that the ability to read and write is an essential part of a dignified human existence.

In the course of time, admittedly, this influential idea was subject to a series of noteworthy reinterpretations. Almost in the twinkling of an eye, the concept of Enlightenment was replaced by that of education. According to Ignaz Heinrich von Wessenberg, a German pedagogue of the Napoleonic period: "The second half of the eighteenth century begins a new epoch in the education of the people. The knowledge of that which was accomplished gratifies the humanitarian, animates the priest of culture and is most instructive for the leaders of the community." Not all contemporaries agreed with him. Another educator of the people, Johann Rudolph Gottlieb Beyer, wrote of the reading of books: "Even if tumult and revolution do not always result, it nevertheless produces the dissatisfied and the malcontent who look suspiciously on legislative and executive authority, and do not abide by the constitution of their country."

That sounds familiar. Fear of the Enlightenment has outlasted the Enlightenment itself. It survives not only in the dictatorships of the twentieth century but also in West German democracy. You can always find some parliamentary or government idiot who, more than anything else, would like to suspend the constitution in order to protect it from the pernicious effects of certain printed works.

But conservative cultural criticism has learned few new tricks during the past two centuries. It never stops wagging its finger. "Why," Johann George Heinzmann was already asking in Goethe's time, "should the corrupted species of humanity which eternally desires to be diverted, eternally flattered, eternally deceived, be printed and written for before the rest?" "The consequences of such tasteless and thoughtless reading are . . . foolish extravagance, insuperable aversion to every exertion, boundless proclivity to luxury, a curbing of the voice of conscience, weariness of life and an early death," complains Johann Adam Bergk in his pamphlet, *The Art of Reading Books.*

I am quoting from these long-forgotten works because their arguments have continued to haunt us down to the present day. Anyone listening to our panel discussions and weekend speeches must gain the impression that virtually no new argument has occurred to us in the course of two hundred years.

Nevertheless, as far as the project of literacy itself is concerned, we have made great progress. Here, so it seems, the philanthropists, the priests of culture, and the leaders of the community have achieved decisive successes. Who would want to contradict Joseph Meyer, one of the most industrious publishers of the nineteenth century, who invented the slogan "Education makes free!" The Social Democratic Party elevated this slogan to a political demand. Knowledge is power! Culture for all! Up until the present day it fights tirelessly against educational privilege and for equality of opportunity. Since Bebel and Bismarck, one piece of good news has followed the next. In Germany, the illiteracy rate had already dropped below 1 percent by 1880. In some other European countries, it took a little longer. But the rest of the world has also made enormous advances since UNESCO took up the cause of the struggle against illiteracy in 1951. In short, light has conquered darkness.

Our job at this triumph remains within bounds. The news is too good to be true. The people learned to read and write not because they wanted to but because they were forced to. Their emancipation was, simultaneously, a loss of voice. From now on, learning was subject to the control of the state and its agencies, the school, the army, and the law. In 1811, when the children of Ravensburg took their places for a prize-giving, they could already sing a song about it:

> Hard work and obedience are the duties,
> Which sincerely to discharge
> Good citizens do endeavor:
> But to live according to duty,
> Only schools imprint
> Deep into the heart of youth.
>
> That we dedicate ourselves to virtue,
> And rejoice in so much knowledge,
> Thank we the school alone;
> Let us be forever grateful.
> Hail the King, Hail the State
> In which there are good schools!

Making the population literate had nothing to do with enlightenment. The philanthropists and priests of culture who championed it were only the accomplices of a capitalist industry that demanded of the state that it make skilled laborers available to it. The good, the true and the beautiful, which the patriarchal Biedermeier publishers talked about and their descendants still like to quote today, was never the issue. It was never a question of beating a path for "written culture," still less of freeing people to speak for themselves. Quite another kind of progress was at stake. It consisted of taming the illiterate, this "lowest class of people," driving out their imagination and their stubbornness, and from this time on exploiting not only their muscle power and their manual skills but their brains as well.

However, before the illiterate can be disposed of, they have first of all to be defined, located, and exposed. The concept of illiteracy is not old. Its invention can be dated fairly precisely. The word appears for the first time in an English publication of 1876, and then spreads rapidly over the whole of Europe. At the same time, Edison invents the lightbulb and the phonograph. Siemens the electric locomotive, Linde the refrigerating machine, Bell the telephone and Otto the petrol engine. The relationship is obvious.

Moreover, the triumph of popular education in Europe coincides with the maximum expansion of colonialism. That too is not chance. In the encyclopedias of the period, one can read the assertion that the number of the illiterate "compared with the total population of a country is indicative of the cultural state of a nation." "[Literacy] is lowest in the Slavic countries and among the Blacks of the United States. . . . On the highest rung stand the . . . Germanic countries, the Whites of the United States of America and the Finnish race." And the information that "men . . . on average" and "higher than women" is also not allowed to go unmentioned.

Here it is no longer just a question of statistics but of classifying and stigmatizing. It is already possible to discern the figure of the subhuman behind that of the illiterate. A small radical minority has taken out an exclusive lease on civilization and is discriminating against all who don't dance to its tune. The minority can be precisely defined. Men rule over women, whites over blacks, rich over poor, the living over the dead. What the Wilhelmine "leaders of the community" did not suspect should be clear to their grandchildren. Enlightenment can lead to rabble-rousing, civilization can turn into barbarism.

You will ask yourselves why I am addressing you on problems that are now only of historical interest. Well, this prehistory has meanwhile caught up with us. The revenge of the excluded is not without a certain black irony. The illiteracy we smoked out has, as you all know, returned, but in a form that has nothing admirable about it any more. This figure, which has dominated the stage of society for some time, is the secondary illiterate.

The secondary illiterate is lucky. His loss of memory causes him no suffering; if he does not have a mind of his own, then that relieves the pressure on him; he values the inability to concentrate on anything; he considers it an advantage that he does not know and does not understand what is happening to him. He is active. He is adaptable. He displays considerable determination in getting his own way. So we do not need to worry about him. The fact that the secondary illiterate has no idea that he is a secondary illiterate contributes to his well-being. He considers himself to be well informed, can decode instructions, pictograms, and checks, and moves in a world that seals him off from every challenge to his confidence. It is unthinkable that he should be frustrated by his surroundings. They, after all, gave birth to him and formed him in order to guarantee their own trouble-free survival.

The secondary illiterate is the product of a new phase of industrialization. An economy whose problem is no longer production, but sales, no longer needs a disciplined reserve army. It requires skilled consumers. As the classic production worker and office employee becomes superfluous, so does the rigid training to which they were subjected, and literacy becomes a fetter that must be cast off as quickly as possible. However, our technology has simultaneously developed the appropriate solution to this problem. The ideal medium for the secondary illiterate is television.

Most theories that have been formulated about this phenomenon are probably wrong. I know what I'm talking about, for less than twenty years ago I attributed great emancipatory possibilities to the electronic media. Still, such a hope, even if it was unfounded, at least had the advantage of boldness. One cannot say the same of the reflections of the American sociologist Neil Postman which are much-discussed at the moment: "When a population becomes distracted by trivia, when cultural life is redefined as a perpetual round of entertainments, when serious public conversation becomes a form of baby-talk, when, in short, a people become an audience and their public business a vaudeville act, then a nation finds itself at risk; culture-death is a clear possibility." Only the terminology has changed; otherwise the arguments of the American in 1985 are identical to those of the Swiss who in 1795 issued an "Appeal to his Nation" in order to warn it against the impending collapse of culture. Of course, Postman's central argument is correct: television is crap with gravy. It's only curious that he appears to see this as an objection. Television owes its charm, its irresistibility, its success, precisely to its imbecility. Another quirk that can be observed in the apologists of reading culture is even stranger. The means by which imbecility is produced seems to be all-important to them: if it appears printed black on white, then it's obviously a cultural treasure; if it's disseminated via antennae or cable, then "the nation is in danger." Well, those who take cultural criticism at face value have only themselves to blame.

I, at any rate, find it difficult to believe a Cassandra whose prophecies of doom serve to defend her own turnover, and even more so if she is simultaneously and recklessly grabbing at new markets. Let us not forget that it was a printed product, the prophetic *Bild Zeitung*, which proved that it is possible to sell the abolition of reading as reading, and to manufacture a print medium for secondary illiterates. And of course it is the publishers who are scrambling to hook up the nation by cable and swinging their satellite beams, in order to blanket the continent with television channels from which every trace of programming has been erased. And today, just as a hundred years ago, when it was a question of making the population literate, they can rely on the support of the state when that policy is to be reversed. The project of a compulsory cable hookup corresponds exactly to the "compulsory education" to which the relevant laws of those days referred. It is most appropriate that industry has as its negotiating partner a minister who himself perfectly embodies all the characteristics of the secondary illiterate.

Public education policy will have to adapt to the new priorities. A first step has already been taken with the cutting of library budgets. Reforms have also been carried out in the schools. As is well known, it is possible today to go to school for eight years without learning German, and at the universities too this Germanic dialect is gradually becoming an only imperfectly mastered foreign language.

You must not think that I am interested in polemicizing against a situation whose inevitability is obvious to me; I do not intend to lament it either; I merely wish to describe it and, as far as I can, explain it. To challenge the secondary illiterate's *raison d'être* would be foolish, and far be it from me to begrudge him his place in the sun and his amusements.

On the other hand, it is presumably possible to point out that the historic project of the Enlightenment has failed in this respect. The slogan "Culture for all" appears quite comical in retrospect. Still less is a classless culture in sight. On the contrary, one can foresee a situation in which there are ever-more-sharply distinguished cultural milieus, which no longer share any common public. I would even like to risk the assertion that the population will break up into increasingly distinct cultural castes. (I use this term descriptively, of course, without any systematic claim.) These castes can no longer be described with the help of the traditional Marxist model, according to which the ruling culture is the culture of the ruling class. Economic class location and consciousness are pulling further and further apart.

It will usually be the case that secondary illiterates occupy the top positions in politics and business. In this connection, it is enough to refer to the current president of the United States and the current federal chancellor of West Germany. On the other hand, in this country, just as in the United States, it is possible to find, without any effort, whole crowds of taxi drivers, casual laborers, newspaper sellers and social security recipients who with their thoughtful awareness of problems, their cultural standards, and their wide knowledge would have gone far in every other society. But even this contrast misses the real point—that any unambiguous attributions can no longer be made; because it is also possible to meet zombies among unemployed teachers, and people in the office of the federal president who can not only read and write but even think productively.

But that also means that in questions of culture, social

determinism has had its day. So-called educational privilege has lost its terrors. If both parents are secondary illiterates, then the VIP's child no longer has any cultural advantages over the worker's son. In future, the cultural caste one belongs to will depend more on personal choice than on one's origins.

I conclude from all this that culture in our country finds itself in a completely new situation. The claim to universal validity, which it always raised but never met, can be forgotten. The rulers, the majority of them secondary illiterates, have lost all interest in it. The consequence is that it no longer has to serve and no longer can serve any ruling interest. Culture does not legitimate anything any more. It is outlawed; but that nevertheless is a kind of freedom too. Such a culture must rely on its own resources,and the sooner it understands that the better.

Ah, yes—the question of whether you have honored an anachronism—we had almost forgotten that. As far as literature is concerned, I believe it is less affected by the changes I have sketched out than might appear. In reality, it was always a minority affair. The number of those devoted to it has probably remained constant in the course of the last two centuries. Only their makeup has changed. It is no longer a mark of class privilege but also no longer a compulsory badge of class to take an interest in it. The victory of secondary illiteracy can only radicalize literature. It produces a situation in which reading will be purely voluntary. Once it has stopped counting as a status symbol, as a social code, as an educational program, then only those who can't keep away from it will become acquainted with literature.

There may be those who deplore that. I have no desire to do so. Weeds are a minority too, after all, and every gardener knows how difficult it is to exterminate them. Literature will keep on proliferating, as long as it retains a degree of tenacity, a degree of cunning, the ability to concentrate, a degree of obstinacy, and a good memory. You will remember that these are the very attributes of the true illiterate. Perhaps he will have the last word. For he needs no other medium than voice and ear.

1985

17) IN DEFENSE OF NORMALITY

NORMALLY I WOULD NEVER have got mixed up in something like that. . . . On the other hand, I think it's quite normal for him not to put up with it for ever. . . . Under normal circumstances the motion would have been carried without opposition. . . . The situation in Nicaragua has returned to normal. . . . Anyone of normal intelligence would agree. . . . I've always told you that Gudrun's behavior isn't quite normal.

> *Normal/abnormal*: it is hardly possible to think of either of these terms without immediately being referred to the other, and then in such a manner as if the two simply excluded one another. Caught between the Freudian unconscious, Marxist economics and Nietzsche's Will to Power, normality does not have a good name in contemporary philosophy. The perverse is preferred to the holy, the abnormal to the normal, madness to banality.
>
> Normality always seems to have its point of reference in the existing order of things; to that extent it possesses neither the charms of disobedience nor the creative virtues of innovative. But such a dichotomy makes the matter too easy; for whether one becomes an MP or a wolf man one cannot become either without transgressing a norm; even Victor d'Aveyron, the "wild child," even Einstein, only became what they are by submitting to a particular social medium, which swallowed, tamed, drilled, educated them. . . .
>
> *Enciclopedia Einaudi*, Vol. IX
> (entry on *normale/anormale*), Turin, 1979

Mrs. Gretel S., seventy, divorced, two grown-up sons, a younger brother, by profession "daily help," pension amounts to 384 marks a month, says: "I could live anywhere if I had to." Political views: "Always the same shit." Basically works without declaring anything; "I can't afford taxes, I've got my children to think about" (debts, hire purchase, alimony, and so on).

Possesses an outstanding knowledge of bourgeois society, diagnoses marriage crises, stinginess, alcoholism, adultery, opportunism, property relations, and so on at a single glance. Is not at all afraid of catastrophes but is prepared at all times for the outbreak of a war. "Always had what I needed, even after being bombed out: butter, French cognac, bed linen, everything."

Tends toward redistribution: if clothes hangers are needed, she quietly brings clothes hangers from houses that have too many clothes hangers. Extremely tidy, regards dirt as a personal enemy, so has ideal qualifications for her profession. Ideologically unpredictable, from time to time repeats phrases from the Weimar Republic, from the Third Reich, from the postwar years, from *Bild* newspaper; yet she ruthlessly employees this material to her own ends, so that her constructions resemble a series of ad hoc shacks erected overnight with planks stolen from ruined buildings, torn down again in the morning. Overall impression: anarchic spontaneity.

Sleeps from seven in the evening until four in the morning, then listens to the radio in bed. "If there's a war, I'll go to the Stubai Valley on foot. An old friend of mine, a hotel-owner, always has a spare bed for me. My advice is to hold on to a kilo of pepper, I can get that for you cheaply. Pepper is always the first thing that runs out, then you barter that for meat from the butcher, butter from the farmer. One kilo can get you through a whole year."

The concept of normality is a terminological pudding, a pulplike mass that sets hard when one's not looking but remains wobbly and falls apart as soon as it is approached with a sharp instrument. Trying to define it is a hopeless task. You've made your normality, now you must live with it.

The conceptual ABC to be found in the reference books—primary and secondary socialization, repression, early childhood impressions, white pedagogy, black pedagogy, training, social mediation—has itself now become puddlinglike, is itself already normality.

Little Historical Dictionary for describing the ordinary person:*

The ordinary man/woman in the street, the little man, the ordinary consumer, the man on the Clapham omnibus, the average person.
Commonplace, common, plain, ordinary-looking, narrow-minded, passive, apathetic, routine.
Conformist, philistine, backwoodsman, suburban, without a mind of his own.
Vulgar materialism, parochial horizon, lowbrow.
Mass man, consumer idiot, one of the crowd.
Inarticulate, lower instincts, conformist.
Scum of the earth, flock of sheep, dull mass.
Carried along by the crowd, vulgar, shortsighted, manipulated.
Employees, labor force, manpower, laboring masses, workers by hand and brain.
Comrades, colleagues, brothers.

* In English "ordinary" tends to carry the deprecatory connotations which in German are conveyed by "normal"—TR.

> Fug, fustiness, petty bourgeoisie, silent majority.
> Ordinary people, simple people, common people, rabble, mob.

Reversing these designations provides a self-portrait of the person who has invented them. Whoever defines the normal, ordinary person, whoever decides who is and who is not a normal person would be (among other things) active, sensitive, articulate, independent, complicated; would think far ahead, would let himself be guided by noble motives, would live far from the world of consumption in a sphere of leisure, of contemplation; would be touched by greatness; would not appear as one of a crowd, large or small, but always only in the singular, and only one thing could with certainty be said about him: under no circumstances would he be ordinary, common or conformist.

Self-quotation I: To a Man in the Tram Car

Why? I don't want to know about you, man
with the watery eyes, with the parting
of fat and straw, briefcase full of cheese.
No. I don't care for you. You don't smell good.
There are too many of you. On the staircase your gaze
behind the counters is everywhere in front of the cinemas,
in the mirror a greedy face smeared with soap.
And you too (not even hate) turn away
to the walnut cabinets, to Sophia Loren,
go home covered in sweat, full of aspidistras
and diapers.

Verteidigung der Wölfe ("The Wolves Defended Against the Lambs"), Frankfurt, 1957

I haven't the faintest idea who the first person to damn normality was; but I shouldn't be too surprised if it was a poet. (*Odi profanum vulgus et arceo*—after all, that's two thousand years old already.) Presumably what he wanted to let his fellow human beings know was the following:

It doesn't even occur to me to mention myself and you and those like you in the same breath. In future, please regard me as an outsider. Polite as I am, I should like to leave the question open as to whether I merely stand outside normality or whether I am far above it. In any case, I should like to ask you to take account of the fact that I am a dangerous, holy, subversive person who is far from ready to abide by your habits, rules, and agreements. You love security, I love risk; you are satisfied with *common sense*, I am concerned with a much higher meaning. And please, if that doesn't suit you, go ahead and persecute me with your vulgar vindictiveness, your secret envy, you can stone me or poison me. Please don't restrain yourselves. By treating me differently from the others, by treating me worse, in fact, you yourselves provide the proof—if any proof was still needed—that I'm not one of you, not part of the common crowd.

Thus far, the speech of the hypothetical, unknown writer who invented the outsider game. As with all good inventions, word of this one spread very quickly, and it is, if I may be allowed to use the expression, quite normal that it did not long remain the sole property of this unique individual. Disciples clung to his heels, imitators, fans who one and all declined to belong to the vulgar mob and who took it as an insult if someone accused them to their face of being quite normal, ordinary people.

In time, the situation grew ever-more critical, for whole schools, cliques, factions, and parties formed which claimed to stand outside every kind of normality. They had to have their own bars, their own clubs, publishing houses, exhibitions, journals, museums, holiday villages,clothes shops, restaurants. Whole crowds of bohemians, *décadents* and

Dadaists populated the boulevards. With all this pushing and shoving, things didn't always proceed peaceably. Embittered quarrels arose as to who had renounced normality with the most determination, who was more out of the ordinary than anyone else. With increasing competition, standards rose. Sad to say, the compulsion to exaggerate brought a degree of hysteria in its train. The struggle of all these unique individuals was exacerbated by the appearance of umpires with stopwatches. It was no longer just a question of who was more exceptional, more militant, more extreme than the others, but also of who was quicker in his deviation, in setting himself apart. What was decisive was not *that* someone wrote a whole novel without using the letter *e*, not *that* someone crapped into a can and got his work into the world's leading museums, but whether he managed to do it before his rivals. Blows were inevitably exchanged. More and more participants turned up on the avant-garde's racetrack and the din grew louder. At the same time, the persecutions grew ever briefer; to get on everyone's nerves became increasingly difficult; more and more spectators shrugged their shoulders and turned away from the contests. "This novel is a provocation!"—"This production is a radical attempt to break with conventional patterns of behavior"—"This exhibition offends the public's ways of seeing." The public faces up to all these provocative ruptures and offenses with imperturbable composure, just as it does the TV advertisements that promise a completely new shower experience, driving experience, tooth-brushing experience.

However, apart from such paradoxes, which are a consequence of their own success, artists by themselves would never have managed to drive normality into a corner and damage its reputation so thoroughly that for millions of people it became a stigma, a kind of social bad breath. But, meanwhile, quite a different set of people, who had more harmful means at their disposal than brushes or typewriters, had taken a hand. In politics, too, during the nineteenth century, people came to the fore who wanted to be right at the front of things, who loved taking risks, who wanted to show the rest, the normal, ordinary, average people what a spade is, what progress is, what liberation is, the true Germany, the historic moment, the great future, the classless society, the white man's burden, the realm of freedom, and so on and so forth. To achieve these things it was, however, necessary to tear the average man, this creature of habit, this dull-witted, sluggish, ordinary everyman out of his rut, and that was no easy matter. People were required who were not conformists, but outsiders, exceptional, not to say supermen. For as matters stood, the idea of socialism, for example, could only be carried into the working class from outside (Lenin), and equally when the fate of Germany was at stake or the blessings of civilization had to be brought to some dark continent or other, leadership personalities were required; on his own, the herdman, the little man, the average man would never have hit on the idea.

Nothing could have been achieved without an educational dictatorship; without a certain apparatus such enormous projects had no prospect of success. It was necessary to give the course of history a helping hand, and those few who looked more than a day ahead could under no circumstances allow themselves to be squeamish in their choice of means. However, here too it became apparent that outsiderness tends toward a strange dynamic. In a short time all Europe was swarming with supermen. Millions of leadership personalities and extremists contended with one another for a place at the head of the historical cohorts, fought propaganda and street battles, and attempted to make the silent majority shout along, ultimately with decreasing success.

Corporal Mollenhauer from Bad Schwalbach, civilian profession—outworker, exceptionally bad marksman, and of limited use for combat duty because of asthma, during World War II learned to cut hair behind the lines, always carried scissors, combs, shaving soap, razor, eau de Cologne with him. Valued by everyone, including the regimental staff officers. In June 1942 was transferred to the Kharkov area with the 29th Infantry Division, later Stalingrad. After the death of Sergeant Schäufele from Esslingen (bullet lodged in body), the only barber in the encirclement. Last haircut: General Field Marshal von Paulus on 22 January 1943. −28°C in the command bunker (no fuel). Returns home 1956 after thirteen years as a prisoner of war in various camps, finally at Ufa (Bashkir Soviet Republic) where his skills were very useful to him.

1956–59 "Reconstruction." Today, Mollenhauer owns a hairdressing salon in Bad Schwalbach, managed by his son-in-law, a pharmacy and a detached house with a flat, market value 645,000 marks (encumbrances under Section 1 of the property register: none). Mollenhauer votes CDU/CSU. Asked what was the most important experience in his life, he replies: "In my life there have been no important experiences, I was lucky, that's all."

> The 'normal person' is of hardly any importance to us; I would almost say, we can delete him. . . . The 'normal person' (the words put me in a rage) is that residue, that primary element left at the bottom of the retort after the smelting process, when whatever is valuable has evaporated.
>
> André Gide, *Paludes*, Paris, 1895

Self-quotation II: On the Difficulties of Reeducation

When it's time to liberate mankind they run to the hairdresser.
Instead of following along enthusiastically behind the vanguard
they say: it's time for a beer.
Instead of fighting for the just cause
they worry about varicose veins and measles.
At the decisive moment
they look for a letter-box or a bed.
Just before the millennium breaks out
they boil nappies.
Everything fails because of these people.
You can't do anything with them.
They're worse than a bag of fleas.
Petty bourgeois vacillation!
Consumer idiots!
Remnants of the past!
We can't kill them all, can we!
We can't go on at them every day!
Yes if it wasn't for these people
then it would all be over in no time.
Yes if it wasn't for these people
yes then!

Gedichte 1955–70, Frankfurt, 1971

There is only one thing more pitiful than contempt for normality and that is to worship it. Since each of these attitudes is only the reverse of the other, it's not surprising that they usually grow on the same dungheap. The attempt to glorify normality is not only a nonsense logically—because every halo loses its shine if it becomes normal headwear—it is also a political lie that is not very convincing. Demagogues, populists, know-it-alls have always declared that ordinary folk are noble, man is good, the simple countryman unspoiled, and many other similar inanities.

The normal person rarely falls for such attempts to curry favor, and he immediately sees through the cheap irony with which a prince of the spirit talks of the delights of ordinariness. The *Proletkult*, germ-free "workers' literature" and the prints produced by socialist realism met a similar fate. It's not only the breakfast roll that's normal but marital conflict; not only slippers but the massacre on the evening news; not only health but also dying in hospital; not only the rubber plant but the assembly line; not only cosiness but also fear and trembling.

Regional Postal Director Thalmayr's project

In 1923 in Germany several thousand women are busy connecting long-distance telephone calls. Local calls are, by this time, already largely automated (rotary selector Strowger System). Graduate engineer Thalmayr, at that time a director of telegraphs, thirty-one, single, monthly salary 414 Rentenmarks plus local allowance, is entrusted with a study whose aim is to explore the technical possibilities and problems of automatic long-distance dialling. At the end of 1924 he installs the first experimental circuit in southern Germany at the Freising (Upper Bavaria), a long-distance telephone exchange operating between two district central exchanges, though at first still with a confidential code.

In 1957, one day before his retirement—two sons from a second marriage have meanwhile completed their studies, and as Regional Postal Director he now earns, according to the pay scale, 1,720 marks—Thalmayr opens the Cham (Upper Palatinate) district network. The latest Siemens EMD units are being brought into use. The lost Bavarian local network has now been connected to the subscriber trunk-dialing system.

Thalmayr's life's work, begun at the height of the inflation, was continued through four political systems: the

Weimar Republic, the Third Reich, the US Military Government, the Federal Republic of Germany. The total cost, at 1981 prices, can be estimated at approximately 28 billion marks. Impediments arose as a result of the financial crisis of 1923–24, the depression of 1929–31 (emergency decrees), the armaments priorities of the Four Year Plan, 1936, and of the war economy 1939–45. Further disruptions to Thalmayr's work: allied air attacks (1942–45) and restrictions on production in the electrical engineering industry (1945–49, shortage of materials, dismantling of plant).

Thalmayr joined the Nazi Party in 1934. Political activities: none. In 1941 his post placed in the reserved category. Thalmayr sabotaged the Führer's order of February 1945 to blow up his life's work. On 3 March 1945 he was arrested by the Gestapo and on 21 April 1945 liberated by American troops. Demoted to telegraph work in June of the same year because of his membership of the Nazi Party, Thalmayr could nevertheless continue his task. In 1946 he was classified as a nominal party member, and in 1952 promoted to Regional Postal Director.

After the inauguration of the Cham central exchange, the reception took place in the "Randsberger Inn" in the presence of a State Secretary from the Ministry, Thalmayr was interviewed by a journalist from the "Upper Palatine Messenger" [*Oberpfälzer Bote*]. The conversation turned to the historical conditions of his work. Asked how he rated the social significance of his work, Thalmayr replied: "Everyone wants to talk on the phone."

Every one of society's norms—of course!—has a definable social location. But no such location (I'll take bets on this) can be found for normality in general. Certainly, it's always already predetermined—well, by what? By class prejudices, feelings of inferiority, projections, resentments. Well, there you are! Without such cribs we would be quite unable to say what we think is normal and what's not. But wait a minute! That hardly means that the category of normality can be reduced to class conflict. Well, perhaps category is a bit too grand. At any rate, it was quite normal for the high nobility to beat each other up, get drunk and argue about gambling debts and for our original geniuses to darn their socks after the day's work was done; while the Bavarian peasants kept to their etiquette more strictly than the king, and the revolutionary working-class movement of Germany disapproved heartily of premarital sex. It can't be helped, normality occurs in the best circles. And word that the intelligence of ordinary people is only surpassed by the ordinariness of intellectuals must have spread even in academic circles. It's just as clear, at least to the initiated, where normality can be studied in its most naked, shameless form: among those who consider themselves to be outsiders.

That is why we now rise from our seats and pronounce the following sentence in the first instance: anyone who wants to investigate the riddle of normality is condemned to look in the mirror. We quote the following from the summing up: the principle according to which normality is always in the majority is true not only in an objective but also in a subjective sense. Experience of life indicates that the validity of the 95 percent clause can be assumed. A deviation of one-twentieth is already the height of emotion. Depending on class position, profession, age, background, gender, status, and milieu, you shall find in your own breast what you try in vain to ignore, to deny, to split off from yourself: reserves of normality that are bondless, inexhaustible, inescapable. Before all you unique individuals assume an injured expression we would like to say: enjoy it! As long as a remnant of *com-*

mon sense still glows within your breast, as long as you stumble through each day as a dull mass, you are not quite lost. All in all, a degree of common humanity cannot be denied.

Soon after being called to the Bar, R. A. Weinert, a beginner in criminal cases, discovers that his clients—pimps, burglars, conmen, most already with a criminal record—are intent only on shortening the procedure in every possible way, regardless of a whole series of rights which the criminal code grants every prisoner on remand. "Let's get out of here!"—even though time spent on remand is automatically deducted from the prison sentence.

Weinert can't understand it and talks to his colleague Bachmann, an old hand. "Just imagine, Weinert, that you move into a tenement block and find out that the tenants change every few days. Never-ending commotion in the house, no idea who lives next door and who you'll meet in the lift; apart from that constant snooping by the landlord, the neighbors, the caretaker's wife, etc."

Weinert rejoins that the comparison isn't a very good one. "Why not? Jail is a kind of home for our clients. There are old friends, firm rules for everything, trade flourishes, enmities develop, friendships, pecking orders, favors are exchanged, cosy habits, movable feasts. . . . In a way, once sentence has finally been passed then nothing else can happen: no more interrogations, no more uncertainty, no judge, no public prosecutor, no police. In other words, you know what to expect. That's something at least! More than you think . . . !"

Three strategies for normality:

1. *Silence* It is always only minorities who speak out in public. The majority, every majority, remains silent. It is difficult, strictly speaking it's impossible, to say if it pays any attention at all to what the minority says. Does it reject everything it sees, hears and reads? Rejection would already be putting it too strongly. It's more a matter of a specialized, highly developed ability to ignore, of perceiving things "as if," of an almost ironic inclusion and exclusion, of a silent reserve, which is ultimately unbreakable.

That, of course, grieves all those who "have something to say," the politicians and the opinion-makers, the educationers and publicity men, the artists and preachers. Even though the majority by and large tolerates them, feeds them, and even flatters them without rebelling, they do find it disturbing that the majority ignores their pronouncements, is deaf to them. The "dull mass" simply waves it all away. For example, it hears "Side by side with the glorious Soviet Union" or "The people's computer is here!" and replies, if at all: "Excuse me, but first I've got to heat up a bottle for my little Tommy." The response to the catchwords "mankind's dream" is: "Maybe, but my pension. . . ." If someone says "no future," or "apocalypse," then expect the majority, after nodding politely, to change the subject and turn to the question of what's happening to their favorite sports team this season.

Because this is all so damned annoying, masses of questionnaires are distributed, meetings called, polls conducted: "Would you be prepared to make sacrifices for future generations? Would you buy blue toothpaste? How many books have you read during the last year? Which position do you prefer during intercourse? Whom would you vote for if national elections were held on the coming Sunday?" Evasive phrases, laconic lies, refined forms of silence are the reply.

(Last year a third of those interviewed by a public opinion research company willingly confirmed the popularity and high profile of a named Bonn minister who never existed.)

One can easily feel sorry for the eager opinion-makers who, day in day out, announce the trends, give out slogans, evoke the current mood, sell beliefs, create fashions, direct appeals, make predictions. Sixty-five years of manipulation, pedagogy, censorship, monopoly of information in the Soviet Union, the dream of every pedagogic dictatorship, and what's the result? An imperceptible shrug of the shoulders, a hint of resignation around the mouth, an invincible silence. This *silentium populi* is the limit of all consciousness industries, all media, all propaganda.

2. *Regression.* A liking for the garden gnome and for pinball, for skittles, disco, horoscopes, and Suzuki is not, as the enlighteners believe, willful ignorance or the systematic stupefaction of defenseless masses. No historic lag is crying out to be made up. It's the poor victims of manipulation who are silently but energetically refusing every kind of instruction. Not for any price do they want to be raised to a higher level of culture, of taste, of political consciousness, that is, to where the particular spokesman of the day is standing.

The majority doesn't turn away to superstition, sport, and entertainment by mistake, because it doesn't know any better; it does so quite intentionally. Escapism is a well-defined strategy. The illusory is systematically and deliberately sought out. Regression is a staple food. A tabloid newspaper is indispensable because it is meaningless, not despite being so; for the important things we call history have always confronted us, in our capacity as majority, in only one form: as impositions.

3. *Persistence.* The good and the bad habits of normality are only for the smallest part a product of that "system" which stands on the historical order of the day. They are above all sediments, in which for good or for bad, immeasurably old experiences have been deposited. Normality is collective memory in its most solid form, and to that extent it is always out of date. There's something disturbing in that, a scandal that must deeply embitter anyone aiming to change the world. In the mouths of those who have something to say, the word "change" has taken on a peculiar pathos in the course of the last hundred years, as if it always stood for something desirable. The majority is not so sure about that; with its elephant's memory, it has presumably understood very well that the result of the furious transformations it has experienced has often enough been catastrophic.

Its silence can also be interpreted as a delaying resistance to the dizzying speed with which the so-called lifeworld is changing. To everyone for whom uncompromising modernization is an inner need, the normality of everyday life can only be perceived as a declining remnant, as a hindrance to be planed away as quickly as possible.

This is in marked contrast to the recalcitrance of the majority, a recalcitrance that is all the more difficult to overcome as it is not rooted in an idea but functions quite materially, not to say materialistically. An obvious example can fairly easily demonstrate the doggedness with which normality pursues its goals. German fascism can be understood as a large-scale attempt to make a clean sweep. At the end of World War II, this experiment seemed to have succeeded: the whole country was a *tabula rasa.* That Hitler's (and Morgenthau's) calculation nevertheless did not work out was the fault of the women who cleared away the rubble, the returned prisoners of war, the Ami-girls, cellar children, blackmarketeers, coal thieves, allotment gardeners, denazification certificate holders, people who stared building their own homes, handymen, a silent majority who insisted on reconstructing Germany.

To our social sciences, which until now have failed to colonize it, normality appears as a dark continent, an impenetrable black hole, which swallows up the light of curiosity, of criticism, of dominant rationality. Normality is a defensive power, but it is incapable of resigning. Opinions, philosophies, ideologies will never be able to get to grips with it.

In its small life—but can life ever be something small?—there are enormous reserves of labor power, cunning, readiness to help, vengefulness, stubbornness, energy, prudence, courage, and savagery. Fear of the future is not its strength. If the species is capable of surviving, then it will presumably owe its persistence not to some outsiders but to quite ordinary, normal people.

1982

18) THE ZERO MEDIUM

or,

Why All Complaints About Television Are Pointless

TELEVISION MAKES YOU STUPID. No matter how finely spun or crudely worked they appear to be, virtually all current theories of the media come down to this simple statement. As a rule, this conclusion is delivered with a melancholy undertone. Four principal variants can be distinguished.

The manipulation thesis points to the ideological dimension that is ascribed to the media. It sees in them, above all, instruments of political domination and is of venerable age. Originally deeply rooted in the traditions of the Left, but when required also gratefully adapted by the Right, it has directed its entire attention to the contents that supposedly determine the programs of the major media. Its critique is based on ideas of propaganda and agitation, as they have been passed down from earlier times. The medium is understood as a neutral vessel, which pours out opinions over a public regarded as passive. Depending on the position of the critic, these opinions are considered to be mistaken; according to such a cause and effect model, they must necessarily produce false consciousness. Refined methods of ideology critique extend this "effect of distortion" by furnishing the opponent with increasingly subtle and insidious intentions. In place of direct agitation, there is a seduction that is difficult to recognize for what it is; the unsuspecting consumer is won over by the wire-pullers, without ever realizing what's happening to him.

The imitation thesis, on the other hand, argues primarily in moral terms. According to it, media consumption leads above all to moral dangers. Anyone who is exposed to it, becomes habituated to libertinism, irresponsibility, crime, and violence. The subjective consequences are blunted, callous, and obstinate individuals, the objective ones are the loss of social virtues and general moral decline. This form of media critique draws, as is obvious at first glance, on bourgeois sources. The motifs that recur in it can already be identified in the eighteenth century, in the vain warnings that early cultural criticism sounded against the dangers of reading novels.

More recent is the simulation thesis, which is informed by an epistemological assumption. It is also more modern insofar as it takes account of the technological development of the media, therefore also takes the existence of television seriously, which one cannot say of its predecessors. According to it, the viewer is rendered incapable of distinguishing between reality and fiction. The primary reality is rendered unrecognizable or replaced by a secondary phantomlike one. A further version of this thesis, which occasionally is even put in positive terms, reverses this relationship and asserts that the distinction between reality and simulation has become meaningless in the given conditions of society.

All of these converge in the stupefaction thesis, which condenses into an anthropological statement. According to it, the media attack not only the ability to criticize and differentiate, and the moral and political fiber of its users, but also their ability to perceive altogether, yes even their physical identity. They produce, therefore, if one lets them, a New

Man, who can, according to taste, be imagined as zombie or mutant.

All these theories are rather convincing. Their authors consider proof to be superfluous. Even the minimal criterion of plausibility doesn't worry them at all. To mention just one example, no one has yet succeeded in putting before us, outside a mental hospital, even a single viewer who was incapable of telling the difference between a family quarrel in the current soap and one at his own breakfast table. This doesn't seem to bother the advocates of the simulation thesis.

Another common feature of the theories mentioned is just as curious but has even more serious consequences. Basically, the user of the media appears as a defenseless victim in them, the program makers, on the other hand, as crafty criminals. This polarity is maintained with great seriousness and considerable thoroughness: manipulators and manipulated, actors and imitators, simulants and simulated, stupefiers and stupefied face one another in a fine symmetry.

The question, on which side any particular theorist is to be found, has to remain open. Either he makes no use of the media at all, in which case he doesn't know what he's talking about; or he subjects himself to them, and then the question arises, through what miracle he has escaped their effects; because unlike anyone else, he has remained completely intact morally, can distinguish in a sovereign manner between deception and reality, and enjoys complete immunity in the face of the idiocy he sorrowfully diagnoses in them. Or could—fatal loophole in the dilemma—his theories themselves be symptoms of a universal stupefaction?

However, one can hardly say they have failed to have any effect. It is true that their influence on what is broadcast is severely limited, which may be considered distressing or noted with gratitude, depending on one's mood, but it can hardly be denied. On the other hand, they found ready listeners among the makers of media policy. That is not surprising either, for the conviction that he is dealing with millions of idiots "out there in the country," is part of the basic psychological equipment of the professional politician. Quite the opposite impression is confirmed, when one watches how the veterans of the trade fight each other and the media functionaries for every single minute, when it comes to displaying their limousine, their historic appearance before the guard of honor, their hairstyle on the platform, and above all their speech organs. The number of broadcast minutes, the camera angles, the degree of devotion on the part of the reporter, the level of applause are registered with a touching enthusiasm. They have been particularly taken by the good-old manipulation thesis. That explains the obstinate bickering about governing bodies, the never-ending political patronage, and the fierce desire to gain control of the whole shop once and for all.

The industry shares neither the passionate longing nor the barren theories. Its considerations are of ascetic sobriety. They circle, on the one hand, around frequencies, channels, formats, cables, beams, parabolic antennas; on the other hand, around investments, participations, distribution keys, costs, quotas, advertising revenue. From this perspective, the really new thing about the new media appears to be the fact that none of the promoters has wasted the least thought whatsoever on any kind of contents. Every single economic, technological, legal and administrative aspect of their activity is thoroughly analyzed and bitterly contested. Only one factor plays no role in the industry's thoughts and wishes:

the programs. Who pays and who collects when, where, how, from whom is debated, but never ever what is transmitted. Such an attitude would not have been conceivable with any previous medium.

That might seem strange, even bold. Millions are expended to shoot satellites into space and cover the whole of Central Europe with a cable net; an unparalleled expansion of "means of communication" is taking place, without a single person raising the question of what is actually supposed to be communicated. However, the solution to the puzzle is obvious. The industry knows that it has the full agreement of the decisive social figure in its game—that of the television viewer. The latter, far from lacking a will of his own, is determinedly steering toward a state one can only describe as programlessness. In order to come closer to this goal, he makes virtuoso use of all the available buttons on his remote control.

Nothing is a match for this intimate alliance of customers and suppliers. The embittered minority of critics has difficulty explaining such firm harmony, because it contradicts their own identity.

What if the majority had their reasons, reasons that cannot simply be derived from the idiocy ascribed to them? What if programs really were dispensable, and if the concept of the medium itself proved to be useless, a mere mystification? Perhaps it's worth pursuing such conjectures a little further.

The concept of the medium is an old one; it indicates first of all simply something middling, mediating; a means; in Greek grammar a specific voice of the verb which is suited to emphasizing "the interest of the active subject or the effect of an action on him"; further "in the spiritualist philosophy, someone who mediates the intercourse with the spirit world"(!); finally, in the physical sense, an agency such as the air, through which light or sound waves can travel; subsequently also applied to social communication, to its technical tools, for example printing.

The concept of the program is also derived from writing. The word originally means nothing more than what has been previously dictated or already written; "really a public written announcement, public notice, now (1895) usually a notification or invitation which is issued by universities or other establishments of higher education. In public life one speaks of the program of a party, of a newspaper, of a society founded for particular purposes, also of a government, when the principles of intended action are announced in advance in more or less binding form."

What, on the other hand, the leading television companies announce in advance reads like this: Magic Booth. Mini-ZiB. Eye-eye, look who's here. You again (8). At sunset, when the heather dreams. Music the Alpine Way. Men's World Cup Super G. Helmi X-Large. The Golden Shot. Gobstopper. Till the Trap Snaps Shut. Simply Wicked. Bet that . . . ? Long Live Love. Mrs Miller Never Sleeps Without a Thriller. Just Another Pretty Face. Tintifax and Max. I Want You to Love Me. Well, did you Evah? Hulk (31). Musi and Metty. At Home Today. Hard as Diamonds. Am, dam des. Barbapapa. Texas Jack (12). Look In and Win. Superflip. She-He-It. Love International. Tough, but Friendly. 1-2-X. Who'll Offer More?

The fact that such phenomena can no longer be grasped with anachronistic concepts such as "medium" or "program" presumably requires no further explanation. What's new about new media is that they no longer depend on programs. They achieve their true destiny to the extent that they approach the condition of the zero medium.

In retrospect, it can be seen that this tendency was already familiar to the old media. Printing, too, has not been lacking in attempts to rid itself of the burden of contents. Pioneering successes on this difficult path were obtained by the tabloid press, picture novels, and illustrated magazines. A triumphant record, still unsurpassed in the printing industry, reaching the dream boundary of illiteracy, has been set by the tabloid.

However, it was only with the electronic media that the decisive advance was made. It has turned out that insuperable obstacles stand in the way of creating a printed zero medium. Anyone who wants to free writing from any meaning has to reach for extreme solutions. The heroic proposals of the avant-garde (Dada, Lettrism, visual poetry) were ignored by industry. That's presumably because the idea of zero-reading is self-contradictory. The reader, any reader, has the fatal tendency to make connections and to poke around in even the thickest stew of letters for something like a meaning.

One might expect less, and in this context that means more, from a younger medium like radio. Emancipation from writing at least opened up a new perspective. In practice, however, it turned out that there was quite a lot to be read out on radio. Yet even where free speaking made a way for itself, in announcements and discussions and even with pure babble, the words again and again established something like meaning. As we all know, it is very difficult and demands practice and concentration to produce, over longer periods of time, sentences that are complete nonsense, to which no meaning of any kind can be ascribed. It is language itself that here produces something like a minimal program. In order to get rid of this interference factor, the innovators who have been at work in radio for some time now, have consistently cut back spoken broadcasts. However, a certain residue of chatter is left: for economic reasons at least the names of idols and other brand-name goods must be put out at regular intervals.

Only the visual technologies, television above all, are in a position to really throw off the burden of language and to liquidate everything that was once called program, meaning, "content." The proof of the undreamed-of potential of the zero medium is provided by a simple experiment. Place a six-month-old child in front of a video. Given the physiological development of the brain, the infant is simply incapable of resolving and decoding the pictures, so that the question, whether they "mean" something or other, cannot be posed at all. Yet independently of what is appearing on screen the bright, colored, flickering patches unfailingly arouse a lasting and intense, one might say, a sensual interest. The perceptual apparatus of the child is kept wonderfully occupied. The effect is hypnotic. Impossible to say what is going on inside; yet the infant's eyes, in which the television picture is reflected, takes on such an entranced expression that it is tempting to call the child happy.

It will cost the humanist little effort to condemn such an experiment as a barbarous outrage. He should not only consider that the experiment is part of everyday routine millions of times over; he would do well to ask himself, to what extent his condemnation also concerns a culture that he perhaps values. The zero media would be inconceivable without the pioneering achievements of modern art. The colored spots and patterns that delight our six-month-old human guinea pig are not so unlike abstract painting. From

Kandisky to action painting, from Constructivism to the low points of Op Art and computer graphics, the artists have done what they could, to purge their works of every "meaning." To the extent that this minimalization has been successful, they can rightly be considered the forerunners of the zero media. This role becomes directly comprehensible in video art, where in the more advanced productions as good as nothing can be made out any more.

Of course, the authors and apologists of this art are very far from regarding themselves as paving the way for the industry. In order to maintain their status, and presumably also their prices, they have developed a "philosophy" of their own which, however, relies more on shamanlike invocations than on arguments, and which they probably believe in themselves. This belated avant-garde obstinately imagines itself to be in the minority and cannot believe that, in the shape of zero medium, it long ago conquered a mass audience.

Nevertheless, the approach to perfection is always a wearying, protracted process. That is also true of television. A further difficulty is that the zero medium has to overcome small but influential minorities, who are out to defend either remaining historical assets or cherished hopes for the future. On the one hand, figures from the political parties and media managers tenaciously cling to the belief that television could be harnessed to stabilize their own positions of power; on the other, there is no shortage of educational and critical theorists who continue to suspect productive forces in the electronic media which only need to be unfettered in order to set in motion undreamed of social learning processes.

In the course of time, an extremely odd coalition of feuding brothers has formed around such conceptions. They have only one thing in common, what one might call the program illusion.

In the Federal Republic, this illusion even has the force of law behind it; it is anchored in state treaties, agreements, broadcasting laws, statues, and guidelines, and is cherished, in defiance of all the evidence of one's eyes, by all responsible parties. Broadcasts, according to them, "must be informed by a democratic spirit and loyalty to the constitution . . . by a sense of cultural responsibility. They should promote freedom, justice and truth," "encourage peace and social justice," "serve the cause of peaceful reunification of Germany and freedom and understanding among peoples." One is left speechless. The producers of shows and shockers, clips and advertisements are supposed to provide not only "education, useful knowledge, and entertainment," but also "humanity" and "objectivity," "diversity of information," "comprehensive and unbiased reporting," and always, of course, a broad "cultural palette."

These fantastic obligations imposed by the legislators are related to the history of the establishment of the broadcasting companies. They derive from a time when it was not yet possible to foresee what a fully developed zero medium is capable of. The "program makers" who doggedly, but impotently, hold on to the "mission" they have inherited from their fathers, present a melancholy sight. They are fighting a losing battle in their tenured posts, struggling for television as a pedagogic province, as a moral institution.

The program illusion is not only the product of legal and institutional factors; it derives directly from the phylogenesis of the media. It is a rule of their evolution that each new medium first of all orientates itself toward an older one, before it discovers its own possibilities and comes to itself, as it were. This external determination can also be observed with television. The idea that it exists to transport forms and contents, that is "programs" like those produced by earlier media, is consequently hard to eradicate. Technically it is by no means out of the question. It is also not impossible to dig a trench with a teaspoon or to transmit the Bible by telex; only the purpose of teaspoons or teletypers does not lie in such efforts.

The evolutionary eggshells that television trails behind it are particularly noticeable in certain genres that have maintained themselves in transmission schedules. So displaced forms such as the sermon, opera, the chamber concert, the comedy of manners, and the leading article haunt the zero medium here and there where they don't belong. Radio forms such as the news bulletin, the discussion, and the radio play, in which the presence of the camera seems like a superfluous luxury, are also conserved.

Some television veterans, who have not recognized the signs of the times, also suffer from the notion that they could run out of material. The obsession that something rather than nothing must be broadcast, causes them to exploit the old media. This leads above all to the cannibalization of film, a medium that one might believe was related to television. Of course, it soon turned out that this is a mistake. The aesthetic fascination of the cinema cannot be repeated on the television screen; it is destroyed by the ridiculous format, the interruption of advertising breaks, and the indifferent endless repeats; the viewer's secret weapon, the dreaded channel-surfing, gives the film the coup de grâce.

And what about the viewer! He knows exactly what he's dealing with. He is impervious to every program illusion. The legislators' guidelines burst like bubbles of soap in the face of his practice. Far from allowing himself to be manipulated (educated, informed, enlightened, admonished), he manipulates the medium in order to enforce his own wishes. Anyone who does not acquiesce to them, is punished by the withdrawal of love at the push of a button, anyone who fulfills them is rewarded with wonderful viewing figures. It is quite clear to the viewer that he is dealing not with a means of communication but with a means for the refusal of communication, and he does not allow anything to disturb this conviction. In his eyes, it is exactly what it is accused of that constitutes the attraction of the zero medium.

This also explains a characteristic of television which would be puzzling given any other premise: its transcultural range. The same series, the same promotional video, the same show develop the same attractive force, irrespective of all social conditions, in Bradford, Hong Kong, and Mogadishu. No content can be so independent of every context, so irresistible, so universal.

The zero position is television's strength, not its weakness. It constitutes its use value. The viewer switches the appliance on in order to turn off. What politicians consider to be politics is, for this reason, absolutely unsuitable for television. While the pitiful minister imagines he is influencing the opinions and actions of the viewer, the viscous emptiness of his statements only satisfies the public's need to be spared meanings.

By contrast something like image disturbance occurs, as soon as anything resembling a content surfaces in the broadcast flow, a genuine item of news, or even an argument that is a reminder of the real world. The viewer starts, rubs his eyes, and reaches for the remote control.

This extremely purposeful utilization deserves to be taken seriously at last. Television is employed primarily as a well-defined method of pleasurable brainwashing; it serves as personal hygiene, as self-medication. The zero medium is the only universal and widely distributed form of psychotherapy. It would be absurd to question its social necessity. Anyone who wants to abolish it should take a good look at the available alternatives. First of all, there's drug consumption to consider, from the sleeping pill to cocaine, from alcohol to the beta-blocker, from the tranquilizer to heroin. Television instead of chemicals is surely the more elegant solution. If one thinks of the social costs and of the so-called side effects, it has to be admitted that the users of the zero medium have made a wise choice—to say nothing of all the other possible solutions, like the flight into motorway madness, violent crime, psychosis, running amok, and suicide.

There is help for anyone who finds this negative argument too gloomy. He only needs to direct his gaze away from the unpleasant facts toward higher spheres, and look for advice to mankind's oldest philosophy, which is so popular again today. For when our concentration is at its maximum—this is the incontestable conclusion to be drawn from any mystical paperback—it can no longer be distinguished from absentmindedness, and the other way round: the most extreme absentmindedness turns into hypnotic absorption. To that extent, the cotton wool in front of one's eyes comes rather close to transcendental meditation. So the quasi-religious veneration that the zero medium enjoys could also be easily explained: it represents the technological approximation of nirvana. The television is the Buddhist machine.

Admittedly, this is a utopian project, which like all utopian projects is hardly to be realized without an earthly remnant clinging to it. Only with difficulty will the adult attain the state of complete forgetfulness of self which is granted the infant. He has forgotten how to employ his perceptual apparatus without interpreting what he sees. Whether he wants to or not, he tends to produce meaning even where absolutely none is to be found. This involuntary focusing constantly interferes with the use of the zero medium. In case of doubt, I can always maintain that I am not after all a zombie, and in what I'm looking at, there is nevertheless *something* to be seen, something or other definite, something like the smouldering remnant of a content. Consequently, it's unavoidable that even the practiced television viewer now and then succumbs to such a mystification.

The ideal situation is therefore unattainable. Like the point of absolute zero, one can only approach complete emptiness asymptotically. This difficulty is familiar to every mystic: meditation does not lead to nirvana, oblivion is possibly only momentarily and not finally, the little death is not the great one. A minimal signal, the murmuring of reality always modulates the "experience of pure abstraction" (Kasimir Malevich).

Nevertheless—the achievements of recent decades have been remarkable, even if the screen will never catch up with its great precedent: that *Black Square* of 1915 which, strictly speaking, makes all transmissions of the zero medium superfluous.

1988

19) THE STREET THEATER OF RAGS

An Obituary for Fashion

I RATHER LIKE TO REMEMBER the tyranny of fashion. In those days long ago, the trend-setting magazines were studied with rapt attention at the hairdresser or the café, the pronouncements of the Parisian fashion "creators" and "popes" were respectfully accepted and, observing the proper distance, punctually followed: waistline or no waistline, hemlines up or down, and then, again and again, "the new line." Legendary names, now long-forgotten, like Poiret, Baleciaga, or Schiaparelli went from mouth to mouth. In old films one can occasionally sense a tiny aftershock of those distant excitements; otherwise, one must go to the museum, where one can admire, with repressed emotion, the high-buttoned shoes, ornate undergarments, hats, and gloves, all bizarre inventions that once embodied something like a style, a longing, or at least a whim of the season, and now are entombed in glass cases.

In the shifting flow of these various forms of appearance there was at least one thing that stood firm: the certainty that everything fashion forced upon its willing victims was destined for rapid disappearance. Hotly desired must-haves one season, the "creations" were already inconceivable the season after that. The rule of change ensured that the outré would not be permanently damned to the hell of the unworn. And the appeal of fashion, as Georg Simmel wrote, resided in "its rapid and thorough transience."

This calming prospect is now essentially lost to us. The current fad sticks like chewing gum to a public that has resigned itself to the idea that the misnamed "trend" is a curse impossible to escape during the average human lifetime. Only reckless optimists can allow themselves to hope that the eternal leather jacket and jeans will ever disappear. The "new" casual look has now achieved lifelong validity. Once fashion had breathed its last, things came to a grinding halt. No more shoes, just shit-kickers, broad, clunky, scruffy, and ugly as a strip development. Tromping becomes second nature to anyone who wears them. People who have stumbled through life as mindless as a rock concert will never learn to walk properly. The olive-green parka, too, the khaki bush-jacket, the camouflage gear and the army boots, the parade-ground get-up of all good pacifists, not only provide external uniformity; they have become a psychic necessity.

Just as peculiar is the view one gets when one goes out into the street, especially in Germany, Scandinavia, and the United States, but also in other parts of the world—to say nothing of countries of the former East Bloc. For in those lands the ordinary passer-by has decked himself out as a deep-sea fisherman, a parachutist, a circus clown, a top athlete, a mercenary combatant, a proletarian, a jester, a pimp, or a bomber pilot, all without reference to gender, class, or actual profession. The following intentions seem to guide this masquerade:

1. The body should be presented as amorphously as possible, as a gigantic sausage, a blimp, or a potato sack. However, the required mass should look strangely pumped-up in a way that makes one wonder whether the filling is air or hormonally enhanced flesh.
2. One's actual identity must be categorically denied. The tax official sees himself as a small-time hood, the preppie girl as Rambo, and the illiterate wears a T-shirt displaying the inscription UNIVERSITY OF

SOUTHERN CALIFORNIA. Sons of millionaires present themselves as unemployed bums, and hard-driving officials run around in outfits that proclaim that they have gone on a permanent vacation.

3. If we can say that those who wear what we justly call rags are customers, they are no longer wooed; on the contrary, they have placed themselves at the service of advertisers. They are walking billboards. There is hardly anyone who has not pasted himself with labels and logos advertising something, whether it is a rock band, a brand of cigarettes, or a worldview.
4. Special favor is shown to colors reminiscent of kindergarten. It is well known that humans reach the height of aesthetic anesthetization around the age of five. Consumers of fashion hold fast to this ideal—to glaring bonbon colors, to hideously eye-catching styles, up to the age of retirement. The more infantile, the better.

In this vile circus, the bank employee who dresses like a bank employee by now seems as though he were the one wearing a costume. In his upstanding suit, his white shirt, his striped tie, he stands out as an extremist. His quiet protest does the heart good. Anyone who remains true to a wardrobe that conforms to their actual life, whether he is a waiter or a government minister, a baker or a major general, makes a comforting impression in the desolate costume ball of our streets and shopping malls. One imagines that he still enjoys the use of all five senses. It is the nerd, accused a thousand times over of conformity, who has become the true rebel, as far as his external appearance is concerned.

One does not have to look far for the ideological perquisites for our street theater of rags. They are obvious. For one thing, the foolishness we find everywhere is a form of rot eating at the so-called youth culture, which has, as anyone knows, reached a respectable age and is most accurately represented by fifty-year-old guitarists. What began as shock and provocation a half-generation ago has triumphed so thoroughly that only a vicious, motley layer of slime remains. We inherited another aspect of this everyday aesthetic from political protest. The cults of the proletariat and militarism have disappeared; only their emblems remain, crowding shop windows at every price level.

Feminism, too, has done its bit by producing the slob, an unachievable but often-imitated ideal, who goes to any amount of trouble to conceal whatever charms she might possess under a protective layer of shabbiness. This play at ugliness has achieved its greatest triumphs in the United States, where there are well-paid designers who do their best to come out with exclusive variations of the essentially immutable Scruffy Look.

Finally, the contribution of the creators of culture to the demise of fashion should not be underestimated. In art, too, the Garbage Cult has reigned for a long—an unbearably long—time.

Archeologists of the future could be aided by a ubiquitous fossil, in the form of pieces of garbage that has grown, in the works of countless imitators, into veritable landfills. Even the screaming color that goes limping through the shoppers' paradise (but is usually associated with wind-surfers, race-car drivers, hang-gliders, and skiing champions) can be traced easily back to Pop and Op, hard-edge painting, primitivism, neo-geo, and other darlings of gallery art. Further, the products of artistic industry have for some time been designated only as "Works" or "Installations." This apparently is due to the fact that their creators are working less and less, and that much of what is produced by the market is reminiscent of the mess left behind by badly trained plumbers.

Horrors are bubbling, as we see, from many sources. But it

would be unfair to leave unmentioned the contribution of the theater. Everywhere German is spoken, at least, directors have distinguished themselves with trailblazing work for the past thirty years. They surprise opening night audiences night after night with Hamlet as heavy-metal rocker, Orestes in a Gestapo trenchcoat, Nora as Playmate of the Month, and Tasso as a soccer hooligan. Generous subventions allow our set designers to produce, at $100,000 a pop, colorful spaceships, marble-floored battlefields, and rubble-filled cartoon landscapes, in which the entire ensemble can throw off their carnival costumes and, bellowing, relieve themselves of their hearts' blood and other bodily fluids. In this way, the municipal theater has contributed decisively to the development of that sort of taste that invariably sets the tone for boutiques calling themselves *Fun* or *Riot* or *Ecstasy*.

The person, who despite decades of exposure, is still rubbing his pained eyes at the sight of this eternal festival, can receive comfort from only one source—the poet. The words of salvation came to Robert Gernhard in his poem, "After he Walked through Metzingen":

> Thy praises I'll sing, ugliness,
> On you our confidence can rest.
> Beauty dwindles, takes leave, flies—
> It almost hurts our ravaged eyes [. . .]
> Beauty gives us grounds for grief;
> In ugliness we find relief.

1993

20) THE FUTURE OF LUXURY

IS IT EVEN WORTH DISCUSSION? Wasn't the issue settled long ago? It seems that the debate has finally played itself out after two thousand years, and it looks as if luxury has won. It has conquered—no, flattened—the shopping malls and the convenience stores, at least in the so-called Western world (which, in defiance of all geography, includes Japan but not Cuba). It has even spread to the streets of Moscow and the bazaars of Manila. This sounds cynical when one considers that poverty is rife in both East and West; but the buyers and sellers of affluence have never been much impressed by this argument, and today they are even less concerned about it than ever. If a bomb is set off occasionally in front of a delicatessen in Paris, or some confused idiots take out their rage on a fancy Berlin restaurant where the food is too fine for their taste, it is hard to imagine these brutal yet tired forms of protest as anything more than exercises in futility, lacking any popular support.

But the passionate opposition to luxury has a long and dignified past. It is impossible to ignore the long line of philosophers and lawmakers, preachers and demagogues, who have spoken out against extravagance, opulence, and the addiction to pomp. In the course of time, their arguments and the targets of their zeal have varied widely, and to trace this history—even just as recent past—would be the historical task of a lifetime.

For example, the fabled Spartan education had hardly anything in common, as far as its motives and methods were concerned, with the teachings of the Cynics, and it was yet another, quite different set of anxieties that led to the draconian but unsuccessful anti-extravagance and anti-luxury laws of the Romans. The moralist Savonarola wanted to consign everything that did not contribute to salvation to the bonfire of the vanities, but his aim was not the same as that of the classical Utopians, who wanted to ban from their various ideal Republics—under the threat of the most severe punishment—everything that struck them as excessive. And on and on.

Yet the more ground lost over the centuries by the purely religious and moral arguments of the clergy, the more criticism of the wasteful habits of the rich and powerful has entered the political arena. When the Enlightenment put the watchword "equality" on the agenda, it seemed that luxury had finally become a social scandal. To root out luxury and all of those who had succumbed to it became a goal emblazoned on the banners of the revolutionaries.

It is not easy to make sense of the long battle that ensued. But there is a locus classicus where we can find the most important arguments. This is the French luxury debate of the seventeenth and eighteenth centuries, in which almost all of the themes appear that have held the field since then. By the reign of Henry IV in the sixteenth century, the Duke of Sully was infuriated by the urban classes' descent into luxury and all of its attendant vices: sloth, effeminacy, lechery, and extravagance. He argued that too much was being spent on "splendid gardens and pompous palaces, the most costly appointments, golden ornament and porcelain dishes, for coaches, cabriolets, festivities, liqueurs, and perfume." Up to this point he restricts his criticism to the suspicion of decadence and traditional notions of morality, which were already old news during Roman times.

But his diatribe was provoked by something concrete. As Minister of Finance, Sully is attacking the contemporary plan to introduce large-scale silk production in France. This project already contained the spirit of the idea of large manufacture, which would subsequently become, especially in Lyon, the engine for industrialization.

A good hundred years after the appearance of Sully's *Mémoires des sages et royales œconomies d'estat*, a pamphlet authored by Abbé Coyer reads like a direct refutation of Sully. "Luxury is like fire, in that it can warm as well as consume. If, on the one hand, it causes the downfall of wealthy houses, on the other, it keeps our manufacturing alive. It feeds on the fortune of the spendthrift, but it also nourishes our workers. . . . If one wanted to ban our Lyonese silk, our gold fittings, our tapestries, our lace, our mirrors, and our jewels, I could imagine the consequences: with a single blow the lives of millions of people would be laid waste, and just as many voices would be crying out for bread."

In *The Spirit of Laws* (1748), Montesquieu puts it more succinctly: "We cannot do without luxury. If the rich do not spend extravagantly, the poor will die of hunger." And Voltaire reduced the problem to a bon mot: "Excess is a highly necessary thing."

These statements might seem rash and naive, but they took a new and definitive step in the battle over luxury. It is true that they do not fully answer the objections of the moralists. Diderot, for instance, offers a decisive rebuttal: "Luxury ruins the rich and doubles the misery of the poor." Condorcet agrees: "It sacrifices the lives and needs of the poor to those who are richer and stronger." But at this point the obligatory criticism encountered, for the first time, economic arguments that are not so easy to dismiss, because they are based on a rational calculation. Such considerations have been perpetuated into the present century. In *Luxus und Kapitalismus* (1913), which describes the origin of the modern world in the spirit of extravagance, Werner Sombart argued that capitalism had actually been created by luxury.

This had always been the view of the emergent bourgeoisie. An encyclopedia of 1815 states with disarming bonhomie: "*Luxury*, splendor, or opulence, is, as a consequence of wealth, the inclination and striving for the beautification of life and ennoblement of existence through the invention and use of ever-newer, more beautiful, and more charming means of pleasure in luster, ornament, décor, and artfully conceived comfort in daily life, in the appearance of apartments and their surroundings, in clothing, coaches, horses, dishes, service, meals, drinks, and many other amenities and pleasures," a list to which one could scarcely add anything today. The anonymous author continues with a daring definition that seems surprising coming from the golden age of German idealism: "Luxury is not only useful and necessary, in that it facilitates the aim of humankind, that is, physical prosperity, but it also extends this prosperity to the largest possible number of people, and thus against the inequality of wealth so detrimental to national prosperity."

Here, in a surprising move, the tables are turned. The apologist for luxury calls upon the same notion of equality used by his critics to attack him. And in his happy materialism he insists on praising an unbridled consumerism that does not shrink from any hedonist consequences:

> Since the highest aim of human well-being is based on sustained prosperity, the government has the duty to restrict luxury only when it places someone in the danger of losing prosperity.
>
> Seen in this light, luxury is not the exclusive privilege of the wealthy, but every person can enjoy it according to his own means, beautifying his life though the pleasures he is able to afford. The frequent complaint of the noble and wealthy about the proliferation and disadvantages of luxury thus seem for the most part to be motivated by a malicious and misanthropic sentiment, arising out of their pride and their resentment of the lower classes, because the higher classes can not yet accustom themselves to the prosperity of the lower classes, which has undeniably been improved though advances in industry.

With astonishing decisiveness, the Biedermeier author takes exception to a cultural critique that sounds familiar to us. He responds to it with a suspicion that has not yet been successfully refuted, even up to our day.

But there is yet another merit in the economic analysis of the production of luxury. It also does away with the archaic concept that supply and demand, production and consumption can simply cancel one another out, as if the demand for justice could be resolved simply through a redistribution of wealth. In his break with this *idée fixe*, by the way, Karl Marx was entirely in agreement with his bourgeois opponents, though the denser among his followers never quite wanted to believe that. The material goods of this world can simply not be imagined as a cake of a fixed size to be divided into equal pieces, though the belief in this model apparently cannot be rooted out. Whatever one might think of luxury, its history in any case proves otherwise.

This can already be seen in the constant shift in its forms. The concept of luxury is just as relative as that of poverty. It was not so long ago that goods like sugar and glass, silk and light, pepper and mirrors, were reserved in Europe for a small minority of the powerful and wealthy. The fact is that much of what is today considered natural for a construction worker or a hairdresser to own would have been unattainable for a prince in the past.

Yet even the materialist theories do not explain everything. They have always underestimated the symbolic power of luxury. They have not seen that luxury represents a driving force not only in economic development but in evolution itself.

As early as the nineteenth century, biologists noticed that extravagance plays an overwhelming role not only in human society, but in nature. The quantitative and qualitative excesses that prevail in nature can hardly be explained completely through a calculation of their usefulness. When evolutionary theorists interpret the exorbitant play of colors in tropical butterflies in Darwinian terms, they only make it difficult on themselves. (The word "luxuriate" is, by the way, a concept taken from botanical terminology.)

Take the tooth of the narwhal, which reaches a length of two to three meters. It is exceptionally ingenious, always turning in a counterclockwise spiral, and it is always on the left, while the corresponding tooth on the right wastes away. Why that is and what purpose it serves is unknown. Zoologists have concluded in resignation that it is a "purely superfluous feature of the animal," which "has brought it nothing but persecution from humans." This was because the narwhal's tooth once was revered as a miraculous horn, a priceless healing agent, because it was said to have the magical powers of the legendary unicorn. Another puzzle is the tusks of the Siberian mammoth. They seem to have contributed not to the survival of the species, but to its extinction. And so the luxury of nature proves too hard a nut for science to crack.

Whether the human inclination toward luxury can be traced to biological causes must remain an open question. Yet it seems natural to look for social analogies for nature's wasteful tastes. Modern ethnologists have not neglected this comparison. Their most famous—and most debated—example is the potlatch. This was a Native American ritual of the Northwest, in which competing clans of the Kwakiutl and other tribes are supposed to have spectacularly destroyed their most valuable resources. Those who could squander the most were judged the winners of the contest.

Newer studies express doubt about the reality of this custom. But even if the potlatch proves to be nothing more than a scholarly myth, its case will be far from closed. Like the legend of the unicorn in the medieval period, it will haunt the European imagination. It is convincing to us, because it provides a symbol for waste: the potlatch makes clear that every act of ostentatious consumption is a demonstration of power, and it shows that luxurious overspending is always dependent on spectators who allow themselves to be impressed.

The philosophical interpretation of luxury was finally taken too far by Georges Bataille. It is no coincidence that he had just finished a long career as ethnologist when he began to meditate on his *Concept of Overspending* (1933) and *The Accursed Share* (1949). He came, as was his wont, to a radical conclusion: "The history of life on earth is above all the effect of a mad exuberance: the dominant event is the development of excess, the production of ever-more expensive forms of life." One need not share Bataille's metaphysics of waste to agree with him on one point—that despite all of the world's poverty, there has never been a human society that survived without luxury.

One could even argue, with just cause, that people always save less during hungry years. It is precisely the most traditional societies, those constantly threatened with shortages, that put on insane displays of wealth in their celebrations. It was not narcissism or the megalomania of their rulers that determined this but the exigencies of representation. The best examples of such excess are the courtly pageants of the Baroque period. Any excuse sufficed for the princes to put on the orgies of extravagance: a baptism, a birthday, a saint's day, the anniversary of a death, a treaty, or a victory. Even marriage had to be consummated, in a symbolic sense at least, in the public arena: thus the year-long celebration of the bedding of Leopold I in Vienna.

The most celebrated artists of the country and from abroad were engaged for these spectacles. "Houses are erected, mountains moved, forests planted, and ponds excavated. Thousands of workers are occupied for hundreds of hours—only to have their work laid to waste, perhaps in the course of a single night. When the last Habsburg to occupy the Spanish throne, Karl II, aging and weary of life, was shown the new Fountain of Diana in the Garden of La Granja, he remarked gloomily, 'It cost me three million, and it amused me for three minutes.' "

It becomes clear that to believe in the display of splendor and luxury as existing solely for the pleasure of the powerful is a puritanical misconception. It was much more the case of the rich and powerful were obligated, even forced, to offer the world an exorbitant spectacle at any cost, even at the price of their own ruin. Like the lords of the lesser classes, they had to borrow money for the expense, which burdened them and their subjects to the point of threatening their existence. And as far as pleasure was concerned, the participants in these festivities were strictly forbidden to take a step outside the constraints of etiquette. One must imagine the whole affair as an avoidable, horrible strain that left all of the participants in a state of exhaustion.

And what role did the people, or in modern terms, the audience, play in this ritual of waste? They not only had to pay the piper; they also had the right to watch. The fireworks of representation practically depend on the crowd of voyeurs. Even in Haile Selassie's Ethiopia, the lowest beggar could still demand a place at the great celebrations of the ruler. The poor had the right as onlookers to be fed the leftovers from the imperial table.

This co-dependent relationship has survived from the age of absolutism. Even today the audience takes part in the celebrations of "celebrities" through the press and television. Whether it is the Opera Ball in Vienna or Oscars night, the marriage of a top athlete or one of the few remaining royals, there is always a greedy crowd peering through the media keyhole.

The more material forms of public luxury, too, have continued to hold their own. Not only new opera houses, cultural centers, and museums testify to the desire for collective overspending. Science, too, erects colossal monuments to itself. One of these is the Large Hadron Collider, which is presently being constructed near Geneva, an underground high-tech cathedral of such an esoteric nature that the taxpayers of the sixteen participating countries can hardly grasp its purpose. The construction and maintenance of the site will probably cost upwards up two billion dollars.

Not even the researchers and managers want to swear to the fact that this wonder of the world will have come conceivable use, that it will amortize itself, to speak in business terms. To the theologians of pure market economy, the project must be as big a thorn in the side as Neuschwanstein, the fantasy castle of Ludwig II of Bavaria, once was to his treasurers. The officials of Ludwig's time regarded Neuschwanstein as the brainchild of "the sick extravagance of a paranoid." Today, incidentally, ticket sales bring in more than three million dollars every year, the original cost of the entire construction, and this roundabout net yield will doubtless continue to rise into the billions.

Yet the interesting thing about this example is not the numbers. It is the love that is displayed, now as then, for this royal madman, who throughout his lifetime detested the people. It is a sign of the fact that excess, especially when it explodes every normal sense of proportion, hardly meets with spontaneous outrage. This is true today, as well. Every year entire streets are illuminated at Christmas. The municipality of Paris customarily puts up a half-million bulbs every December. This does not seem to disturb anyone, not even the champions of the poor. On the day the Louvre was reopened with the greatest possible pomp, a half-dozen homeless people froze to death in the French capital. And while Mitterand was putting his pharaonic plan of construction into action, a mini-civil war was raging in the suburbs. Unemployed and taxpayers alike respond to the white elephants of our civilization with astonishing tolerance.

In general one cannot avoid the fact that it has seldom been the damned of this earth, but, then, their self-appointed advocates, who have condemned the obscenity of public extravagance. Radical intellectuals on the model of Robbespierre, Lenin, Mao Zedong or Pol Pot were the ones—that is, lawyers, the sons of landowners, sociologists—who saw asceticism as the height of virtue and were ready, if necessary, to enforce it with all the means of terror at their disposal. One has to look a long time for sermons supporting abstinence from the poor, the disenfranchised and the degraded.

In a rather less harmful way, the same has held true for the history of the Federal Republic of Germany. Already in the first years of the Economic Miracle, during the puberty of the Republic, the masses did not want to listen to intellectual warnings about refrigerators and cars, which were at that time still considered luxury items. Later the student movement's protests, too, fell on deaf ears when they tried to protect people from the threat of consumption's terrors. And when East Germany came to its deserved end, virtuous authors had to stand by helplessly and watch as millions succumbed to the temptations of excess in the form of exotic tropical fruits.

This rouses the suspicion that the aversion of all forms of luxury, even the most modest ones, should sooner be ascribed to the scruples and self-hatred of the critics of affluence than to the resentment of those who have no share in it.

So all is right with the world? All scruples set aside, luxury rehabilitated, its prospects for the future bright, the "highest purpose of humankind, affluence, based on sustained prosperity" achieved, as our anonymous encyclopedist of 1815 maintained? Only an idiot could believe that.

Because alongside collective extravagance another kind of luxury has taken hold: a more democratic, more commonplace luxury, freed from all ritual, smaller, so to speak, if not shabbier. It was made possible by the "undeniably improved prosperity of the lower classes through advances in industry." Far be it from us to espouse the "malicious and misanthropic sentiment" that begrudges them these fruits! And we should also leave aside the dark connotations so popularly applied to the social climber. After all, everyone began this game as a nouveau riche.

During the boom years, private luxury, scarcely noticed by its old enemies, took an unexpected and fatal turn. It conquered the field and, in so doing, dug its own grave. In its original form, at least, luxury was vulnerable to entropy, to that regularity that leads to the flattening of extremes, to uniformity and indifference. In every society of the past, waste and excess were rare exceptions to the rule. It was precisely the fact that luxury broke with all of the norms of everyday life that gave it brilliance and prestige. Mass production brought luxury both its greatest triumph and its downfall. An enormous industry, with fantastic growth rates even during recessions, lives off the products of its decay. Emblematic of this development is the trend toward name brands. The names of producers have become a universal code, as the label replaces the object. This has gone so far that customers routinely offer the companies their bodies as advertising space.

"Luxury is not the opposite of poverty out of vulgarity." With these words Coco Chanel pronounced judgment on the industry she pioneered. The morgues of luxury are called "duty-free shop" and "shopping mall." There, the pitiful remains of the dear departed are displayed. The uncanny thing about them is how they replicate, as in a horror film. This flood of sameness claims to represent the exclusive, and arbitrary desire comes at us with the foolish claim that it is a "must." The emptiness of the oft-cited product wars finally becomes clear when the eternal return of the "in" and "out" lists reveals a desolate sameness.

These findings also shed light on the glorious past. In retrospect, we see that there was always an aesthetically questionable side to luxury. Every type of display tends toward excess: too much gold, too much glitter, too much ornament, too much obtrusiveness. Only the dust and patina, the wear and tear of much of our inheritance blur its resemblance to kitsch, make the tastelessness of good taste bearable. In the horror chambers of souvenir shops and upscale furniture stores, tastelessness assails the observer with the force of a fist.

That private luxury has lost even its envious onlookers can come as no surprise. Where there is nothing more to see, the voyeur turns away with a shrug. And it is probably no coincidence that it is mostly pimps, gangsters, and drug lords who place the greatest value on decking themselves out in exclusive crap. Nowhere is the battle of the trademark, the designer label, fought more violently than in the ghetto.

So one must ask if private luxury has any future at all. I hope and fear: yes. For if it is true that the struggle for difference is a part of the mechanism of evolution, and that the desire to squander has its roots in our natural drives, then luxury can never completely disappear, and the question is only which form it will take in its flight from its own shadow.

All we can offer is conjecture. And so I would guess that there will be completely different priorities in our future battles over distribution. Fast cars and gold watches, cases of champagne and perfume are available on every street corner; they are not scarce, rare, expensive or desirable in this age of raging consumerism. Instead, it is the elementary necessities of life that come at a great price: quiet, good water, and enough space.

It is a peculiar reversal of the logic of desire: the luxury of the future will turn away from excess and strive for the necessary; which, it is to be feared, will be available to only a select few. The things that matter will not be sold in any Duty Free Shop:

1. *Time.* This is the most important of all luxury items. Strangely enough it is precisely the elite who have the least say over their own time. This is not primarily a question of quantity, though many members of this class work upward of eighty hours a week; it is much more a matter of the multifarious dependencies that enslave them. They are expected to be on call at all times. Besides that, they are bound to a day-planner that extends years into the future.

   But other professions, too, are bound to regulations that limit their temporal sovereignty to a minimum. Workers are tied to the pace of their machines, housewives (in Europe) to absurd shopping hours, parents to school functions, and almost all commuters have to travel at peak times. Under the circumstances, it is the person who always has time who lives in luxury; time for what he wants to do, and the power to decide what he does with his time, how much he does, when, and where he does it.
2. *Attention.* This, too, is a scarce commodity, with all the media competing bitterly for a piece. Watching the melee of money and politics, sports and art, technology, and advertising, leaves little attention leftover. Only the person who turns his back on these overbearing claims on his attention and turns off the roar of the channels can decide for himself what is worth his attention and what is not. In the barrage of arbitrary information our perceptive and cognitive capabilities decline, they grow when we limit our attention to those things and only those things that we ourselves want to see, hear, feel and know. In this we can see an occasion for luxury.
3. *Space.* As the day-planner is to the economy of time, congestion is to space. In a sense, everywhere and everything is crowded. We have rising rents, housing shortages, and sardine-packed public transport. We feel the press of flesh on sidewalks, public swimming pools, discotheques, and tourist spots. All of this creates a density in living conditions that verges on a robbery of freedom. Anyone who can remove himself from this cagelike existence lives in luxury. But he must be prepared to shovel himself out from under a mountain of

consumer items, as well. Usually our already-too-small living space is jammed with furniture, appliances, knick-knacks, and clothes. What is missing is the excess of space that is required for free movement. Today a room seems luxurious when it is empty.

4. *Quiet.* This, too, is a basic requirement that has become harder and harder to satisfy. Anyone who wants to escape the everyday din must be very extravagant. In general, apartments cost more the quieter they are; restaurants that do not pour musical pollution into the ears of their guests demand higher prices of their discerning clientele. The raging traffic, the howling sirens, the clatter of helicopters, the neighbor's droning stereo, the month-long roar of the street fair—the person who can elude all of that enjoys luxury.
5. *The Environment.* That one can breathe the air and drink the water, that it does not smoke and does not stink, is, as everyone knows, not a given but a privilege enjoyed by fewer and fewer. Anyone who does not produce his own food must pay a premium for nontoxic edibles. It is a problem for most to avoid the risk to life and limb in the workplace, in traffic, and in the dangerous bustle of leisure. In this arena, too, the possibility of withdrawal proves ever-more scarce.
6. *Security.* This is perhaps the most precarious of all luxury items. As the state has become less able to guarantee safety, the private demand for it has grown and driven the prices sky-high. Bodyguards, security services, alarm systems—anything that promises security now belongs to the realm of privilege, and these businesses can count on further growth in the future. If one takes a look around the wealthier neighborhoods, one can already sense that luxury does not promise unmitigated pleasure. As in the past, it will bring with it not only freedom but obligations. For the person of privilege who wants to remain safe does not just lock others out, he locks himself in.

All in all, these speculations revolve on an about-face that is rich in ironies. If there is anything to them, the luxury of the future will depend not on increase, as it did in the past, but on decrease, not on accumulation but on avoidance. Excess will enter a new stage in which it negates itself. The answer to the paradox of mass exclusivity would then be a further paradox: minimalism and abstinence could prove to be just as rare, expensive, and desirable as ostentatious spending once was.

With that, in any case, luxury would relinquish its role as representation. Its privatization would be complete. It would no longer require viewers, but would exclude them. Its reason for being would be, precisely, to be invisible. But even with that kind of withdrawal from reality, luxury would still be true to its origins; it has always been at odds with the reality principle. Perhaps it has never been more than an attempt to flee life's monotony and misery.

New and bewildering, however, is another question that must be posed in light of future prospects: who will count among the beneficiaries of luxury in the future? The original parameters of social position, income, and fortune will no longer be the deciding factors. A top executive, star athlete, banker, or leading politician will quite simply not be able to afford the items discussed here. Such individuals can buy sufficient space and a certain degree of security. But they have no time and no peace.

On the other hand, the unemployed, the elderly, and refugees, who in the future will make up the majority of the world's population, usually dispose of their time as they like. But it would be sheer mockery to call that a privilege. Crammed into crowded living space, with no money or security, many of them can make little use of their empty time. It is difficult to say how the scarce commodities of the future will be distributed, but one thing is clear: anyone who has only one of them enjoys none of them. There can be as little hope of justice in the future as there was in the past. At least in this respect, luxury will remain what it always was—a stubborn opponent of equality.

Maximilien de Béthune, Duke of Sully, published his extensive memoirs under the *Mémoires des sages et royales œconomies d'estat . . . 1638–1662* in Amsterdam and Paris. The quotations, from the sixteenth book of the work, have been cited here from the translation by W. G. Sebald (*Die Ringe des Saturn*, Frankfurt, 1995). *Développement of défense du systems de la noblesse* is the name of polemical treatise, which appeared in Paris in 1757, authored by Abbé Coyer. The citation from Montesquieu is taken from the seventh book of *De l'Esprit des loix* of 1748. Voltaire's aphorism is supposed to have appeared in *Le Mondain*; for Diderot, see the article *"Luxe" in his Encyclopédie* and his discussion in *Salon de 1767*, published in German in the first volume of *Philosophische Schriften* (Berlin 1961). Condorcet's remarks are in *Duhamel*; other sources can be found in Werner Sombart's book *Luxus und Kapitalismus* (Berlin 1913, 1922, 1983). The article "Luxus" appears in the *Conservations-Lexicon oder Hand-Wörterbuch fur die gebildeten Stände*, the first Brockhaus, in the fifth volume (Leipzig and Altenburg, 1815). The most important and pertinent remarks by Georges Bataille are found in *La notion de dépense* (1933) and *La part maudite* (1949); in German, they are in Traugott König's translation, *Die Aufhebung der Ökonomie* (Munich, 1985). The baroque festivals are treated by Richard Alewyn in his book *Das große Welttheater: Die Epoche der höfischen Feste* (Munich, 1959, 1985). Rainer Schauer reports details about Neuschwanstein in an article on "Dividends on Royal Dreams" (*Frankfurter Allgemeine Zeitung*, June 1, 1995).

1995

ACKNOWLEDGMENTS

Chapter 1, "Second Thoughts on Consistency" (1981), originated as a lecture at New York University. It first appeared in German in *Politische Brosamen* (Suhrkamp) and in English in *Political Crumbs* (Verso). Translated and revised by Martin Chalmers.

Chapter 2, "Two Notes on the End of the World" (1978), first appeared in German in *Politische Brosamen* (Suhrkamp) and in English in *New Left Review*, volume 110, and in *Political Crumbs* (Verso). Translated by David Fernbach.

Chapter 3, "The Pastry Dough of Time" (1996), first appeared in German in *Zickzack* (Suhrkamp) and appears here in English for the first time. Translated by Linda Haverty Rugg.

Chapter 4, "My Fifty-Year Effort to Discover America" (1997) originated as a lecture in English at NYU in 1997. It appears here in print for the first time.

Chapter 5, "Las Casas, or a Look Backwards into the Future" (1966), first appeared in German in *Deutschland, Deutschland unter Andern* (Suhrkamp) and in English in *Critical Essays* (Continuum). Translated by Michael Roloff.

Chapter 6, "Reluctant Eurocentrism: A Political Picture Puzzle" (1980), first appeared in German in *Politsche Bro-*

samen and in English in *Political Crumbs* (Verso). Translated by Martin Chalmers.

Chapter 7, "Europe in Ruins" (1990), first appeared in German in *Zickzack* (Suhrkamp) and in English in *Civil Wars: From L.A.to Bosnia* (The New Press). Translated by Martin Chalmers.

Chapter 8, "Brussels or Europe?" (1989), first appeared in German in *Der Fliegende Robert* (Suhrkamp) and appears here in English for the first time. Translated by Linda Haverty Rugg.

Chapter 9, "Billions of all Countries, Unite!" (1988), first appeared in German in *Mittelmass und Wahn* (Suhrkamp) and in English in *Mediocrity and Delusion* (Verso). Translated by Martin Chalmers.

Chapter 10, "Hitler Walks Again" (1991), first appeared in German in *Zickzack* and was partially reprinted in English in the *Los Angeles Times*. It appears here newly translated by Linda Haverty Rugg.

Chapter 11, "Pity the Politicians" (1992), first appeared in German in *Zickzack* (Suhrkamp) and appears here in English for the first time. Translated by Linda Haverty Rugg.

Chapter 12, "The Hero as Demolition Man" (1989), first appeared in German in *Zickzack* (Suhrkamp) and appears here in English for the first time. Translated by Linda Haverty Rugg.

Chapter 13, "The Industrialization of the Mind" (1962), first appeared in German in *Einzelheiten* (Suhrkamp) and in English in *The Consciousness Industry* (Seabury). Translated by Hans Magnus Enzensberger.

Chapter 14, "The Aporias of the Avant-Garde" (1962), first appeared in German in *Einzelheiten* (Suhrkamp) and in English in *The Consciousness Industry* (Seabury). Translated by John Simon.

Chapter 15, "Literature as Institution, or The Aspirin Effect" (1974), first appeared in German in *Mittelmass und Wahn* (Suhrkamp) and in English in *Mediocrity and Delusion* (Verso). Based on a lecture at Cooper Union. Translated by Martin Chalmers.

Chapter 16, "In Praise of the Illiterate" (1985), first appeared in German in *Mittelmass und Wahn* (Suhrkamp) and in English in *Mediocrity and Delusion* (Verso). Translated by Martin Chalmers.

Chapter 17, "In Defense of Normality" (1982), first appeared in German in *Politische Brosamen* (Suhrkamp) and in English in *Political Crumbs* (Verso). Translated by Martin Chalmers.

Chapter 18, "The Zero Medium" (1988), first appeared in German in *Mittelmass und Wahn* (Suhrkamp) and in English in *Mediocrity and Delusion* (Verso). Translated by Martin Chalmers.

Chapter 19, "The Street Theater of Rags" (1993), first appeared in German in *Zickzack* (Suhrkamp) and appears here in English for the first time. Translated by Linda Haverty Rugg.

Chapter 20, "The Future of Luxury" (1995), first appeared in German in *Zickzack* (Suhrkamp) and appears here in English for the first time. Translated by Linda Haverty Rugg.